FORGOTTEN CASTLES
OF WALES AND THE MARCHES

FORGOTTEN CASTLES
OF WALES AND THE MARCHES

PAUL R. DAVIS

LOGASTON PRESS

First published in 2011 by Logaston Press.
This revised edition published in 2021 by Logaston Press
The Holme, Church Road, Eardisley HR3 6NJ
www.logastonpress.co.uk
An imprint of Fircone Books Ltd.

ISBN 978-1-910839-52-2

Designed and typeset by Richard Wheeler in 11 on 14.5 Caslon.
Cover design by Richard Wheeler.

Printed and bound in Poland.

Logaston Press is committed to a sustainable future for our business, our readers and our planet. The book in your hands is made from paper certified by the Forest Stewardship Council.

FSC
www.fsc.org
MIX
Paper from
responsible sources
FSC® C105618

British Library Catalogue in Publishing Data.
A CIP catalogue record for this book is available from the British Library.

CONTENTS

ACKNOWLEDGEMENTS

Grateful appreciation is due to a number of individuals who have helped with the research for this book, and patiently answered my various queries over the years, particularly the staff of the National Monument Record at RCAHMW (Aberystwyth), Will Davies (Cadw), Neil Guy (Castle Studies Group), Philip Hume (Mortimer History Society), Tim Hoverd (Herefordshire Archaeology), Neil Maylan (Glamorgan-Gwent Archaeological Trust), Neil Phillips (APAC Ltd), Rob Scourfield (Pembrokeshire Coast National Park), and in particular the late Rick Turner (Cadw). Many thanks too, to the various landowners up and down the country who allowed me access to survey their ancestral ruins over the years, including David Addams-Williams (Llangybi), Trefor Griffiths (Stapleton), Michael Holloway (Wattlesborough) and Liz Wheedon (Newhouse). All the illustrations belong to the author and OverView aerial photography.

For Martin Davies and the good ship Barbary, long may she sail

INTRODUCTION

There is something in ancient ruins that fills the mind with contemplative melancholy ... they point out to us the striking proof of the vanity of those who think their works will last for ever.

From the 1744 edition of the complete works of Samuel and Nathaniel Buck

Of all the ruined buildings and monuments of the past that lie scattered throughout this land, it is arguably the castle that provokes the most fascination. The thrill of crossing the drawbridge, exploring the dark dungeons and 'secret passages', climbing interminable winding stairs to the dizzying tops of the towers, recalls our childhood games and the memory of swashbuckling Hollywood films, as well as satisfying the most adventurous ego. To be 'king of the castle' for a day probably holds a far greater attraction than to experience the contemplative environs of a ruined monastery.

For centuries these imposing ruins have drawn artists, writers, travellers and inquisitive passers-by, while academics and archaeologists have sought to unravel their histories with pen and spade, and preserve what remains of their shattered walls for posterity. Perhaps it is, as the above quotation suggests, the inherent melancholy of fallen splendour that intrigues and attracts us. Would the castles have the same ambience if they were still intact and occupied, or had been rebuilt in make-believe splendour like many a Continental chateau? Surely it is their very ruined state that makes them so interesting, half-hidden by creeping greenery, devoid of floors, roofs, windows, furniture, decorations and – most importantly – people, to make the buildings live and breathe. The stark walls and stony foundations dare us to imagine what they once looked like, to know the history behind the bare masonry, the fate of the people who built them and the purpose they served.

Wales has an astonishing legacy of castle sites. Six hundred is a conservative estimate, and of that figure some 200 are major stone edifices whose longevity is a tribute to the skills of the original builders. This updated edition of *Forgotten Castles* now includes a number of castles in the Welsh Marches – a richly historic, if rather ill-defined region, incorporating the more westerly parts of the modern counties of Herefordshire, Shropshire and Cheshire. From the late eleventh century onwards, the Norman invaders launched attacks upon the native kingdoms of Wales, striking out from their military bases in the Marches; but they soon found that castles had to be built in unprecedented numbers to retain their grip on the lands they had so readily seized upon.

These innumerable fortifications once symbolised the armed might of a brutal and oppressive class system, and from this safe and distant vantage point that aspect, too, may be part of their attraction. But what of the less well-known sites, the neglected and uncared-for ruins that have avoided wider notice for various reasons, and are located away from busy towns and villages, often hidden from the public gaze? These are the 'Forgotten Castles' explored here.

An apology is necessary for the slightly misleading title of this book. None of the castles included here are really 'forgotten' in the true sense of the word; they have not been obliterated from the face of the earth, nor have they been wiped from all records and memory. In the majority of cases there is still *something* left to see, and they are generally named and marked on Ordnance Survey maps. Furthermore, they will have some documented history preserved in libraries, archives and on internet sites, and anyone with an interest in the history of their locality will surely be aware of them. What this book explores are the castles that have *not* been resurrected as stately homes, nor saved for the nation as visitor-friendly ruins enshrined in landscaped grounds with car parks and ticket office. These neglected strongholds are rarely visited and in many cases are not fully accessible to the public, so you will search in vain for a gift shop, information plaque or an audio guide to elucidate their history; and yet these ruins have a story to tell about the turbulent history of their locality, and of the warlords who ruled it with a grip of iron.

The definition of a castle will be looked at in greater detail below, but the term basically covers the fortified dwellings of the upper classes that were built between the end of the eleventh century and the end of the fifteenth century (roughly 1066 to 1500). Defensive sites from earlier eras, and mock-military structures raised afterwards, are often misleadingly termed 'castles' but are not included here (though they are touched on briefly if they feature in the history of a particular site described in these pages). Nor too are the hundreds of earth and timber forts established in the wake of the Norman invasion of 1066, even though many of these are truly forgotten and survive in overgrown obscurity. Rather, the castles examined here are their successors, the masonry buildings that have left a more tangible legacy in the landscape than grassy mounds and silted-up ditches. They range from minor strongholds like Aberedw, Alberbury, Llancillo, Pennard and Plas Baglan, to substantial fortresses such as Castell Dinas, Clifford, Dinas Powys, Llangybi, Morlais and Penrice.

These are the 'forgotten' castles explored in the following pages: the reasons why they were built, the story of the people who ordered their construction, the architectural development of the various buildings, and the causes of their subsequent decay. Castles selected for inclusion in the gazetteer section of this book are indicated in bold in the following text (to distinguish them from those mentioned in passing or located in other parts of the country). Place-name spellings have been derived from current editions of Ordnance Survey maps, or else are in common use on road signs, to help the motorised explorer. And for the thornier issue of personal names (which not only varied considerably in medieval times, but still causes disagreement among modern-day historians), the more familiar versions have been adopted here, regardless of any inconsistencies that might cause. To help visualise the original appearance of these neglected castles, reconstruction drawings have been used throughout the book, although any such illustration is bound to be a personal interpretation and very much a 'work in progress', subject to revision should any new features come to light in future excavations.

WHAT IS A CASTLE?

a castle was in the nature of things a most important part of its lord's property, often his residence, or one of his residences, by its strength enabling him to hold his position in the world, to enforce his rights and perform his duties.

D.J. Cathcart King (*Castellarium Anglicanum*, 1983)

Fortified residences had been used on the Continent by the ruling elite from the 900s at least, but the appearance and proliferation of the castle in Britain was a direct result of the Norman invasion of 1066. Some brief background history is needed here.

The Normans were descendants of Viking settlers who had colonised a region of France in AD 911. In time, this land became known as Normandy, a name derived from the French word for Norse or 'Northman'. It was a duchy controlled by powerful magnates ennobled at first with the title of Count, and then later Duke, and who exercised considerable independence under the aegis of the king as their overlord. The Norman nobility had been fighting amongst themselves for years, and had to build fortified residences to uphold their status and defend their lands against the incursions of belligerent neighbours. These private fortifications were called 'castles', a term derived from the Latin 'castrum' or 'castellum'.

Across the Channel in Anglo-Saxon England a similar social system existed. The authority and power of the king was not bolstered by a standing army, but depended upon a group of wealthy noblemen and their supporters, who were expected to provide armed might in return for the lands and privileges they had been granted. However, the fortifications here took the form of large walled enclosures, built around major settlements and commercial centres to protect the local populace against Vikings raids. These communal fortifications were known as 'burhs' and appeared in increasing numbers from the reign of Alfred the Great (c.866–99), in response to the dangers posed by the Norsemen.

The penultimate Anglo-Saxon king of England was Edward the Confessor, who reigned from 1042 to January 1066. Much of his youth had been spent in exile in his mother's homeland of Normandy, while England was ruled by a short-lived dynasty of Danish invaders. After claiming the throne, Edward remained on good terms with the ducal court and even allowed some Norman mercenaries to settle in Herefordshire and build castles to keep the Welsh in check. He may also have been trying to counterbalance the ambitions of his more powerful earls by so doing. But these early castles failed to fulfil their promise and the English lords quickly sent the Norman interlopers packing.

To all intents and purposes, it is Duke William of Normandy who must be blamed (or perhaps thanked?) for introducing castles *en masse* in the wake of his successful bid for the throne in 1066. Along with the deployment of mounted knights, the building of castles proved to be a major factor in the rapid subjugation of Anglo-Saxon England.

While castles primarily fulfilled the role of aristocratic fortified residences, they had other uses and functions that changed as society itself changed during the course of the Middle Ages. Most of the first-generation castles were short-lived forts solely designed to gain a foothold in an invaded land, to shelter knights on campaign, and to act as springboards for further advance. Behind the front line, larger and more substantial castles would be built to provide security to the owners and their retinue. They would also serve to protect any settlement that might be established to provide economic stability in a conquered territory and bring in revenues to its founder. A purely military base rarely survived for long once the immediate threat had been quashed.

During outbreaks of unrest the castle was a fortress and refuge for the owner, his family and supporters; a place where soldiers prepared for a siege or gathered for armed conflict in the field. In the longer spells of peace, it was a residence and an administrative centre to run the surrounding estate, a place where rents were collected, courts were held, and wrongdoers punished. Some of the nobility might own a concentration of estates in just one area, but more often their lands were scattered across the country, for it was a sensible policy for a king to prevent any subject becoming too powerful in a particular region, and thereby a potential magnet for any unrest and rebellion. The lands of the Norman conquerors were gained by piecemeal acquisition and through lucrative marriages with other wealthy families, and many of the nobility had estates in Normandy as well as in England. The Anglo-Norman invasion of Ireland in 1176 provided new opportunities to acquire more territories and bring in greater revenues.

The medieval aristocracy spent a good deal of time on the move, travelling on horseback from one manor to another to consume locally produced goods *in situ*. A rich lord might own several castles in his far-flung territories, but he and his retinue could only be in one place at any given time, and so his other properties would be run by an appointed constable with a nominal garrison. When danger threatened, the call went out to the neighbouring vassals to perform their duties and boost the size of the garrison.

But aside from all these practical military uses, a castle had a very important symbolic function as well – it represented the power and dominion of an invader in a conquered territory, and indicated the position of that person in the social structure of the time. By erecting a castle, an invader was saying 'I'm here to stay' and therefore it was essential to capture that castle in order to oust the enemy and remove his symbol of lordship. Once taken, the castle might be retained and garrisoned by the victor, or else destroyed to prevent its reuse by the opposition. Thus, a long chain of taking and re-taking might begin, as fortresses changed hands through the vicissitudes of war.

Exactly how many castles there are in Britain has long been a matter of debate, and any attempt to produce a definitive list is bound to be bedevilled by categorisation into *probable, possible* or *uncertain* sites. Some earthworks which look like medieval castles may actually be Iron Age forts, Prehistoric burial mounds, or even natural geographical features. Many late-medieval buildings have such vestigial defences that they can hardly be deemed castles at all, but must instead be classified as tower houses, fortified manors or stronghouses, according to individual interpretation. Other sites have disappeared altogether so that the researcher is forced to rely on antiquarian accounts of sometimes dubious accuracy.

The historian and castle student D.J. Cathcart King wrote an amusing chapter in his magnum opus *Castellarium Anglicanum* (1983), detailing the various attempts to play the numbers game. His own total of existing sites within the modern boundaries of Wales was 427, but more recent studies have shown this to be an underestimate. For instance, he includes 67 in the county of Glamorgan, but a survey subsequently carried out by the Royal Commission on Ancient and Historical Monuments in Wales pushed this up to 81 extant sites, plus a further 19 vanished or possible castles, and an astonishing 71 rejected entries that were once thought to be castles but are almost certainly not! A more recent total for probable castle sites in the whole of Wales is around 630, though the number increases to about 720 if tower houses, fortified manors and suchlike are included.[1] However, it is important to remember that these figures are just a modern-day tally. There were never that many castles operating at any one time during the medieval period, and a large proportion of sites were short-term military outposts that would have been abandoned once their immediate purpose was served.

The number of castles in the Marches is even more difficult to pin down because there is no official boundary to define that region. The estimated total of probable sites in the three counties of Cheshire, Herefordshire and Shropshire is 277. Even if the more easterly sites are excluded as being 'too far' from the frontier, then the number is still going to be around 200. And so, to bring this numerological diversion to a close, the best 'guesstimate' is that there are over 900 castle sites in Wales and the Marches – at least until the next time someone does the maths.

WHY WERE CASTLES NEEDED?

To meet the danger the king rode to all the remote parts of his kingdom and fortified strategic sites against enemy attacks. For the fortifications called castles by the Normans were scarcely known in the English provinces.

Orderic Vitalis (1075–c.1142)

The Norman Conquest was an act of piracy on a colossal scale. Duke William of Normandy had only a flimsy claim to the throne, for it was alleged that Edward the Confessor had once promised him the Crown and that Earl Harold Godwin-son (the foremost magnate of the realm), had sworn allegiance to William whilst staying as his guest in Normandy. There was also a tenuous link to King Edward's bloodline. These vague promises and half-hearted oaths were conveniently ignored by the English nobility when Harold was chosen to succeed Edward in January 1066 – but the duke was not so forgetful, and when no crown was forthcoming, he took direct action. William was not the only warlord vying for the English throne that year, but he was the one who ultimately triumphed.

After the decisive battle of Hastings in October 1066, William (now king) redistributed vast tracts of confiscated Anglo-Saxon territories among his followers as reward for their services. He and his administrators set about refining the system of land ownership based on the bonds between the ruler and his vassals, and which has since become known as feudalism.

Simply put, the king would reward a nobleman for services rendered by granting possession of territory (thereafter termed a *fee* or *fief*) in return for loyalty, homage and certain obligations. The most important of these feudal obligations was to provide armed support, for a period of up to 40 days a year. This might involve actual fighting on military campaigns, or a spell of guard duty at the nearest castle (and in time that tedious responsibility could be dodged by paying a small fine). A nobleman who held his estates directly from the king was termed a 'tenant-in-chief'. Some of the lands received would be retained by the nobleman himself for his own use; but the larger the territory, the greater the manpower needed to manage it effectively, and so it was subdivided amongst the nobleman's followers as a reward for their services. These 'sub-tenants' would give the same oaths of loyalty and support in return.

The value of fiefs varied considerably. They depended not so much on acreage but on whatever resources could be derived from the land, and were based on a 'knight's fee' (that is, the amount of money or services that would theoretically support one knight). A knight had to be self-sufficient and provide for his family, run a castle, supply his own armour and horses, and pay any taxes out of the income produced from his estate. The border lordship of **Huntington** was held on the service of five knights, while **Penmark** in the Vale of Glamorgan was valued at four. Neighbouring Llantrithyd was so small that it was worth just a half-fee (termed a *moiety*).

Another example from the Vale of Glamorgan shows how complicated the procedure could become. Thirteenth-century documents record that the lordship of St Nicholas was held by William Corbet from the chief lord at Cardiff, and was valued at three knight's fees. Evidently this was a burden for one family to maintain and two sub-fees were created and granted to vassals who built their own castles to signal their status and defend their lands. Today, there are three small earthworks within a kilometre of St Nicholas village. The larger mound near the parish church probably represents the main Corbet seat, while the outlying sites belonged to his sub-tenants. A similar grouping of minor earthwork castles is associated with the defence of the barony of Kington, which was held by the service of five knights and controlled from the major stronghold of **Huntington**.

Although simple in theory, the feudal system could result in complex interconnected relationships amongst the nobility, particularly if a vassal possessed several estates and therefore owed allegiance to more than one magnate. And so it was expected that when the king announced he was going to war, his nobles would be summoned to perform their feudal duty and provide all the armed and mounted knights that their estates were valued at (along with any pitchfork-wielding villagers – the medieval equivalent of cannon fodder).

At the start of William's reign, a series of uprisings demanded his direct intervention, and to prevent any interference from the native rulers of Wales he selected three of his most trusted warriors to police the troublesome border. Firstly, the defence of Herefordshire was entrusted to William fitz Osbern (d.1071), a relative and close confidant of the king. This southern region was of particular concern since the Welsh had carried out devastating raids some years earlier and had burned the fortified city of Hereford. Control of the north-western frontier was initially given to Gerbod the Fleming, but he returned to Normandy within the year and was replaced by the much more dedicated and ruthless Hugh of Avranches (d.1101). Finally, to protect the midlands, Roger of Montgomery (d.1094) was placed in charge of a new castle set on a hill within a loop of the River Severn at Shrewsbury. These three warlords were among the wealthiest and most influential magnates in King William's new realm, and were instrumental in consolidating the initial Norman advance in the border region. The encroachments that they and their followers set in motion, would have serious consequences for the native rulers of Wales.

And so, by 1071, a vast swath of territory stretching from the Dee in the north to the Severn in the south, had been organised into three new earldoms centred upon royal castles at Hereford, Chester and Shrewsbury. Over a period of time, this frontier region became

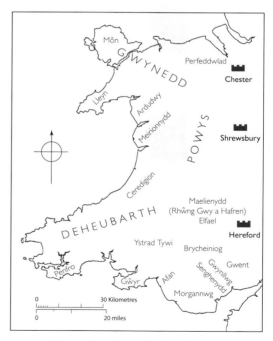

The main native territories of Wales at the start of the Norman invasion

known as the March (a word that has been considered to derive from either the Norman-French *marche*, or the Anglo-Saxon *mearc*, both meaning a border). The lords of the March were given free rein to manage their estates as they wished, so long as the Welsh threat was contained. They could dispense justice and wage war, establish castles, towns and markets, give or take territory as reward or punishment, collect tolls, salvage or court fines – privileges they could not enjoy elsewhere. They were, in effect, kings within their own realms, for the laws of the March differed from those of England, and the monarch could only meddle in affairs or disputes if formally requested by a Marcher lord to do so. As was often stated by these power-hungry lords in medieval times (and repeated by historians ever since), 'the kings writ did not run' in the Marches. And so, from these three capitals, the new Norman aristocracy looked west and saw opportunities to bring more land under their sway.[2]

The ruined enclosure of Llys Bradwen near Dolgellau is traditionally said to mark the site of a native royal court

While the Norman subjugation of Anglo-Saxon England was accomplished in a few short, savage years, the outcome in Wales was very different. The land itself was hardly conducive to easy conquest; even the Romans had found Wales to be a tough nut to crack over a thousand years earlier. The river valleys and broad plains made some regions easy to penetrate, but the network of deep, winding valleys and rugged, inaccessible uplands, served to hinder any coherent attempt at conquest and colonisation. Furthermore, there was the nature of Welsh society itself. The country had long been organised into a number of independent realms made up of administrative units called *cantrefs* and its smaller constituent division known as a *commote*. The administrative heart of each commote was the *llys*, which contained the hall and other domestic buildings of the royal court. Few of these courts survive in any recognisable form today, apart from in place-name evidence; although archaeological remains have been exposed at Llys Rhosyr on Anglesey, and its great hall has been imaginatively reconstructed at the National History Museum at St Fagans near Cardiff.[3]

These territories were controlled by warlords dignified with the title of *brenin* (king), though in later years the title was downgraded to *tywysog* (prince) or *arglwydd* (lord), perhaps due to diplomatic pressure by the English kings, who on occasion wrested some obedience from the Welsh rulers. Most of the country came under the control of three main dynasties – Gwynedd in the north, Powys in the midlands and Deheubarth in the south-west. There were a number of smaller and less powerful houses vying for supremacy, but for much of the medieval period it was these three realms that dominated the political scene.

Warfare was ingrained among the Welsh. The belligerent princes were fiercely competitive and far from paragons of nationalistic pride, for they employed Norman aid in getting rid of opponents and eagerly seized their neighbours' lands if the occasion presented itself. Years of enforced peace alternated with vicious uprisings, as invader embarked on campaigns of conquest, while defender lashed back with fire and sword. The fluctuating fortunes of war changed the map of Wales. Territories grew and shrank according to the outcome of guerrilla battles and dynastic murders. With such a violent and complex situation to contend with, not to mention a topographically challenging landscape, it is hardly surprising that castles proliferated here, and that it was to take a further two centuries before an English king could claim to have pacified the whole country.

THE EARLY CASTLES

With a few rare exceptions, the first castles built by the Marcher lords were relatively simple structures that relied on earthen ramparts and timber buildings, in total contrast to the towering strongholds now familiarly thought of as castles. They were certainly less imposing and durable than what was to come, but it would be misleading to think of them as nothing more than a collection of little wooden huts and flimsy towers. Timber was the cheapest and most convenient building material available in the heavily afforested lands of medieval Britain and was used by almost all levels of society. The deep outer ditches and high inner ramparts would have formed serious obstacles for any attacker to cross, while the stout timber palisades and watchtowers provided the defenders with height and cover to retaliate with spear and bow. Such a simple wooden fort could be erected in a matter of months (and William brought at least one prefabricated castle with him in 1066). Despite their obvious vulnerability to fire, timber castles were the commonest type of fortification used in war zones for the next century or so.

The Normans introduced a completely new type of fortification to Britain known as the **motte-and-bailey** castle, and its most characteristic and unique element was the motte – a conical mound of earth crowned with a timber tower that functioned as the strongpoint and last resort of the garrison during a siege. The scale of the motte would vary considerably depending on several factors – the strategic importance of the site, the wealth and standing of the owner, and the number of locals who could be rounded up and forced into building it. The largest motte in Wales is at Cardiff, which measures almost 12m high with a summit diameter of 23m, and it was perhaps built on the orders of King William himself during a visit in 1081. **Clifford** is another early mound dating from the Conqueror's reign, and this too is quite substantial, being at least 10m high with a 30m summit. It was probably even higher before the stone buildings were later added on top. Yet most castle mottes are far less ambitious in scale, particularly those built in the decades after the initial invasion, and by those feudal sub-tenants who had more modest estates to control.

Top: *An illustration of a Norman motte from the Bayeux tapestry: the building work underway at Hastings.* Bottom: *Example of a motte-and-bailey (Beguildy, Radnorshire)*

The second element of the classic Norman castle was the bailey, and this was an enclosed courtyard beside the motte that served as an outer line of defence and a protective enclave for ancillary buildings. These would include workshops, garrison quarters, stables and stores, the sort of buildings essential to the running of the castle and its surrounding estate. Kitchens were usually freestanding structures positioned a short distance away from the main buildings to reduce the risk of fire. Chapels, too, were commonly found within the castle walls, since religion played a significant role in medieval life; but the most important building within the defensive perimeter was the great hall, a symbol of lordly status and hospitality, where the owner could reside in greater comfort than the cramped confines of a lofty tower. Within the cavernous space of the hall, a fire burned on the central hearth, providing heat and light, the smoke drifting out through a vent in the roof. At the far end of the hall stood the high table, where the lord of the castle and his immediate family would sit and preside over the rest of the company. Doors behind the table led through into the final element of the hall block, the innermost private chamber or **solar**. As an added security measure, many castle halls were located on the first floor (above ground-floor storerooms) and accessed by an external staircase.

The Normans also employed another type of wooden castle, known as a **ringwork**, which consisted of a massive rampart and ditch encircling the main buildings. Although there is no obvious strongpoint like a motte, some excavated ringworks have produced evidence of timber towers over, or beside the

Example of a ringwork (Waun Gynllwch near Builth Wells)

gateway. Whenever possible the builders saved time and labour by constructing the castle earthworks out of natural features like ridges and promontories, scarping the slopes and piling up the surplus earth from the ditches to create suitable mottes. Nor did they ignore the advantages of pre-existing fortifications – the mottes at Cardiff, Caerwent and Longtown were built within derelict Roman forts, while the enormous bailey enclosures of **Caus**, Twmbarlwm and Wiston are almost certainly reused Iron Age hillforts dating from before the Roman invasion. Evidence from excavated sites, and timber-framed buildings that survive from later periods, suggests that the early castles were quite formidable structures, strongly constructed and well-suited to the needs of the time.

A number of churches in the Welsh Marches have detached timber belfries that give a very good impression of how strong these early castle towers would have been. Pembridge has the largest and most impressive example, and was constructed from massive upright posts with a latticework of interlocking struts forming a square tower 7m a side and standing almost 11m high. Although it was built at the start of the thirteenth century and was subsequently modified, the primary timber structure of Pembridge reveals the carpentry skills of the local craftsmen that would have been utilised by the Anglo-Norman warlords as they made their conquering way through the land.

THE ANGLO-NORMAN CONSOLIDATION

Gerald, the steward of Pembroke, founded the castle of Cenarth Bychan where he settled and there deposited all his riches, his wife, his heirs, and all dear to him; and he fortified it with a ditch and a wall and a gateway with a lock on it.

Brut y Tywysogion (trans. John Williams 1860)

From their bases at Chester, Hereford and Shrewsbury, the Normans pushed into Wales and strengthened their hold by building numerous castles, from Chepstow in the south to Rhuddlan in the north. The vast frontier territories created by the chief lords were soon fragmented into smaller and more manageable estates that were granted in fee to their subordinates. Thus, within a few decades of the Norman Conquest, a scattering of independent lordships had appeared along the border, controlled by dynasties whose surnames appear again and again in the turbulent history of the region – Braose, Clare, Fitzalan, Lacy and Mortimer, to name but a few. In time, the number and extent of these lordships increased as more territory was seized and consolidated in the face of native opposition, so that by the later Middle Ages there were over 40 Marcher lordships in Wales and the borderlands.

The threat posed by the Norman freebooters seems at first to have been under-estimated by the Welsh. The native princes carried on fighting for supremacy amongst themselves, even using Norman mercenaries to bolster their own forces on occasion. After a particularly bloody period of civil war, Rhys ap Tewdwr (d.1093) emerged as the main leader of the south, while Gruffudd ap Cynan (d.1137) ruled the north.[4] King William I travelled through south Wales in 1081 and met with Rhys to receive homage and tribute in return for acknowledging the Welshman's position. The king also took the opportunity to establish a castle and mint at Cardiff, which at that time was the most westerly foothold in the south.

In 1085 William carried out an assessment of his realm to find out how much money could be wrung from his subjects. Men were sent men all over the coun-tryside to find out who farmed the land, and to work out its relative value; 'So very closely did he let it be searched out that there was not a single hide nor rod of land – nor, further it is shameful to tell … not an ox, a cow, a pig was left out' as the *Anglo-Saxon Chronicle* records. The outcome of that exhaustive survey was collated the following year into what has become known as the Domesday Book. It provides historians with a snapshot of property ownership two decades after the invasion and reveals that the predominant land-owning class at the time was Norman, rather than Anglo-Saxon.

William I's son and successor, William II (r.1087–1100) appeared to have had less interest in maintaining the status quo, and led several punitive raids into the wilds of Wales, though with little success. However, the relentless drive of the Marcher lords proved key to the Norman takeover of the southern Marches. One of William fitz Osbern's successors was Bernard de Neufmarché (d.c.1125), who had been granted extensive lands in Herefordshire by 1087, with the promise of more plunder further west. It was while extending his control into Brycheiniog in 1093 that he defeated and killed Rhys in battle, and established a new castle and lordship centred on Brecon. The last obstacle to a full-frontal invasion was removed, and the Marcher lords descended in force upon the kingdoms of Gwynedd, Morgannwg and Deheubarth. This sudden onslaught provoked a series of violent counterattacks the following year, and the invaders were driven out of Gwynedd and Deheubarth; however, despite a further series of uprisings the Norman grip proved too tenacious to be shaken off. Areas such as Pembroke and south Glamorgan were to remain more or less firmly under foreign control through the establishment of new lord-ships backed by a proliferation of castles.

King Henry I (r.1100–35) adopted a less confrontational approach to ruling Wales than his predecessors had, and installed trusted Welshmen in control of certain territories as vassals under his terms, rather than relying on the driving force of the

Marcher lords. Warring dynasties were left to weaken themselves by infighting, lands were given or taken away as reward or punishment, and the occasional show of military strength was used to frighten any overbearing prince into submission. Inroads were made in Ceredigion by Gilbert fitz Richard (d.1117) of the Suffolk dynasty of Clare; Henry de Beaumont (d.1119) earl of Warwick, was allowed to seize Gower; while Ralph de Mortimer (d.*c*.1115) of Wigmore, and Philip de Braose (d.*c*.1134) of Sussex, began to consolidate lands around Builth and Radnor.

This slow, steady encroachment was reversed during the troubled reign of King Stephen (r.1135–54), when civil war broke out between the supporters of Stephen and those of Henry's designated heir, the haughty and imperious Matilda Plantagenet. Ambitious and self-seeking lords added to the confusion, changing sides for material gain and boosting their own power at the expense of others. The Welsh too, were not slow to exploit the weakness in the English Crown and the divisions that had arisen among the Marcher lords.

The accession of Matilda's son Henry II (r.1154–89) ended the anarchy of Stephen's reign and brought about a measure of stability to the Marches. King Henry was a far shrewder and more energetic monarch than his dithering predecessor, and quickly set about restoring royal authority and putting the princes in their places. In 1157 an invading army wrested homage and obedience from Owain Gwynedd (d.1170), prince of north Wales. The following year another campaign humbled Rhys ap Gruffudd (d.1197) of Deheubarth. Yet an even greater expedition in 1165 ended in dismal failure when Henry's huge army was brought to a standstill in the Welsh mountains by the appalling summer weather.

Henry never again tried to crush the native rulers with force. Because of his subsequent complicity in the murder of Archbishop Becket in 1170, and the disastrous loss of prestige this incurred, the king was more amenable to a rapprochement with the opposition. Owain died in that year and the authority of Gwynedd waned as civil war amongst his heirs fragmented the realm. Powys too had weakened since the glory days of Madog ap Maredudd (d.1160) who

A fourteenth-century tomb effigy traditionally identified as the Lord Rhys ap Gruffudd

had extended his dominions beyond Offa's Dyke as far as Oswestry, and expelled William Fitzalan (d.1160) from the seat of his lordship for almost a decade. With an exposed border facing England, Powys was always vulnerable to Anglo-Norman incursions, and after Madog's death the land was split in two and controlled by separate dynasties.

For the remainder of the twelfth century, Rhys ap Gruffudd was the foremost leader of the native princes and, through his diplomatic alliance with the Crown, ruled virtually undisturbed as lord of Deheubarth. Welsh literature and arts flourished under the largely benevolent reign of the Lord Rhys, culminating in a celebrated contest between bards and musicians at a Christmas feast in 1176 (the first recorded Welsh Eisteddfod). Rhys also took up practice of castle building with some enthusiasm, rebuilding the conquered Norman stronghold at Cardigan to enhance his standing, and using military bases at Aberdyfi, Nevern and Rhayader to secure his territorial conquests.

CASTLE ARCHITECTURE IN THE TWELFTH CENTURY

For all the convenience and thrift of building in timber, masonry was a far stronger material, and better at withstanding damage from fires and sieges. A few strategically important castles had been built in stone soon after the Norman invasion, but these were the exception rather than the rule, and it was not until the beginning of the twelfth century that the use of masonry became more widespread. It is, however, worth noting that an understanding of the development of early stone castles is hampered by the fact that the vast majority of mottes and ringworks have never been properly excavated. Antiquarians and local historians have frequently claimed certain earthwork sites were more substantial than they might now appear, and three of the sites included here – **Aberyscir, Castell Pen-yr-allt** and **Mynydd-brith** – may look like grassy mounds, but they display tantalising remains of masonry buildings. There are doubtless many more sites that retain buried structures, which will only ever be fully revealed through archaeological excavation.

Building in stone was a time-consuming and expensive business, so it was only indulged in by the king and his richest lords. Specialist workers such as miners, diggers, quarrymen and masons, had to be employed. The raw materials would be obtained from the nearest quarry, but good freestone for shaping into doors, windows and other decorative details might have to be sourced from further afield and carted to the site. Limestone was rendered into powder to make mortar, and used as limewash to cover the walls inside and out, thereby brightening the gloomy rooms and creating a striking impression when seen from afar. Blacksmiths had to produce hinges, bolts and nails (43,000 nails were required at one stage during the building of York Castle). Plumbers were needed to fix lead sheets and flashing to ensure the roofs were watertight. Carpenters were still an essential part of the workforce since timber was required in large quantities for scaffolding and temporary defence works, as well as for floor beams, roof trusses, doors, panelling and furnishings for the completed interiors.

Building generally took place between April and October, and the usual estimate is that medieval workers could raise walls up to a height of 3m per season. This average could, however, vary considerable on the size of the workforce. Orford castle in Suffolk was built from scratch by Henry II over an eight-year period and cost just over £1,400, an enormous sum by the standards of the day. The castle has a three-storey tower 30m high, surrounded with an outer wall studded with additional towers and a gateway. Because few building accounts survive from this period the actual process and cost of constructing a major stone castle are rarely known, but the king at least had an army of clerks on hand to record the expenditure with bureaucratic efficiency.

And so, within the protection of temporary wooden stockades, new stone towers began to rise. Usually of rectangular plan, with a turret on each corner and shallow buttresses strengthening the flanking walls, these forbidding structures came to symbolise the brute power of Norman authority. They were known as 'great towers' or *donjons*, a word that symbolised their importance and status among the castle-owning nobility, and derives from the Latin *dominarium* (lordship). The term donjon was later downgraded to mean a basement

Examples of square keeps: Goodrich (left) *and Rochester* (right)

prison (dungeon) and was replaced by 'keep', an anachronistic word that is still in popular usage today.[5] The keep was capable of resisting attack even if the rest of the courtyard had been overrun by an enemy. Access was often through a fortified porch, or forebuilding, which might contain a drawbridge and portcullis to defend the approach to the main apartments. The ground floor of the tower was used for the storage of food and goods, and might contain a well dug below the foundations in search of water (essential if the garrison was to endure a long siege when no supplies might be obtained from outside). The principal chambers were invariably situated on the upper levels for security.

It is now appreciated that great towers had other roles to play in the feudal society of the time, rather than just for defence. Aside from providing secure accommodation for the lord and his immediate family, they contained a hall or audience chamber where matters of state were dealt with, where envoys could be met in suitably impressive surroundings, and where honoured guests were entertained in splendour. The towers also reflected the wealth and status of the builder, and displayed to all the authority of the Anglo-Norman ruling class.

Recreated medieval castle interior (Dover)

Originally these rooms were a far cry from the dark echoing stone cells that have resulted from long years of decay and disuse. The floors were usually of timber and strewn with rushes or furs, but if the rooms had a solid stone surface then decorative ceramic tiles might be used instead. The rough masonry walls were concealed with smooth plaster and limewash, and enlivened with painted decorations or fabric hangings. Research has shown that medieval tastes in interior decor bordered on the garish (as can be seen by any visitor to the keep at Dover, which has been restored to its twelfth-century polychromatic glory). The main rooms of the keep would be heated by fireplaces in the side walls, but a chamber located on the topmost level might have had an open hearth set on the stone floor, with the smoke escaping through a louvre in the roof above. There were few windows in the massively thick walls, just splayed openings secured with metal bars to allow in some light and air. Glass was an expensive luxury few could afford in medieval times (nor was it very practical in a building liable to be attacked) and so wooden shutters were used to control draughts.

As for sanitary arrangements, the usual method of waste disposal consisted of a hole in the floor discharging down a shaft into a cesspit. These latrines were known as garderobes (literally 'mind-your-clothes') a euphemism that is matched by today's use of the word 'cloakroom'. Some claim that the ammonia fumes from the latrines deterred moths, hence the habit of hanging clothes there. Garderobes were small rooms within the thick outer walls and reached by dog-leg passageways that helped cut down smells. Sometimes the latrine chamber was built jutting out from the castle wall on stone brackets (corbels) which offered a draughtier, but less odoriferous option for the user. The thick walls of the keep also contained passageways, fighting galleries and stone stairs leading to the upper levels. The stairs might be arranged in straight flights, but more usually spiralled up around a central newel post and rose above the battlements within a small turret.

The small square holes that are often dotted about the exterior faces of walls and towers are *putlog holes* into which scaffolding poles were inserted during construction. Other holes would have served to drain excess water from the roofs, or else marked the position of vanished timber fighting galleries, referred to as *hourds* or as *brattices*. These structures jutted out from the battlements so that defenders could oversee the base of the walls and drop missiles on any attacker below. When compared to the level of comfort enjoyed by today's householders, these medieval buildings seem basic, unhygienic and claustrophobic, but could be palatial residences by medieval standards.

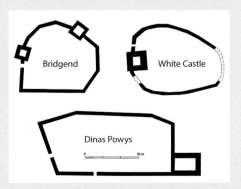

The outline plans of three Welsh castles showing the location of keeps and square towers as part of a circuit of defences

Monumental examples of Anglo-Norman keeps can be seen at Corfe (Dorset), Dover (Kent), Hedingham (Essex), Rochester (Kent) and – largest and most iconic of them all – the White Tower of London. In Wales and the Marches, keeps are much smaller and rarely contain more than two floors. They can be seen at Chepstow, Goodrich, Ogmore, Manorbier, Monmouth and **Wattlesborough**. The towers at **Hay**, Ludlow and **Usk** were built to serve as the main gateway into the castle, but their entrances were later blocked up for security.

Although the rectangular plan was commonly adopted by the keep builders, there were no hard and fast rules to dictate its overall design; indeed, most of the towers show a considerable degree of variation in scale, layout and detail. The sheer size of the average tower-keep meant that it was unwise to build one on top of a motte (unless the mound was massive and stable enough to take the weight) and so in most cases, they were erected on level ground within the bailey. A more lightweight alternative was to crown the motte with a *shell-keep*, which was basically a walled enclosure containing lean-to buildings ranged against the inner sides, and overlooking a cramped central courtyard or lightwell. The shell-keep might be round, oval or polygonal in plan, and the enclosing wall was sometimes strengthened with buttresses or turrets. Good examples can be seen at Cardiff, **Kilpeck**, Restormel (Cornwall), Totnes (Devon), and Wiston.

Example of a shell-keep (Wiston Castle in Pembrokeshire)

At Launceston (Cornwall) and Tretower – and possibly **Lyonshall** as well – the internal buildings were subsequently replaced by a free-standing tower; while at **Llancillo**, **Snodhill** and Wigmore, it is likely that the enclosure on top of the motte was completely roofed over, so that it would have looked more like a squat tower, than a true shell-keep as such.[6]

As mentioned above, there is a great variety in the detail of castle keeps, and the architects (or *ingeniators* as they were known at the time) seemed to delight in creating fanciful variations for their patrons. The motte at **Richards Castle** was crowned with a tower-keep of octagonal plan, and the buried remains at **Huntington** may share the same design. The builders of the royal castle at Orford (1165–73) took this multangular plan to the extreme, for it has so many sides as to be practically round. The near-contemporary tower at Conisbrough (Doncaster) was truly cylindrical and foreshadows the next generation of keeps (to be described in the next panel).

Whatever its shape, the keep did not stand alone. The earthworks and timber stockades of the earlier bailey defences would have been retained, or improved with the addition of stone gates and curtain walls. Twelfth-century castles relied on fairly unsophisticated layouts with straight lengths of walling following the line of the outer ramparts, while a few small square towers improved the defensive strength of the enclosure. Examples of twelfth-century enclosure castles can be explored at Bridgend, **Castell Dinas**, Coity and White Castle. As the thirteenth century dawned, the modest castles of the Anglo-Norman period began to be refined and improved, as new concepts in fortification design spread to Britain, and more efficient castles were needed to withstand the appearance of powerful native rulers who challenged the authority of the king and the Marcher lords.

Top: *Orford Castle, Suffolk, built over an eight-year period at a cost of just over £1,400.* Bottom: *The twelfth-century enclosure castle at Bridgend*

The enemy that the castle faced was not exclusively Welsh. There were episodes of civil war amongst the upper classes, and rebellions against the misrule of monarchs; however, by and large, castles in Wales and the Marches were there for one thing – to protect the Anglo-Norman landowners from the fury of the dispossessed Welsh. The belligerent nature of the native princes is well attested by contemporary scribes and chronicle histories, none more so than *Brut y Tywysogion* ('Chronicles of the Princes'), a year-by-year account of events in Wales from the Dark Ages to the beginning of the fourteenth century.

Another valuable source is Gerald of Wales (*c*.1145–1223), born of mixed Norman and Welsh parentage at Manorbier in West Wales, who pursued a long and often turbulent career in the Church. He was a tireless traveller, writer, raconteur and self-publicist, and his surviving works – particularly *The Journey through Wales* (*c*.1191) and *The Description of Wales* (*c*.1194) – provide us with a unique glimpse of life in late twelfth-century Wales. 'They are fierce rather than strong, and totally dedicated to the practice of arms. Not only are the leaders but the entire nation is trained in war', wrote Gerald about his own countrymen. 'They are passionately devoted to their freedom and to the defence of their country; for these they fight, for these they suffer hardships, for these they will take up their weapons and willingly sacrifice their lives'.

Yet he did not shrink from the less praiseworthy aspects of the Welsh nation – their cowardice in the face of determined, well-organised attackers, greed of land acquisition, and endemic in-fighting. He went on to write 'If the Welsh would only adopt the French way of arming themselves, if they would fight in ordered ranks instead of leaping about, if their princes could ... unite to defend the country – or, better still, if they had only one prince and he a good one – I cannot see how so powerful a people could ever be completely conquered'.

The fragile peace that had lasted for almost 20 years ended abruptly when King Henry ii died and Richard i (r.1189–99) acceded to the throne. Lord Rhys ap Gruffudd had no particular regard for the new monarch and broke out in revolt, capturing and destroying a large number of Anglo-Norman strongholds. Before his death in 1197 the aged prince had the misfortune to suffer from the treachery and ingratitude of his offspring (just as Henry himself had in his last years). Rhys was even briefly incarcerated by one faction of his rebellious kin. The power of Deheubarth waned as the surviving heirs imprisoned, dispossessed or murdered each other, fatally wounding Rhys' hard-won unity. Once again, the king and the Marcher lords moved in to encroach on native territory and exploit any weaknesses among the lesser rulers. And yet, within a few short years, Gerald's plea for a united Wales ruled by an effective leader was destined to come true.

And the King has heard and in part seen that Llywelyn's ancestors and himself had the power within their boundaries to build and construct castles and fortresses and set up markets without prohibition by anyone.

from a letter by Llywelyn ap Gruffudd to Edward I, July 1273

When Owain Gwynedd died in 1170, his realm fragmented as civil war broke out amongst his successors. One of the dispossessed heirs, Iorwerth, sent his young son Llywelyn to be raised by relatives in Powys away from the bloodbath that inevitably accompanied native power struggles. When Llywelyn came of age he took back his birthright by fire and sword, seizing the lands of one of his deceased uncles and defeating another in battle. From relative obscurity, Llywelyn ap Iorwerth (*c.*1173–1240) rose to become the most powerful and successful native leader, and one of only two figures in Welsh history to earn the posthumous designation 'The Great'. The unsettled reign of King John (r.1199–1216) gave Llywelyn plenty of opportunity to fight back against the shaky royal authority in Wales, and bring more native rulers under his sway, whether they wanted to or not. He took southern Powys from its rightful ruler, ousted his cousin, and reined in the squabbling princes of Deheubarth. Llywelyn entered into a politically motivated marriage with King John's daughter to help consolidate his position, and formed several alliances with Marcher lords opposed to the king. The dominions ruled directly by Llywelyn the Great, or controlled through his vassals, comprised the whole of north Wales, Powys and Deheubarth, and the territories held by the Crown and Marcher lords were pushed to the periphery. The bards lauded him as 'Prince of Wales', yet Llywelyn contented himself with the less provocative title of 'Prince of Aberffraw and Lord of Snowdon'.

Llywelyn ap Iorwerth tried to establish a Welsh feudal state united under one ruler, but despite obtaining formal recognition of his legitimate son Dafydd (d.1246) as sole heir and successor in place of his elder son Gruffudd (d.1244), all his efforts were in vain. Once death had removed his forceful presence from the political scene, the princes fell to their usual infighting. Dafydd himself died unexpectedly early and the English recovered most of Llywelyn's territorial gains.

Dolwyddelan Castle, one of the fortresses built by Llywelyn to impose his authority on Wales

CASTLE ARCHITECTURE IN THE THIRTEENTH CENTURY

By the start of the thirteenth century, new trends appeared in military architecture, probably introduced by knights returning from abroad where more advanced buildings had long been used. Rather than relying solely on the intimidating strength of a tower-keep, there was a move towards creating a more effective and integrated defensive circuit, with the layout reflecting geometrical shapes such as rectangles and polygons. High curtain walls were built in straight sections with the angles capped by rounded towers that boldly projected out beyond the *enceinte* (enclosing wall). The defensive advantage of a round tower is that it lacks awkward angles that might be susceptible to ramming or undermining, and the curved shape also helped deflect missiles. Inside, the towers had strategically placed loopholes that enabled archers and crossbowmen to provide flanking fire along the line of the walls and target anyone approaching the castle, without exposing themselves to the enemy. The older form of arrow loop with its restrictive deep splay was replaced by a more effective opening set into a rectangular recess, which gave greater freedom for an archer to manoeuvre and take aim.

One of the Continental castles that inspired a long line of similar designs was the Louvre (Paris), built by King Philip II of France around 1190. It was a relatively simple, square enclosure with round towers on each corner, and additional half-round towers on the intermediate walls. Two of these towers were set close together to guard an entrance between them, and within the

The preserved walls of the Louvre, Paris, built to a square plan with round towers at each corner, which proved to be an influential design

central courtyard stood a round keep. In Wales, a similar layout was adopted at Skenfrith in the 1220s by Hubert de Burgh (d.1243), chief advisor to the young King Henry III. Both Hubert and his older contemporary William Marshal (d.1219) earl of Pembroke, were at the forefront of the new trends in castle design, and these ideas were put into practice at the key Marcher strongholds of Chepstow, **Clifford**, Grosmont, Montgomery, Pembroke and **Usk**. They also featured in the many baronial and royal castles that were being built in Ireland in the wake of the Anglo-Norman invasion of that country in the 1170s

The old concept of a single strongpoint was not abandoned despite the introduction of more advanced designs, and in fact a change of shape from square to round gave the donjon a new lease of life in the thirteenth century. Again, the inspiration probably came from across the Channel, where cylindrical keeps had been built in the twelfth century and were a particular feature of King Philip's innovative castles. William Marshal was an active campaigner in France and, at the seat of his lordship of Pembroke, built one of the earliest (and certainly the largest) circular keep in Britain around 1200.[7]

The effigy of William Marshal, earl of Pembroke in the Temple Church, London

Round keeps soon gained a vogue amongst the southern Marcher lords, and appeared at Bronllys, **Bryn Amlwg**, Caldicot, **Lyonshall**, **Penrice**, Skenfrith and Tretower. Other vanished examples are believed to have stood at Brecon, Cardigan and Monmouth. They were still being built at the latter end of the century – **Blaencamlais**, Flint and **Hawarden** are notable late examples. None of the towers are exactly the same, and there are subtle differences in detail – some are completely cylindrical while others have flanking turrets; some have newel stairs while others have stair passages curving up within the walls. These variations may be the result of chronological changes in fashion, a fad of the architect, or of a specific requirement on the part of the patron. There may have been

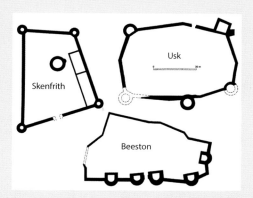

Castle plans of the early thirteenth century showing the preference for angular enclosures and rounded corner towers

Examples of round keeps: Rouen (left, with hourd) *and Pembroke* (right)

a social or military reason that we can no longer discern after all this time. It is noticeable that round towers are generally smaller than those of square plan and fit very neatly on the circular summits of pre-existing mottes; so maybe it was simply a case of making the best use of the available space when a Marcher lord commissioned an expensive makeover of his castle.

The Welsh princes also adopted round towers at **Castell Meredydd**, Dinefwr, Dryslwyn and Dolbadarn, but on the whole native castle design was far less forward-looking; probably the comparative lack of resources was a major factor, as well as the difficulty of employing skilled designers from outside their realms. The rectangular keep remained a firm favourite with the Welsh well into the second half of the century, although the princes of Gwynedd did develop a curious hybrid form of keep – square at one end, round at the other (like an elongated letter D in plan). The foundations of one can be seen at **Carndochan**, although the best-preserved example is at Ewloe.

Aside from the increased use of flanking towers, the other notable development of the early thirteenth century was an improvement in gatehouse design. Gates were the most vulnerable part of any castle since they offered the enemy a way in. Early gateways tended to be fairly simple structures – at its most basic just an arched opening in the wall, or else a passageway through the ground floor of a small tower. Stout wooden doors, a portcullis and perhaps a drawbridge spanning the outer ditch, would be all that stood between the enemy without and the defenders within. As the keep was the most characteristic feature of twelfth-century castle design, it could be said that the gatehouse was the defining architectural element of the thirteenth century. Recent research suggests the trail was blazed unexpectedly early by William Marshal at Chepstow, where the outer gate was built in the 1190s as an 'advance guard' of the type of structure that became much more commonplace as the new century progressed.[8]

The classic form of gatehouse consists of a heavily defended entrance passageway between two round or D-shaped towers boldly projecting out from the walls. Each tower usually contained guardrooms on the ground floor with larger residential chambers above. Beeston (Cheshire), Montgomery and probably White Castle, are early examples dating from the 1220s or '30s and which served to inspire Llywelyn the Great to build something similar at Criccieth. The plan was further refined by Gilbert de Clare (d.1295) at Caerphilly around 1270. The latter also relies on an imaginative use of water defences to keep enemy siege machines well away from the walls, a concept Gilbert surely copied from the huge Midlands fortress of Kenilworth that he had helped besiege a few years earlier.

Caerphilly also has a second defensive perimeter surrounding the inner enclosure, effectively creating a 'castle within a castle'. Even if the invaders had managed to break into the outer circuit, they would be exposed to the garrison defending from the more massive inner ring. This type of defence in depth is known as a concentric castle, and some of the finest examples were later built in north Wales for King Edward I by his favoured mason from Savoy, Master James of St George. Edward had returned from the Crusades in 1274, having seen the large and elaborate fortifications in the Middle East, and was

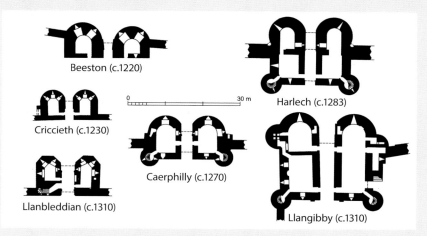

Beeston (c.1220)

Criccieth (c.1230)

Caerphilly (c.1270)

Llanbleddian (c.1310)

Harlech (c.1283)

Llangibby (c.1310)

0   30 m

Comparative plans of various gatehouses.
The position of portcullises is indicated by broken lines

perhaps also inspired by Gilbert's work at Caerphilly. From 1277 onwards, the king subdued the rebellious heartland of Wales and embarked on the most ambitious and costly scheme of castle-building ever carried out by the English Crown. A few, like Conwy and Flint, have a strangely old-fashioned layout, but Aberystwyth, Beaumaris, Harlech and Rhuddlan display an almost scientifically precise concentric design.

By that date, gatehouses had reached massive proportions and incorporated a whole host of defensive features aimed at stopping an enemy dead; arrow loops sweeping the approach and passageway, multiple portcullises, thick wooden doors, and 'murder-hole' slots in the roof through which the defenders could drop rocks or pour boiling water on an enemy below. The last great gatehouse in Wales was built around 1310 at **Llangybi**, a monumental edifice whose carved stone decorations and abundance of garderobes proves that it was not merely a gate to let people in or out, but one of the principal residential buildings at the castle.

From the top: *Caerphilly (with gatehouse to left); the gatehouse at Chepstow; and at White Castle*

The struggle for Welsh supremacy was rekindled by Dafydd's nephew, Llywe-lyn ap Gruffudd (d.1282). Like his grandfather and namesake, Llywelyn clawed his way to the top by first defeating his relatives in battle and seizing their lands, then spreading out from the mountainous heartland of Gwynedd to stamp his authority on the other native princes. King Henry III (r.1216–72) was a less dis-liked monarch than his father John, but his long reign was nevertheless fractured by a major uprising, in this instance headed by the earl of Leicester, Simon de Montfort (d.1265), with whom Llywelyn had become closely allied. Even after Simon's death and the collapse of the revolt, Llywelyn succeeded in forcing King Henry to recognise his title of Prince of Wales and acknowledge his territorial conquests over his fellow countrymen and Marcher lords. But whether lacking the shrewd ruthlessness (or the sheer luck) that had gained his grandfather so much, Llywelyn could not deal effectively with the many enemies his progress had made.

The accession of Edward I (r.1272–1307) marked the turning point of Llywelyn's fortunes. In 1274 his own brother Dafydd (d.1283), along with Gruffudd of Powys (d.1286), plotted his overthrow; but when the coup failed, they fled to England. Llywelyn persistently refused to pay the expected homage to the new king and feared for his safety should he leave Wales to do so. The situation continued to deteriorate, and in 1276 Edward finally opted for military action to bring the rebel prince to heel. As the royal army moved against Gwynedd, the usual ploy of retreating into the mountains and launching guerrilla attacks failed, because English ships patrolled the Menai Strait and prevented the Welsh from harvest-ing the vital Anglesey grain supply. Llywelyn was forced to surrender and make what peace he could. By the terms of the Treaty of Aberconwy (1277) Llywelyn was deprived of much of his former territories except for Gwynedd, although he was allowed to retain the hollow title of Prince of Wales.

King Edward safeguarded his position by building a number of major new castles on the edges of native territory, and rewarded his allies (including the treacherous Dafydd) with land confiscated from the prince. With so much pres-sure from the Marcher lords and royal officials it is hardly surprising that rebellion broke out again after only a few years; what is surprising is that it was Dafydd who sparked it off, perhaps fed up with all the interference from his English overlords, or maybe wanting to be Prince of Wales in place of his brother.

Edward swiftly retaliated and used the same military tactics as before. Angle-sey was blockaded and Llywelyn was forced to head south to rally troops, where, in December 1282 he was killed in a skirmish near Builth. Dafydd continued the war to its bitter end. He was hunted down and betrayed by his own men, and in October 1283 he was disembowelled alive in the marketplace at Shrewsbury.

Edward was determined to stamp out the princely House of Gwynedd forever; any immediate kin disappeared into prisons and even Llywelyn's little daughter Gwenllian was effectively incarcerated for life in a remote Lincolnshire nunnery.

The king was now free to consolidate his hold on the county and complete his ambitious scheme of encircling Gwynedd with a ring of powerful castles. As the walls went up, so the lands previously seized by the Welsh passed swiftly back into the firm control of the Marcher lords. Most of Llywelyn's forfeited territories became Crown lands (and formed the basis of the English-style shires of Anglesey, Caernarfon, Cardigan, Carmarthen, Flint and Merioneth); while the rest was parcelled out as rewards amongst Edward's supporters, who were expected to build new and effective fortifications to defend those lands. And so, a member of the Mortimer clan started Chirk Castle, Henry de Lacy (d.1311) built Denbigh, John de Warenne (d.1304) built Holt, and Reginald de Grey (d.1308) completed **Ruthin**. Another of Edward's supporters, Gilbert de Clare (d.1295), had already constructed Caerphilly, arguably the largest non-royal castle yet built in Britain. The rest of the Marcher lords had breathing space to regroup and strengthen their castles against any possible future threat that might arise from the wilds of Wales.

At Rhuddlan in March 1284, the future administration of the country was formalised. Restrictive legislation was set in place and English law prevailed over Welsh rights and traditions. Even the title 'Prince of Wales' was reserved by the king as a hereditary honour for the eldest son (as it is to this day). Edward could be magnanimous to those who had joined the winning side; Llywelyn's brother Rhodri had long since turned his back on the political quagmire and lived out his days as an obscure English landowner; Rhys ap Maredudd (d.1291) was allowed to rule in what was left of Deheubarth; Gruffudd of Powys returned in triumph to Welshpool, for all intents and purposes an English baron rather than Welsh prince. His heir Owain (d.1293) even adopted an English surname, de la Pole after the place-name, Pool (as Welshpool was then known). The native rulers of Afan, once at the forefront of resistance in the south, also bowed to the inevitable and restyled themselves the Lords de Avene. A few descendants of once noble dynasties were left in possession of some ancestral lands in mid Wales.

Yet the destruction of the House of Gwynedd did not completely eradicate Welsh resistance. Rhys ap Maredudd lost patience with the constant interference of royal officials and rebelled in 1287. His uprising did not gain widespread support and after several years on the run, he was hunted down and brutally executed. A far more serious and widespread revolt took place in 1294–95 and was headed in the north by Madog ap Llywelyn, a distant relative of the late prince. The southern insurgents were led by Morgan ap Maredudd, son of the last ruler of Gwynllŵg ousted by Gilbert de Clare. Despite the damage caused to English castles and towns, Edward was surprisingly lenient to the captured leaders (Madog was imprisoned for life and Morgan released to serve in the royal army); perhaps the king realised that the revolt was just the last flickering of a dying flame. A further uprising in 1316 by Llywelyn Bren (d.1318) was restricted mainly to Glamorgan but thereafter for almost a century the castles of Wales were used only in the petty squabbles of the new ruling hierarchy.

The territorial divisions of Wales and the Marches around 1300

... All Carmarthenshire, Kidwelly, Carnwyllion and Iscennen be sworn to Owain
yesterday, and he lay last night in the castle of Dryslwyn ... and there I was and spoke
with him upon truce, and prayed of a safe conduct, under his seal, to send home my wife
and her mother ... and he would none grant me.

from a letter written by the constable of Carreg Cennen
during the rebellion of Owain Glyndŵr, July 1403

During the early years of the fourteenth century, the role of the castle in Wales and southern England changed dramatically due to the combination of several factors. Most obviously the defeat of the Welsh princes meant there was no further need for a widespread system of mighty fortifications, and the costly business of castle-building slowed to a trickle. Several of the hugely ambitious fortresses started by King Edward and his lords in the aftermath of the wars were never completed. Other castles located in remote areas and serving no purpose except as military bases were abandoned once their *raison d'être* had passed, to save on the costs of upkeep and maintaining garrisons. The long-established feudal system was also beginning to break up, and instead of the old practice of granting land in return for armed support there was a shift towards paid military service and financial contracts.

Within a few generations there was a further change in the need for defence as the enemy came not from within the kingdom, but from overseas. King Edward III (1327–77) started an interminable series of conflicts with France in order to press his claim to that kingdom through his mother's line of descent. Many Welsh warriors found lucrative employment in the royal armies ransacking French towns and villages. The king built new castles in England and made sure that older fortresses and town defences near the coast were capable of repelling raiding fleets. Robert de Penres earned the wrath of the king by failing to properly garrison and stock his castles at Llansteffan and **Penrice**. Increasingly though, any building work to castles was geared towards improving the domestic comforts rather than upgrading the defences. The revenues from a lord's estate that would once have financed the building of strong walls to keep his life and belongings safe, was now being used to make that life as comfortable as possible. There are many records of repairs and alterations to existing structures, but after 1320 virtually no new castle was built in Wales – there was very little need in truth, since the country had an embarrassing surfeit.

The appearance of a new weapon – gunpowder – on the battlefields of Europe altered the perception of a castle's usefulness in war and led to a gradual change in military architecture. Small cannons or 'bombards' cast from bronze, began to be used from the 1320s onwards; but their small size coupled with poorly mixed quantities of powder meant that they were more effective at frightening and demoralising the opposition rather than inflicting serious harm. As the century progressed the manufacturing process was refined, so that larger and more efficient guns could be made from cast iron. The lofty walls and towers that had for so long kept the military aristocracy safe and sound were soon to prove inadequate.

Yet despite the incipient signs of slow decay and changing needs, the medieval castle was far from redundant, and with the start of the new century war once more spread out from the hills and valleys of Wales to threaten security of English rule. What began as a minor border dispute between two landowners rapidly escalated into a national uprising. Owain Glyndŵr (1359–1415?) was provoked into rebellion by the tactless and underhand actions of his neighbour, Lord Grey of Ruthin (d.1440) and the suspicious Henry IV (r.1399–1413). The initial uprising in September 1400 was not an immediate success, and after a retaliatory attack the Welsh leader was forced to spend the winter hiding in the mountains; but the ball had been set rolling, and the tensions simmering in Welsh hearts for many long years were violently released. Rioting quickly spread to all parts of the Principality. A flurry of building activity occurred as King Henry ordered the Marcher lords to ensure that their castles along the border were adequately supplied and prepared for war. Yet even the seemingly invincible royal strongholds of Aberystwyth, Conwy and Harlech fell to the Welsh. By 1404 Owain's dominions extended over most of the country and native parliaments were held at Harlech and Machynlleth.

Glyndŵr allied himself with a number of powerful and single-minded English lords opposed to the regime of the Lancastrian king, and an unfeasibly ambitious plan was drawn up, dividing England and Wales into three parts. Owain was to rule a swollen Principality extending well beyond the traditional boundaries. A Welsh army bolstered by French mercenaries even marched into England as far as Worcester in the summer of 1405. But the momentum of the uprising could not be sustained; support fell away, the successes turned to defeats. By 1408 most of the ringleaders were dead or imprisoned, and the following year the last of the captured castles were back under royal control. Despite the generous offer of a pardon from King Henry V (r.1413–22), the fugitive Glyndŵr disappeared from the pages of history into the realms of folklore.

Within a few generations war had broken out again as rival claimants for the throne engaged in a long drawn-out series of skirmishes and full-scale battles popularly known as the Wars of the Roses. The strife between supporters of the Yorkist and Lancastrian dynasties took place over a 30-year period, although it is estimated that the actual amount of fighting in all that time totalled no more than three weeks. Many castles were utilised in the struggles (Harlech being the most famous example, captured in 1468 after a seven-year siege), and at least one (Carreg Cennen) was deliberately wrecked to prevent any future use; but by and large the outcome of the wars was decided by pitched battles rather than long sieges, and the main conflicts took place outside Wales.

CASTLE ARCHITECTURE IN THE FOURTEENTH AND FIFTEENTH CENTURIES

In the settled years between sporadic bouts of warfare, new castles were built in England that displayed a far greater emphasis on domesticity rather than defence. They have the moats, gatehouses, towers and battlements of the true castle, but rarely share the scale or structural strength of their predecessors. Though looking like castles, they are in reality grand, fortified houses dressed up in the paraphernalia of the recent past. Acton Burnell near Shrewsbury is a forerunner of this type and dates from the 1280s, but probably the best-known example is Bodiam in Sussex, a photogenic collection of symmetrical towers reflected in the waters of an encircling moat for added effect. It was built in 1385 by a veteran of the Hundred Years War, to a design possibly influenced by the more ornate chateaux of France. Behind the playful military facade of Bodiam lies a compact and lavish suite of domestic apartments. Old Wardour

Castle architecture at its most picturesque: fourteenth-century Bodiam in Sussex

in Wiltshire (c.1393) has a similar level of luxury, although here the rooms are contained within a hexagonal tower-like structure.

Within a few generations more of these large 'show castles' were being built across England, in some cases utilising the newly fashionable building material of brick. Herstmonceux in Sussex (c.1440) and Kirby Muxloe in Leicestershire (c.1480) have residential suites of rooms grouped around a central rectangular

Nunney Castle in Somerset (c.1373)

courtyard. Castle-like on the outside, a country house within, these are fortified manor houses rather than the feudal strongholds of the previous centuries. The antiquated concept of the donjon was revived with enthusiasm too, not so much as a gloomy bolt-hole but rather a lavishly appointed private tower, containing numerous suites of comfortable rooms with expansive windows and ample garderobes. Nunney in Somerset (c.1373), Tattershall, Lincolnshire (c.1434) and Ashby de la Zouch, Leicestershire (c.1474) are just three examples of architectural one-upmanship.

Wales has a single (but exceptionally fine) monument to this late flowering of castle design – Raglan, built between 1435 and 1469 for the ascendant Herbert family. The fortress-like exterior, complete with louring octagonal keep, shelters an extensive and complex group of residential apartments within. The walls have narrow loops for archers and crossbowmen, but the designers of Raglan found it prudent to provide gunports as well (even though some were probably for display rather than practical use). The Vaughans of Tretower were

Raglan Castle, Monmouthshire, built between 1435 and 1469, included gunports and contained an extensive residential complex

related to the Herberts, but chose instead to abandon their twelfth-century stronghold for a spacious manor house close by, which was totally undefended apart from a token gatehouse and a battlemented wall to spice up the facade. And perhaps the most forceful image of the declining importance of the medieval castle is provided by **Cefnllys**, where the constable Ieuan ap Philip chose to reside in an undefended timber hall, and built it for prestige beside the crumbling walls of the old fortress.

However, the situation in other parts of Britain was very different to Wales. In the northern counties of England, raiders from the independent kingdom of Scotland remained an ever-present danger for years to come. In this border region a distinctive type of fortified dwelling appeared, consisting of a suite of rooms stacked up vertically in the form of a tower. Called tower houses, these miniature keeps offered a flexible and cheap alternative for those not of the castle-owning class. There was a basement store (usually vaulted in stone to safeguard against fire), several upper floors of cramped living quarters, and a battlemented wall-walk from where the

A typical Scottish tower house (Clackmannan near Stirling)

inhabitants could mount some defence against a small-scale attack. All the different levels were connected by spiral stairs within a projecting turret, and there was usually another turret for the essential privies. This basic layout was subject to a surprising variety of design, with additional rooms and chambers housed in jutting wings that could result in some very odd-looking buildings. The tower house sometimes stood alone, but was more often associated with a walled courtyard containing ancillary buildings.

For homeowners further down the social scale, then the sort of protection they might expect would be a stone-walled farmhouse with a hall on the first floor, reached by a removable ladder. In northern England this type of simple defensible building is termed a *bastle*, though elsewhere it is usually known by the more flexible term 'stronghouse'. In the event of trouble all the occupants could do was round up their valuable livestock for safekeeping in the undercroft, retire to the passive security of the upper chamber, and sit things out. Such awkward and inconvenient dwellings were considered a necessary feature of everyday life in the north; and so too it would seem in parts of Wales, where a number of such buildings appeared for no very clear reason (see pp. 59–64).

A LINGERING END — THE CASTLE IN POST-REFORMATION TIMES

... in England there is no great reckoning made of castles and fortresses, for they do willingly let them go to ruin and instead thereof build them stately pleasant houses and palaces.

Sir Thomas Wilson (*The State of England*, 1600)

By the early years of the sixteenth century the stable, centralised government of the Tudor dynasty had ensured that there was no need for the aristocracy of southern England and Wales to rely on private armies and personal fortifications. King Henry VIII (r.1509–47) continued his father's policy of sweeping away over-mighty subjects and potential rivals to the throne with ruthless efficiency. The power and prerogatives of the Marcher lords was a particular source of concern to this formidable monarch, who saw the differences in law and language as a barrier to a realm united and at peace beneath the royal thumb. The Marches were considered to be a place of lawlessness and strife, where 'rude and ignorant People have made Distinction and Diversity between the King's Subjects … [and] whereby great Discord, Variance, Debate, Division, Murmur and Sedition hath grown'.

And so, between 1536 and 1543, Parliament passed a series of laws that are today commonly known as the Acts of Union. Wales was united with England and divided up for administrative purposes into 13 English-style shires, an arrangement that survived almost to the present day. The country could now be represented in Parliament and the people had the same rights as all the king's subjects. Some 60 years later the Pembrokeshire historian George Owen rhapsodised over the 'happy reforming' of the Government, and the passing of 'sweet and wholesome laws'; 'I find ourselves now in far better estate than any other part', he wrote. But many would not have found the situation so rosy; anyone representing Wales in Parliament had to speak English and that language (alien to most) was mandatory in the Welsh law courts.

The process of administrative unification and cultural marginalisation has roots back in the thirteenth century, when King Edward I created a number of shires out of the Principality lands seized from Llywelyn. The patchwork quilt of Marcher lordships still remained, even though their very purpose had been undermined by the conquest of native Wales; but ownership was increasingly held by a smaller number of aristocratic families, who were often little more than absentee landlords with more valuable estates elsewhere. Consequently, many of their castles lost their strategic purpose and were left to decay. When the duke of Lancaster ascended the throne as King Henry IV in 1399, all his Marcher possessions passed into Crown ownership. The same thing happened when the Yorkist heir of the

Mortimer dynasty, Edward, earl of March, became King Edward IV in 1461. The lordship of Ruthin passed into royal hands in 1508 to pay off the debts incurred by its owner. But now, at a stroke of a quill, Henry VIII brought the reign of the Marcher lords to an end. Most of the old lordships were amalgamated into the new Welsh shires, while the remaining pieces went to swell the county boundaries of Gloucestershire, Herefordshire and Shropshire.

The relatively peaceful conditions enjoyed by most were in marked contrast to the Continent, where warfare was endemic, and fortifications remained an essential aspect of life for a long time to come. Sir John Meldrum observed that 'France, Italy and the Low Countries have found by experience during these three hundred years what losses are entailed by places being fortified, while the subjects of the Isle of Britain, through absence thereof, have lived in more tranquillity' (Meldrum was doubtless reminiscing over happier days when he penned those words in 1644, for at the time Britain was being torn apart by civil war, and he was to be killed in action the following year).

The widespread use of gunpowder drastically reduced the efficiency of the medieval castle in warfare, and to beat the enemy it was necessary to adapt and improve. Facing the threat of a French invasion in the 1530s, Henry VIII ordered the construction of up-to-date artillery forts at key positions along the south coast of England. Good examples can be seen at Deal (Kent), Camber (Sussex), Southsea (Hampshire) and Falmouth (Cornwall). A more modest fort was built to guard the mouth of the Milford Haven waterway against enemy shipping, but unfortunately, coastal erosion has reduced this sole Welsh example to a precarious fragment on the cliff top. The initial design of Henry's forts was clearly influenced by earlier castle architecture, for they resembled dumpy, round keeps with concentric outer bastions, even being

Cannons (such as this restored Tudor example at Mount Orgueil, Jersey) were now the deciding factors in siege warfare

Example of a Henrican fort (St Mawes, Cornwall)

provided with water-filled moats, portcullises and murder holes – but by necessity the walls were massively thick to support the heavy cannons and withstand the impact of incoming shot. Within a generation or so, such faux-medievalism was replaced by startlingly different designs. Long and low earthen ramparts were built in straight sections to create spacious enclosures to geometrically precise plans. Any vulnerable corners were capped by arrowhead-shaped bastions allowing gunners to provide enfilade firepower along the walls and keep practically every line of attack in sight.

Most of the old castles proved too cumbersome and costly to maintain, and those that had outlived their purpose and could not be adapted for residential use, were left to decay. Strongly mortared walls could last undamaged for many years, but once the slates or lead sheets were stripped from the roofs, then rain and damp would quickly crumble the interior plasterwork and rot the beams and floorboards. Within a few generations a more or less intact building could be reduced by natural decay to a gutted shell. Add to this, stone-robbing for building materials, or even deliberate demolition, then a once mighty stronghold could disappear completely within a relatively short period of time.

The accelerating redundancy of the castle during the Tudor period finds a surprising parallel in the present-day decline in church and chapel. Few would say that religion now has the same place in society and daily life that it had just 60 years ago, and the dwindling congregations would have seemed unthinkable at the start of the twentieth century. Yet the end result of centuries of ecclesiastical construction is a surplus of buildings when the original need for such establishments wanes. The upkeep proves too much of a strain on local communities and empty buildings are sold off and converted into houses, offices or workshops. Although responsibility for castles rested with the Crown and individual owners rather than parishioners, there was still the same basic problem of what to do with an unwieldy building once it has become redundant.

The best picture we have of the state of castles at the close of the Middle Ages comes from the work of one man, the antiquarian John Leland, who was born in London sometime around 1503, of Lancastrian descent. Leland was fortunate to receive a good education at Cambridge and Oxford, he was a scholar of Latin and Greek and gained a privileged position as tutor to the son of the duke of Norfolk, one of the most influential men at Henry VIII's court. After returning from studies in Paris in 1528, he secured the patronage of the king's ambitious minister Thomas Cromwell, received various ecclesiastical benefices, and used his literary skill to pen flattering verses in praise of Anne Boleyn. In 1533 the king rewarded Leland with 'a most gracious commission' to record the historical documents and books that were held in the monastic houses of England. This was on the eve of Henry's religious reforms, and most of the books ended up in the royal collection when the abbeys were closed down a few years later.

As the 'King's Antiquary' Leland now began to pursue an interest in topography and history, and between 1536 and 1543 he travelled through a country wracked by the upheavals of the Reformation. He inspected any building or monument that drew his attention, and his observations are frequently quoted in the following pages (although the quaintly archaic spellings have been modernised for the benefit of the modern-day reader). The results of these epic treks were outlined in a long letter presented to Henry around 1544, in which the antiquary boasted that he had travelled all around the country, 'sparing neither labour nor cost' and in so doing noted a 'whole world of things very memorable'. Modesty was never part of Leland's nature, and a contemporary historian

A 1772 engraving of a bust of John Leland, the King's Antiquary

noted that he was 'a vainglorious person who would promise more than he could ever deliver'. Sadly, this proved to be true: in 1547 (soon after the death of his royal master) Leland suffered a nervous breakdown and spent his remaining years confined to his brother's care. He died, still insane, in 1552. His extensive library was dispersed, and his copious manuscripts ended up in the Bodleian Library at Oxford where they were collated and published in nine volumes as 'The Itinerary of John Leland the Antiquary' in 1710.

The exact sequence and dates of Leland's visits are not known for certain, but it is thought that he had undertaken several excursions through Wales and the Marches before 1540. Given the distances involved and number of places visited, it is inevitable that Leland's notes tend to be on the lean side, and it is not always possible to interpret the condition of a building from his sparse comments. His descriptions of **Cefnllys** and **Richards Castle** are comparatively detailed, but more often his observations are restricted to a few throwaway comments such as: 'all in ruin, no big thing but high' (Castell Coch); 'a part of it yet stands' (St Fagans) or the completely unhelpful 'a little pretty pile' (Narberth). In a few cases he seems to have relied on second-hand information and missed out some places altogether; but despite the brevity of his notes the overall picture that emerges is of a countryside filled with ruined or decaying castles. Of particular interest is his description of the broken towers of Elmeley castle on Bredon Hill, where he 'saw carts carrying stone thence to amend Pershore bridge about 11 miles off'. This was a clear case of recycling building materials, a fate that was to increasingly befall many abandoned castles in the future.

Leland noted a small number occupied in a residential capacity, patched up and altered as needs dictated. Carew had not long before been 'repaired or magnificently rebuilt by Sir Rhys ap Thomas' (d.1525) and Newcastle Emlyn had been spruced up by the same Tudor magnate. The medieval buildings at Cardiff, Chepstow, Chirk, Holt and Powis Castle were still occupied at the time, and a few other castles lingered on as administrative centres or local prisons. At **Caus**, **Llangybi** and Montgomery, grand new houses were built within the old walls, and where it was not possible to 'make do and mend', then wholesale reconstruction was carried out. Oxwich Castle on the Gower peninsula had been the seat of the Penres and Mansel families from at least the fourteenth century, but was completely rebuilt as a lavish mansion more suited to the complexities of life in Tudor times. An equally ambitious scheme was undertaken by the Morgans at **Pencoed**, although here at least a bit more of the old fortress was retained. Similarly, at **Hay-on-Wye** parts of the medieval castle were retained to add a bit of antique respectability to the imposing Jacobean mansion that still overlooks the marketplace today.

Thirteenth-century Powis Castle near Welshpool, which was transformed by the Herbert family into a palatial residence in Elizabethan times

THE CASTLE TAMED

Many of the grand new houses that appeared during the Tudor and Elizabethan ages had their roots in the not-too-distant past, when the towers and gatehouses that had once served a purely military need were used instead as architectural embellishments, proudly recalling the feudal ancestry of the homeowner. Cresswell Castle in Pembrokeshire is a typical example of this fashion and could have been a contender for inclusion in this book were it not for the fact that it was a castle in name only and had no defensive capabilities whatsoever. This overgrown ruin on the banks of the Cleddau river consists of domestic buildings ranged around a courtyard, with each corner capped by a tiny round tower, variously serving as a staircase, dovecot or privy. The river frontage was originally left open to benefit from the view and accessibility to river traffic, but at a later date was filled in by a substantial domestic block. Cresswell was built by the enterprising Roger Barlow (d.1553), one of the self-made men who benefited from the break-up of the vast monastic estates at the Reformation, and invested their wealth in stone and mortar.

An altogether more ambitious design, but still adopting the same basic idea, was built in 1608 for Lord Bindon at Lulworth (Dorset). It was just a square-plan house, but was dressed up as an idealised castle with four great round towers on the corners. Lulworth may well have been the inspiration for the almost identical design of Ruperra near Caerphilly, begun in 1626 for Sir Thomas Morgan (d.1642). The battlements, though, are a later embellishment replacing what was originally a gabled roofline. However, unlike the carefully restored facade of Lulworth, Ruperra is in a dreadful state of ruin, though a Trust has been set up to try and preserve what remains. Another somewhat similar design, though with square towers rather than round, was adopted at Plas Teg near Mold in 1610, which fortunately is still intact.

These grand edifices stand at the zenith of the mock-medieval building style that flowered during the Elizabethan and Jacobean periods, and was not to be repeated on such a scale until the appearance of the fake castles of the Victorian age. Smaller houses, such as **Stapleton**, Tregate Castle and **Urishay**, sat on top of earlier mottes either because they were

Lulworth Castle, Dorset, is a typically grand Elizabethan mansion that clearly derives its appearance from medieval castle architecture

A reconstruction of Stapleton Castle, Herefordshire, as it might have appeared in the seventeenth century. By then all that remained of the medieval fortress were the enclosing walls

the culmination of years of occupation and rebuilding, or else were purposely placed there because the builders wanted to emphasise their status and noble ancestry. They might just have easily been built in more convenient situations, rather than squeezed onto a lofty mound, but it seems that for some home-owners it was location that mattered most.

Another near-contemporary of John Leland was Rice Merrick (*c*.1520–87) of Cotterell in the Vale of Glamorgan. His manuscript collection *Morganiae Archaiographia* was compiled around 1578–84 and provides a wealth of information on the customs, genealogy, history and society of Glamorgan at that period. A similar survey was undertaken of late-Elizabethan Pembrokeshire by George Owen of Henllys (*c*.1552–1613), a member of the local aristocracy. Owen wrote that 'all the buildings of the ancient castles were of lime and stone, very strong and substantially built, such as our masons of this age cannot do the like; for although all or most of the castles are ruinated and remain uncovered, some for diverse hundred years past, yet are all the walls firm and strong and nothing impaired'

(*The Description of Pembrokeshire*, 1603). Owen listed 19 castles in his survey, but of these only three were still inhabited at the time.[9] Nevertheless, the inherent strength of the medieval masonry enabled many castles to survive substantially intact, as Owen had noted. Mighty Pembroke may have been a roofless shell, but it was still strong enough to play a major role just 40 years later in the wars between king and Parliament.

Visual rather than verbal depictions of castles and historic buildings are very rare in this early period, but John Speed's *Theatre of the Empire of Great Britain* (1611) provides a valuable resource for the appearance of the main towns of Jacobean Britain. Speed's county maps and bird's-eye views can be used by historians to build up a picture of the pre-industrial townscape of Wales. The drawings of the major castles may be heavily stylised and lack any reliable detail, but they are still useful in depicting buildings that have since disappeared, such as the round keeps within the courtyards of Cardigan and Monmouth castles, and the Shire Hall at Cardiff.

REVIVAL AND DESTRUCTION

I have taken to acquaint your Lordships with what, in my apprehension, I conceive may be both dangerous and unprofitable to this state, which is to keep up forts and garrisons which may rather foment than finish a war.

Sir John Meldrum (report to Parliament, 1644)

The slow decline of the castles into venerable old age was hastened by the social and political upheavals of the seventeenth century. King Charles I (1625–49), like his father James before him, had never been on good terms with Parliament and believed in the divine right of the monarch to rule unopposed. By 1642 the worsening relationship had spiralled out of control. Skirmishes between opposing supporters of the king and Parliament led to a major confrontation in October at Edgehill (Warwickshire), and the country was plunged into nine intermittent years of civil war. At first many of the Welsh aristocracy placed a greater value on their lives and estates rather than the rights and wrongs of the opposing forces, and tried to stay out of harm's way; but it proved impossible to avoid taking sides as the war progressed. Lacking the Puritan fervour of the English, the people of Wales by and large supported the king's cause.

In order to maintain control over strategic areas various buildings were pressed into use as military strongpoints, often changing hands as the fortunes of war ebbed and flowed. The old castles were the most obvious contenders for use and over 40 were sufficiently intact to play a role in the conflict. However, many large houses and churches were also utilised – even the shell of Abbey Cwmhir (gutted at the Reformation a century earlier) was put to use. Although lacking the precision that contemporary military engineers strove for, the old castles did have the advantage of robust construction. Thick walls could hamper the worse onslaught of artillery and the profusion of arrow slits could be adapted for use with muskets. The defences might be greatly enhanced by the addition of earthen ramparts and angular bastions, to serve as gun emplacements and help deaden the impact of missiles. At Aberlleiniog on Anglesey, the Royalist Sir Thomas Bulkeley of Beaumaris (d.1659) used a large castle mound that had been built over 550 years earlier as the foundation for a new artillery fort to defend the Menai Strait. The square stone enclosure on the summit has round towers on the corners and looks far more like a medieval castle than the geometrical earthworks generally used during the conflict.

Few sieges were as long drawn-out as they had been in medieval times and the threat of artillery bombardment was often enough to make the garrison lose heart. The siege of Laugharne in 1644 lasted about five days, with the Parliamentarian forces changing their artillery positions twice before the town was entered. Once it was realised that the end was inevitable, the defenders arranged a truce and agreed to surrender the castle peaceably, so they were allowed to march away and join another garrison nearby. Such chivalrous behaviour happened on many occasions, but there were also times when the rules of war were taken to the bitterest extreme and no quarter was given. When Hopton fell in 1644, the defeated garrison were reputedly all slaughtered; the only kindness being shown to an old servant who was given a chair to sit in while having his throat cut.

After several years of indecisive fighting, the Royalists forces suffered a major defeat in June 1645 at Naseby (Northamptonshire), which marked the turning point of the war. A few isolated pockets of resistance held out for two more years, but the surrender of Harlech in 1647 brought the fighting in Wales to an end. Charles sought refuge with the Scots but was handed over to the Parliamentarians and placed under house arrest. Even so, he persisted by duplicitous means to regain power with Scottish aid. A Royalist resurgence in 1648 (known as the Second Civil War) was sparked by uprisings in south Wales, Essex and Kent, and provided the more radical members of the government with sufficient reason to abolish the monarchy and put the king on trial. Charles was condemned as a 'tyrant, traitor, murderer and public enemy to the good people of this nation' and was executed early the following year. Cromwell's armies did not bring about a cessation of hostilities until 1651, but in the meantime, Parliament gave orders for certain key fortifications to be *slighted* (disabled) to prevent them being used again as strongholds of resistance against the State. Along with the Dissolution of the Monasteries, this government-sponsored demolition job ranks as the greatest act of architectural vandalism ever suffered by this country.

The extent of punitive slighting varied considerably from castle to castle. Carpenters, masons and miners would be employed to hack away and undermine the walls, and any stubborn part of the fabric would be helped on its way down with gunpowder. In some cases, it was enough to breach the gate or knock off a few battlements; at other sites complete and savage destruction was the order of the day. Parliament was particularly ruthless to those castles that had proved hard to take or where the garrison had put up a stubborn and bloody resistance. Corfe Castle in Dorset was bravely defended by Lady Mary Bankes (d.1661) for almost two months before capitulating. The besieging army took their dented pride out on the castle itself (one of the oldest and mightiest in England) and blew it to pieces. Aberystwyth castle was one of King Edward I's great fortresses and once stood as proud and imposing as Harlech; but it too, was shattered into fragments.

However, not all the castles ruined in this period can necessarily be ascribed to state-sanctioned ruin. There is no record of anything being done to Caerphilly, **Penrice** or **Llangybi** for instance, and yet these buildings show clear signs of deliberate demolition. Recent excavations at the latter have revealed a backfill of shattered stonework within the stunted towers. It cannot be said with certainty whether that was done as a precautionary measure to deny the use of the strongholds to the opposition, or the result of punitive demolition carried out after the castles had been captured.

Less uncertainty remains with other key sites utilised in the conflict. Montgomery castle was subjected to a well-documented slighting carried out between June and October 1649, a task that required 180 labourers and cost £675 (a substantial sum in those days). Thanks to the thoroughness of the workforce the large mansion of the Herbert family that stood within the walls has completely disappeared. Similarly, the Marquis of Worcester's palace at Raglan was reduced to a shattered ghost of faded splendour. A later account of the destruction mentions the lead being stripped from the roofs, the great tower tediously picked apart from the top (before being undermined by a collapsible tunnel) and the deforestation of the parklands. Even the fishponds were drained, enabling the hungry locals to make off with the carp.

A few lucky castles managed to escape the general wreck: Beaumaris and Caernarfon were slated for demolition, but the order was fortunately never carried out. Picton was spared, so the story goes, because the Parliamentarian commander felt guilty about the dishonourable way it had been taken (a nursemaid incautiously leant out of the window to take a message from a passing soldier, and the baby was snatched from her arms and used to bargain for the surrender of the castle).

The demolition of fortifications was to a certain extent an economic measure as well as a practical one, for the government was saved the cost of garrisoning them in future. The process continued even after Cromwell's Puritan reign ended in dismal failure. Chirk was partially slighted in 1659 when the owner, Sir Thomas Myddleton (1586–1666), supported a premature rising in favour of the exiled heir to the throne. Denbigh was slighted in March 1660 just two months before the king's return, and the main buildings at Conwy were unroofed in 1665. Once the damage had been done, the shattered castles were subjected to a further round of depredations over succeeding years. The sudden abundance of useable materials was a boon for builders – why pay for stone to be carted from a distant quarry when there might be plenty to hand? Bits of castle found their way into local houses just as the despoiled monasteries had been recycled 100 years earlier.

ROMANTIC RUINS

The evening sun was gilding the whole place with wonderful brilliancy, and as I looked at the old towers gleaming in it, and the wooded banks and the shining river … the scene very much resembled an evening on the Rhine.

William Makepeace Thackeray on Chepstow castle (*Cockney Travels*, 1842)

When antiquarians looked again at the architectural heritage of the countryside following the Restoration of the Monarchy in 1660, the condition of many historic ruins had changed drastically since Leland's day. A survey as ambitious as his *Itinerary* was undertaken in the closing years of the seventeenth century by the Keeper of the Ashmolean Museum in Oxford, a Welshman by the name of Edward Lhuyd (1660–1709), or Llwyd, according to modern spelling. Llwyd's results were as wide-ranging as Leland's, but differed significantly in the approach to fieldwork. While Leland did most of the legwork himself, Llwyd used local correspondents to provide information on the antiquities in their neighbourhood. Questionnaires were sent out to informants in every county in Wales. A few were never returned, others came back with the barest details, while some provided a veritable treasure trove of antiquarian knowledge.

Only a few hardy travellers dared to brave the vagaries of the road network during the seventeenth century. In 1684 Thomas Dineley accompanied the duke of Beaufort on a tour of his estates in Wales, describing the places they stopped at and accompanied by a few simple illustrations of the main places of interest. The Dutchman Johannes Kip (1653–1722) specialised in engravings of country mansions, and William Dugdale (1605–86) produced illustrations of antiquities to accompany his published works.

However, it was not until the middle of the eighteenth century that a more concerted effort was made to depict historic ruins with pictures, rather than words. From about 1711 until 1753, the Yorkshire brothers Samuel and Nathaniel Buck specialised in providing detailed copperplate engravings of the most important and outstanding ruined buildings in England and Wales. Their work not only indicates the condition of the castles and abbeys at that point in time, but also provides us with valuable information on those places that have since deteriorated further, or have disappeared altogether. The etchings can hardly be considered works of art, and they have about as much realism as a stage set (criticisms often levelled at their work), yet they are an invaluable source for the local historian. It would be unwise to study the architecture and history of a particular castle without recourse to their meticulous drawings.

THE SOUTH VIEW OF NEWPORT-CASTLE, IN THE COUNTY OF PEMBROKE.

Many of the castles depicted by the Bucks were shown as romantic ruins, as here at Newport in Pembrokeshire

The Bucks relied upon advance subscriptions from wealthy landowners who wished their ancestral relics to be depicted for posterity. Samuel (who was the main creative force behind the venture) and his younger brother Nathaniel, would tour a selection of ruins in a particular part of the country during the summer months, making drawings with pencil, pen or wash. The sketches were then worked up into detailed copperplate engravings at their London studio during the winter. They brought out a series of Welsh antiquities between 1739 and 1742, and their complete collection of etchings depicting the 'Venerable Remains of above Four Hundred Castles, Monasteries, Palaces etc' was published in 1774. An accompanying portrait depicts two well-to-do periwigged figures, Samuel looking rather portly and not as energetic as he must have been on his earlier travels. According to the blurb they were employed for over 32 years on this huge task, snatching 'from the inexorable Jaws of Time, the Mouldering Ruins of each lofty Pile'. Their achievement would not be surpassed until the advent of the camera.

The Buck engravings bring us about halfway from Leland's time to our own, through the long years of neglect and military depredations. By the second half of the eighteenth century the improving road system in Wales made it easier for people of means and leisure to explore the countryside. The Romantic movement flourished as artists and writers went in search of the wild and sublime landscape to eulogise on paper and canvas. Literary potboilers inspired a revival of medieval architectural styles and the ruined castle became something of a fashionable asset for any large country seat. Those estates lacking a genuine ruin, often made do with a gothic folly tower or 'viewstopper' to grace their lawns, and in a short time the style migrated from the garden to the house itself, resulting in the grand castellated mansions that proliferated throughout the reign of Victoria.

The growth of the railway network in the first half of the nineteenth century allowed access to almost all areas of the countryside, leading to a wider appreciation of genuine architectural and historical remains. Amateur archaeologists and land-owners dug away at local antiquities with ample enthusiasm and varying degrees of scientific thoroughness. Compared to today's exacting methods their work often bordered on vandalism. Articles and reports on various historic buildings appeared in the pages of learned journals such as *Archaeologia Cambrensis,* which was founded by the Cambrian Archaeological Association in 1846 and is still going strong. So too are other publications, such as *The Archaeological Journal* (which first appeared in 1844), and more localised works including the *Journal of the Chester Archaeological Society* (since 1850), *Transactions of the Woolhope Naturalists' Field Club* (from 1866), and the *Transactions of the Shropshire Archaeological Society* (from 1878).

In 1882 the Ancient Monuments Protection Act was passed, giving statutory protection to our national heritage; but even as late as the First World War sites were excavated with shockingly cavalier attitudes, simply by stripping away large areas of rubble to uncover as much of the walls as possible, with little consideration given towards the preservation of the exposed remains. Thus, **Llangynwyd** and **Morgraig**, both dug in the first decade of the twentieth century, are still surrounded by the rubble and collapsed stonework left behind when the archaeologists moved on to greener pastures.

The Royal Commission on Ancient and Historical Monuments in Wales (hereafter referred to by the acronym RCAHMW) was established in 1908 to record and survey the built heritage of the country. At its headquarters in Aberystwyth the RCAHMW maintains the National Monument Record, a vast repository of information relating to archaeological and historical sites in the country. The records are available to view on the Coflein website. The Royal Commission on the Historical Monuments of England (RCHME) was founded later in the same year, and its National Monuments Record (now known as Historic England Archive) is housed in Swindon. The responsibility for conserving and promoting the heritage of Britain lay with the Department of the Environment (formerly the Ministry of Works). Then, in 1983, the government's National Heritage Act created three new departments: Historic Scotland, Cadw: Welsh Historic Monuments, and English Heritage (which absorbed the RCHME in 1999 and became Historic England in 2015). These organisations have the responsibility for preserving, running and maintaining historic sites that are accessible to the public, as well as providing advice and grant aid for the restoration of buildings in private care.

Virtually all of the historic castles have been granted the status of Scheduled Monuments, which puts them under statutory protection, and no works can be carried out on them without prior consent. Paradoxically there is no mechanism to safeguard their condition and the landowner is not legally responsible for their preservation and upkeep. However, grants are available for their conservation. A Scheduled Monument could, in effect, be left to fall down of its own accord should the authorities not step in and carry out essential repairs at their own cost. On the other hand, Listed Buildings (which are often still inhabited) can be restored or modified within certain parameters by the owners, and grant aid is available to help with the cost. As Cadw's former chief inspector Richard Avent pointed out, 'owners who may be willing to apply for grants to keep a historic roof over their heads are generally far less altruistic when it comes to parting with money to prop up a ruin at the end of the garden or at some remote location on the estate. Often these structures are regarded as nuisances, a protected hazard which they would rather be without'.[10]

Prior to the introduction of the Ancient Monuments Act, any restoration work carried out on historic buildings in private ownership was down to the enthusiasm and financial benevolence of the landowner. In 1844 the duke of Beaufort commissioned George Grant Francis (1814–82), a founder-member of the Cambrian Archaeological Association, to provide detailed drawings of Oystermouth Castle near Swansea as a prelude to a course of restoration work. Francis skilfully reconstructed the delicate traceried windows that now form such a conspicuous feature of the castle. The Second earl of Cawdor patched up the ruinous walls of Carreg Cennen in the 1870s, while around a decade later, the antiquarian Joseph Richard Cobb (1821–97) leased Manorbier and Pembroke castles, and bought Caldicot in 1885 as a family home. He carried out repairs to the fabric of all three (particularly the latter, which was extensively rebuilt by Cobb and his descendants). However, officials expressed disparaging views about his work, since it involved replacing large sections of old materials with new and (where details were missing) the substitution of inaccurate and cheap replacements, resulting in 'a most inharmonious and offensive piece of patchwork'. Cobb took umbrage at this harsh criticism and defended his actions in a letter to the Cambrian Archaeological Association. He subsequently stated that he would never 'remove an ancient stone, except to put a similar sound one in its place' and 'never to add anything without evidence that it had existed before'.[11]

The official approach has long been to 'preserve as found' rather than to 'restore', but such cautious sentiments did not extend to the castle-owning aristocracy. Perhaps fortunately, Britain possesses far fewer reconstructed ruins than Continental Europe. The keep at Dolwyddelan was a ragged shell until the splendidly named Lord Willoughby de Eresby completely rebuilt it in 1848; but even that is a very modest example of what could have been done by someone with vast wealth and unstoppable enthusiasm – and such a person was John Patrick Crichton-Stuart, the Third Marquis of Bute (1847–1900). In the 1870s he commissioned the slightly eccentric architect William Burges

Romantic Victoriana: Castell Coch by William Burges

(1827–81) to transform Cardiff Castle and Castell Coch into idealised Gothic strongholds. Whatever their picturesque merits, the two buildings have far more to do with romantic Victoriana than genuine medieval building styles.

In total contrast, his son the Fourth Marquis of Bute (1881–1947) undertook a very lengthy and generally accurate restoration of Caerphilly, rebuilding the towers, walls and battlements that had been lost for hundreds of years. Even the houses and cottages that had grown up around the ruins were swept away as part of an ambitious restoration scheme costing £100,000 and lasting from 1928 until the outbreak of the Second World War. The vast moats, that now form such an impressive feature of the castle, were not dug out and reflooded until the 1950s. At Caerphilly, the intention was to preserve the castle as a medieval relic rather than resurrect it as a fairy-tale mansion; but even so, the work went far beyond what was considered acceptable at the time. Yet few can now deny that, in the case of Caerphilly at least, the end justified the means.

As this book reveals, there are many substantial, ruined castles not looked after by Cadw, Historic England, the National Trust, or suchlike organisations. The proprietor of an ancient monument may want Cadw to take their ancestral relic into Guardianship (thereby making the State responsible for maintenance, whilst retaining ownership of the property), but the offer is not always taken up. Many sites are too fragmentary or considered too historically insignificant to justify the financial outlay of restoration and the burden of ongoing maintenance.

Preservation work is a very expensive and time-consuming process. Any potential disturbance to sensitive archaeological layers in the ground must be thoroughly investigated; crumbling walls have to be stripped of vegetation and carefully repaired with suitable materials; stairs and walkways may need to be built to allow access to parts of the site; and any necessary modern buildings must be designed to complement the ancient fabric and cause as little disruption to the historic environment as possible. The archaeological excavation and masonry consolidation of Laugharne in Carmarthenshire lasted over 20 years and, although actual figures are not available, the cost seems to have been in the region of £3 million. The more modestly sized Oystermouth underwent a £1 million phase of restoration in 2011, including the addition of a rather incongruous glazed walkway to allow the public to access the upper floor of the chapel tower. Even the consolidation of the little tower house at **Candleston** in 2007–8 cost approximately £60,000.

The story is not all doom and gloom though, and had this book been written just 30 years ago then several more major castles would have been included. Ancient Dinefwr, capitol of the Welsh rulers of Deheubarth, was only then in the process of being cleared from centuries of undergrowth and transformed from a little understood and mythologized ruin in a private park. Llywelyn's castle at Dolforwyn was being uncovered for the first time by archaeologists. The imposing ruin of Llanbleddian near Cowbridge was taken over by Cadw only after a protracted legal battle with the owner, before the process of making the remains safe and accessible to the public could begin. Historic England acquired the Mortimer stronghold of Wigmore in 1996 and spent almost £1 million in preserving the overgrown and deteriorating fabric. Similarly, the crumbling tower of Hopton was purchased by a Preservation Trust in 2006 and finally reopened to the public in 2011, after essential work costing over £1 million; and in the Golden Valley near Hereford, ongoing excavation and tree clearance is revealing more of the unexpectedly large Marcher fortress of **Snodhill**.

The extensive ruins of Snodhill have recently been subject to conservation work and, at the time of writing, ongoing excavations are revealing more of the buried structure

The increasing threat to historic sites by modern developments was addressed back in the 1970s by creating four independent Archaeological Trusts to cover the then-current administrative divisions of Wales (Clwyd-Powys, Dyfed, Glamorgan-Gwent and Gwynedd). The Trusts carry out rescue excavations, watching briefs and risk assessments in advance of proposed building works. Although it would be impossible now to excavate a castle with the same carefree attitude as in the past, the damage caused by vandalism or off-road vehicles, and the unauthorised use of metal detectors, can be just as detrimental. Archaeological sites in rural locations may escape the worse depredations, but in urban areas the threat of redevelopment is far greater. Sully Castle was wiped off the map in the 1970s; Rumney Castle near Cardiff was built over in the 1980s; Maesglas in Newport is now an insignificant lump in the middle of a children's playground; Rhoose Castle went after 1910 and Aberafan way back in 1895.

Historic England maintains a *Heritage at Risk Register* which, as its name implies, is a list of 'buildings, places of worship, monuments, parks and gardens, conservation areas, battlefields and wreck sites that are listed and have been assessed and found to be at risk'. The annual list is accessible on the Historic England website and shows all the buildings and structures that are deemed to be vulnerable to severe decay or damage, and includes several sites described in detail in the following pages. Other sites, such as **Clifford** and **Snodhill**, have recently been taken off the list following essential conservation work. For Wales, Cadw has published *Managing Listed Buildings at Risk* (available on the Cadw website), outlining the various procedures and responsibilities that define 'the critical relationship between a building's use, ownership and condition, and how the careful balance between these elements can be managed to ensure a sustainable future'.

As population levels rise and increasing pressure is put on the utilisation of greenfield sites, more will undoubtedly go. While preservation orders and Listed status may save the actual fabric of a building, its unique position within the surrounding landscape will have been changed forever. Certainly, in the case of smaller buildings, this often happens: many old farms or manor houses that once stood in rural isolation have ended up in the middle of a housing estate, as the modern world impinges on their location. This prompts the question, how much can be lost before a historic building ceases to have any historical significance at all, other than its very fabric? Is there any worth in preserving an old building that is totally out of place with the environment that it once formed part of; or, worse still, when only a facade is preserved and everything beyond the front door is a wholly modern structure?

One might also ask how a structure as grand and imposing as a medieval castle, an image that figures so prominently in the national consciousness, could disappear from the landscape. But for those castles that lack the grandeur and substance of say, Caernarfon, Harlech or Pembroke (and do not enjoy the level of care expended upon them), then the answer is very simple.

EPILOGUE

And so, what can be done with these 'forgotten' castles?

Many of the sites looked at in the following pages, such as Castell Dinas, Caus, Cefnllys, Huntington, Mellte Castle, Morlais and Plas Baglan, are so remote and covered in debris and soil that the best thing to do would be to leave them alone, unless erosion or unexpected damage necessitates remedial work. Some minor consolidation may be necessary to preserve the few upstanding remains of Kenfig and Morlais (the south keep was capped in concrete some years ago to preserve the vault beneath). Soil erosion is undermining the flaky walls of Aberedw and Castell Pen-yr-allt, and the potential task of conservation work is hampered by the presence of mature trees. In fact, tree-growth is a major problem facing any restoration scheme: Castell Meredydd, Cas Troggy, Llancillo, Llanfair Discoed, Llangybi and Morgraig are six notable sites where tree roots are buckling the stonework far more effectively than any medieval siege machine (though admittedly at a much slower pace). It is not enough just to strip the ivy away and cut down the trees, for the damage caused by the root growth has to be repaired and any unsound masonry taken down and replaced. This could result in quite major restoration work, and in the case of Dinas Powys proved to be the undoing of a well-intentioned local group that had attempted to conserve the ruin in the 1980s.

Excavation would be highly desirable to clarify the structural development of several key sites, and to ascertain how much of the fabric still remains intact below ground. Cas Troggy, Cefnllys, Llanfair Discoed, Newhouse and Painscastle are good candidates for exploratory work, and re-excavation of Llanhilleth with modern techniques would gather more precise information than that unearthed by the 1924 dig. Minor excavations (the archaeological equivalent of keyhole surgery) have been carried out at Castell Bryn Amlwg in the 1960s, and more recently at Llangybi by Channel 4's *Time Team*. In 2020 Cadw started a long-term programme of excavation and conservation at the privately-owned site of Blaenllynfi.

Excavations by *Time Team* at Llangybi in 2009

In the following pages, some 65 'forgotten castles' have been selected for inclusion, and the entries have been arranged into six geographical areas. The comparatively small number of entries in north-east and west Wales is not due to a lack of castles in those areas, simply that there are fewer sites that meet the criteria for inclusion in this book. A further 11 castles that were omitted for various reasons from the main section, make brief appearances in the appendix for the sake of completeness. All place-name spellings have been taken from current editions of the Ordnance Survey (OS) maps, and each entry is provided with location and access information (which, to the best of my knowledge, was correct at the time of writing). It should be noted that most of the sites described here are on private land and there is no automatic right of public access. Permission to visit should therefore be sought from the landowner and, in all circumstances, please remember the Countryside Code (see www.gov.uk for details). For anyone requiring additional information on a particular site, then the abbreviated references can be used in conjunction with the bibliography at the back of the book. Further details may also be obtained from the Historic Environment Records (HER) of the four Welsh Archaeological Trusts and from the online database (Coflein) of the RCAHMW.

OPPOSITE: The Old Rectory at Angle, one of the best-preserved tower houses in Wales

1 WEST WALES

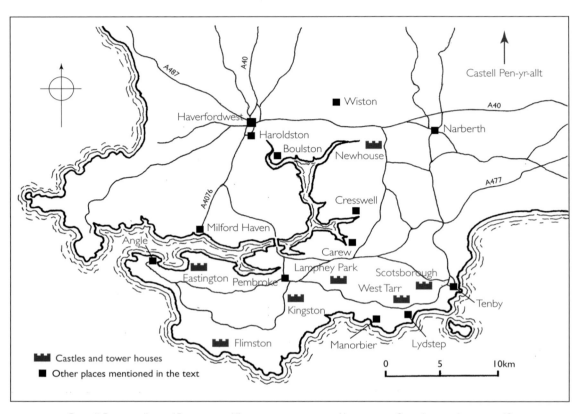

Castell Pen-yr-allt

Wiston

A40

Haverfordwest   Narberth
Haroldston
        Boulston   A477
                 Newhouse

                 Cresswell

Milford Haven

Angle   Carew
Eastington   Pembroke   Lamphey Park   Scotsborough
                                 West Tarr
                Kingston   Tenby

        Flimston   Manorbier   Lydstep

■■■ Castles and tower houses   0   5   10km
■ Other places mentioned in the text

1

West Wales

The fortified houses of Pembrokeshire

Tower houses, stronghouses and *pele* (or peel) towers, are terms used to describe the smaller fortifications that proliferated in the unsettled regions of northern England, Scotland and Ireland between the fourteenth and seventeenth centuries. In a relatively lawless society plagued with endemic infighting, cattle raiding and piracy, anyone who could afford it sought to protect their lives and belongings behind securely locked doors. The classic form of tower house resembles a scaled-down keep, invariably containing a basement store and several floors of cramped living quarters stacked up above. For those nearer the lower end of the social scale the only affordable protection might typically be a stone-walled farmhouse where the residential hall was on the first floor above a vaulted undercroft, and accessed only by a movable ladder.

Although these buildings form a major part of the architectural heritage of northern Britain, there is a far from insignificant number to be found in Wales, and the greatest concentration is in south Pembrokeshire. Why they should be needed at all is something of a mystery, for there is no evidence to suggest that the same level of unrest existed here as in Scotland, or that Pembrokeshire was subject to greater discord than other areas of Wales in the later medieval period. In fact, this part of the country was controlled by the Anglo-Norman settlers from an early date. After several raids on the old Welsh territories of Deheubarth and Penfro, the Normans undertook a more permanent settlement in 1093. Penfro was split into the Marcher lordships of Pembroke and Haverford, and controlled from a series of major castles. King Henry I even introduced Flemish settlers to the region in order to strengthen the takeover through ethnic colonisation, and the ultimate success of this move can be gauged by the many English sounding place-names that survive to this day.

Pembrokeshire retains some of the most architecturally and chronologically diverse castles in the country, ranging from the primary timber forts to early-Norman keeps, massive fortresses of the Edwardian period and defensible houses of the Tudor age. Most of the major castles are accessible to the public, and a few have been restored as residences and are still occupied. However, being far less notable than their larger kin, the tower houses have not fared so well. Only two sites – Carswell and Angle (see below) – have been taken into official care and have had preservation work carried out so that public access is possible. The others remain as overgrown ruins or patched-up buildings in agricultural use.

The question that still remains unanswered, is why there was a need for these towers at all. One possibility is that they were built as precautionary measures against the threat of piracy, for the exposed coastline of Pembrokeshire and the navigable waterway of Milford Haven offered many opportunities for a seaborne enemy to get far inland. Owain Glyndŵr's French mercenaries landed in the Haven in 1405 and 80 years later Henry Tudor's invading army used the same route. The towers may also have had some relevance as status symbols among the local landowners, much in the same way that many manor houses in lowland areas of Britain were surrounded with water-filled moats of negligible defensive strength. Another reason may simply be the result of local building traditions. Pembrokeshire did not have an abundance of good trees for carpenters to create the timber-framed halls in which most people lived during the medieval period. The 'black-and-white' houses that form such a conspicuous feature of the Marches (and were once far more widespread across the country) are absent from the western regions of Wales, where building in local stone was the norm.

The historian George Owen noted in 1603 how 'most castles and houses of any account were built with vaults very strongly and substantially wrought'. And so, if a house has a hall set above a vaulted and fireproof ground-floor storeroom, then there is already some element of defence otherwise lacking in a single-storey timber house. If that upper chamber is accessed only by an external wooden stair or ladder (which could be hauled up inside during an emergency), then the defensive aspect is further increased. Clearly, such a building could never withstand a major assault for long, but it would be very useful in deterring a raiding party or an opportunistic gang of robbers.

Carswell near Tenby is just such a building. Barely 6m square inside, this little house of tower-like proportions contains a vaulted ground-floor kitchen with a separately accessed living room on the floor above, both chambers heated by fireplaces set into a typically massive Pembrokeshire chimney. Only a few metres away there is another vaulted building of similar proportions to the first, although this has undergone considerable alterations. The main house has been preserved by Cadw and so is freely accessible, but just a kilometre away at **West Tarr Farm** is another group of buildings in a far poorer state of repair. The main house contains vaulted chambers on both floors and originally had an external doorway providing access to the first-floor room. After the building was abandoned as a dwelling, the entrance was blocked off and a more convenient doorway was knocked through the fireplace on the uphill side. The West Tarr tower is rather unusual for it seems to have formed part of a larger building that now survives only as a fragmentary ruin alongside. The ground floor undercroft extended well beyond the tower and was accessed by a mural stair from the upper chamber. The relationship between the two buildings might be made clearer by removing the undergrowth and carrying

One of the two diminutive towers at West Tarr Farm

out small-scale excavations. In 1326 West Tarr and Carswell farmsteads were held from the earl of Pembroke and valued at a meagre one tenth of a knight's fee each, although the existing buildings do not appear to be that old.

Another tiny tower stands in the courtyard of **Kingston Farm** near Pembroke, which has a main first-floor chamber above the vaulted basement, measuring barely 3m by 4m. The external appearance has been greatly modified by the removal of the chimney stack, and also by having a doorway knocked through the fireplace on the ground floor. This Listed building has been downgraded from domestic use and is now part of an agricultural range.

These dwellings appear so pathetically small on their own that it must be suspected they were once part of a larger complex, and were served by other buildings close by that have not survived. They have been likened to the 'ten-pound towers' of Ireland, modest little fortified dwellings that landowners were encouraged to build for their own protection in 1429 with the aid of a £10 royal grant.[1] The towers were to measure 6m by 4.8m and stand

Reconstruction of Kingston Farm

at least 12m high, dimensions that tally with the Pembrokeshire houses. Whether these examples actually belong to the fifteenth century is less certain, for they have almost no dateable features, and excavations at Carswell produced finds no earlier than the sixteenth century. Kingston has a window hood that would not be incompatible with a Tudor date. Anyone wishing to explore these curious little houses in further detail, should visit the National Museum of History at St Fagans, where one discovered in a back street of Haverfordwest has been reconstructed and furnished as a merchant's house of the 1580s.

On the Castlemartin peninsula beyond Pembroke there are a number of early farmsteads that were abandoned when the army requisitioned the area as a military training ground in 1938. The most obvious of these is the rambling wreck of **Flimston,** which can be seen from the churchyard when the road to Stack Rocks is open on non-firing days. It may look like a roofless Victorian farmstead, but embedded within the main range is a late-medieval hall with a vaulted cross-wing at one end, clearly distinguished by a prominent round chimney (an architectural feature common in this region). An external doorway seems to have been the original access way into this first-floor chamber. Here at Flimston the tower-like structure is integral with the house, and not free-standing as at Carswell and Kingston.

The extensive ruins of Flimston, incorporating a late medieval hall with cross-wing

Scotsborough near Tenby incorporates a similar defensible wing in its layout, although this is clearly an addition to the older, undefended house. This large mansion of the Perrot family is now in a very fragmentary state and heavily overgrown, but the most substantial surviving part is a rectangular vaulted building with a projecting turret (probably for a garderobe). The first-floor chamber has a fireplace with the usual round chimney, but the tiny loopholes are quite unexpected for a domestic chamber and point to some defensive purpose. Evidently, this wing was a bolt-hole into which the occupants might retreat in case of emergency. There are many more ruined houses all across this region, which incorporate vaulted structures in their make-up, and Boulston, Haroldston, Lydstep, Minwear and Penally are notable examples for the enthusiast armed with an OS map to track down.

One question already touched upon is whether these houses were intentionally planned with defensive needs in mind, or were simply the by-product of the layout and materials favoured by the builders. It may not be possible to give an answer to that when considering the likes of Flimston or Scotsborough, but there are other buildings in Pembrokeshire that employ architectural features derived from castles to create more obviously fortified dwellings. The best example is the Old Rectory at Angle (see chapter frontispiece), a tiny keep-like tower containing four cramped rooms and sporting a drawbridge, winding stair and machicolated battlements. The tower stood at one corner of a square, moated enclosure fed by the tidal reaches of the Haven. This castle-in-miniature is in the care of the Pembrokeshire Coast National Park and can be visited at reasonable times.

The well-maintained fabric of the Old Rectory only serves to highlight the poor state of many other neglected historic buildings, and a particularly sad example is the Listed tower at **Upper Lamphey Park** near Pembroke. It is still in private

The remnants of the tower at Upper Lamphey Park, with surviving winder stairs within

ownership, and no work has been carried out to preserve the crumbling walls since it was identified in 1994. However, it lies close to the medieval palace of the Bishops of St Davids (which is in the care of Cadw). It is doubtful whether any passer-by would recognise this dilapidated structure as a historic building at all, so great have been the changes inflicted upon it – and that may be the reason it took so long to be discovered. It was much more substantial in earlier years, and even appears as a background detail in the Buck brothers' 1740 engraving of the palace. This shows something that looks like a little church with a central tower and adjoining wings. Only the tower still stands today, though it has been incorporated into an agricultural range and has lost its battlements. A stair turret and a corbelled chimney stack are among the few details that reveal this ruin to have a much more complex architectural history than first appearances would suggest. There are also blocked doorways and stone corbels that indicate that a near-contemporary building (presumably a hall) stood against the upper end of the tower. It may have been built as a hunting lodge for the bishops of St Davids, who would have been able to gaze out from the battlements across the parklands stretching around their sumptuous palace in the valley below.

Location & access

Scotsborough lies 1 km west of Tenby off the B4318 to St Florence. A signposted public footpath starts where the road crosses the Ritec marshes (OS map reference SN 117 011). To reach West Tarr, return towards Tenby, take the A4139 to Penally, then turn off to St Florence along the Ritec valley. After 3.5 km there is a sharp right turn (which leads to Carswell) but continue on, and where the road dips into a little valley the Tarr towers can be glimpsed through the trees on the right (no public access) SN 089 009. Upper Lamphey lies 1 km north-east of Lamphey village on the A4139 to Pembroke. Pass the turning to the Bishop's Palace and after crossing a little bridge there is a narrow lane (a public footpath) signposted to Lower Lamphey Park. The tower is near the top of the hill on the right-hand side (SN 026 014). Kingston Farm lies south-east of Pembroke town centre off the A4139 and along Grove Hill Road. After about 2 km there is a layby and a fork in the road, the turning leading down to the farm (there is no public right of way) SR 994 994. Flimston lies on the way to Stack Rocks off the B4319 Pembroke to Castlemartin road. Vehicular access is limited to non-firing days and the ruin is strictly off-limits to the public (SR 924 957).

References

Smith (1988); AW (1990); Austin (1994); Davis (2001)

CASTELL PEN-YR-ALLT, *CARDIGAN*

This is a very innocuous looking site when seen from afar: just a circular earthwork marked by a horseshoe of mature trees. However, a closer examination reveals that this was a substantial little stone castle defended by massive ditches and square towers. Ongoing erosion is revealing heaps of buried stonework under the rampart, constructed from poor quality slate quarried on site and bonded with clay, rather than mortar. This cheap and easy building method is one of the reasons why so little remains of Castell Pen-yr-allt today; another is that in 1950 the landowner deliberately flattened a section of the rampart. What survives is now slowly crumbling away, and in desperate need of some archaeological care and attention.

The innocuous and fast-deteriorating remains of Castell Pen-yr-allt, Cardigan

The site consists of a roughly hexagonal walled enclosure, between 40m and 44m across, surrounded by a rampart and a rock-cut ditch. There was an additional outer bank on the northern side facing the likely direction of attack, and the southern quadrant was protected by steep natural slopes, further enhanced by quarrying. On the western side of the rampart, erosion has revealed a series of wall faces that indicate there was a rectangular stone building set against the curtain wall, with an adjoining square flanking tower. It can be conjectured that the missing rampart was provided with further towers and a simple gateway giving access into the castle. Within the courtyard a grassy mound marks the remains of a collapsed stone tower, presumably of circular plan, though only excavation would confirm this. The presence of the mound has led to the classification of Pen-yr-allt as a motte-and-bailey; but it is clearly not, and is more accurately described as a ringwork. It has also been suggested – not unreasonably – that it is a reused Iron

Age fort (there are several in the locality), but again that would only be proven by excavation. Another question that needs to be answered is whether it started life as a timber castle and was only later refortified in stone, or whether it was stone-built from the start – the latter would be quite feasible given the amount of material that would have been produced as the ditch was dug.

The castle has no documented history, but it lay within the Marcher lordship of Cemais in northern Pembrokeshire, which had been established by Robert Fitzmartin in 1108 as part of a campaign to annexe native lands in West Wales. There had already been Norman incursions in this area, and a major castle at nearby Cardigan had been established 15 years earlier. Robert set up his headquarters at the ancient ecclesiastical centre of Nevern, some 8 km away, where his castle has undergone extensive excavation and is now accessible to the public. In fact, the two sites share many similarities and their history must be closely entwined.

Pen-yr-allt was among a dozen or so minor castles established either by Robert Fitzmartin, or his sub-tenants, to strengthen the Anglo-Norman grip on Cemais. The presence of a small church nearby may indicate that there was an attempt to establish something less fleeting than a military outpost; but if a village was planned, the scheme certainly didn't succeed and there is only a single farm here, while the redundant Victorian church has recently been converted into a private house. In 1165 the region fell under the control of the Lord Rhys when he captured the neighbouring strongholds of Cardigan and Cilgerran. After reaching an accord with King Henry II, the Welsh prince was obliged to return some conquered lands, and so Cemais passed back to Robert's heir, William Fitzmartin (who, incidentally, had an arranged marriage with Rhys' daughter). In 1176 Rhys rebuilt Cardigan in stone according to the *Brut y Tywysogion*, and the remains excavated at Nevern are likely to be near-contemporary work of William, or possibly Rhys himself. The buildings had slate walls bonded with clay to make cheap but fairly durable structures, and included several rectangular towers and a round keep. The same materials have been discovered at other sites nearby, including Cardigan and Cilgerran, and point to a local building technique favoured in the late twelfth century. The refortification of Pen-yr-allt may therefore have taken place around this time.

Gerald of Wales must have passed the castle on his way from Nevern to Cardigan in 1188, but makes no mention of it – so perhaps it had not been built by that time, or else it wasn't deemed noteworthy enough to be included in his travelogue. The following year Rhys renewed hostilities against his Anglo-Norman neighbours and in 1191 he captured Nevern. Four years later it was deliberately destroyed by the retreating Welsh. When the dust of battle had subsided, William Fitzmartin chose not to rebuild Nevern, but establish a new base further along the coast at Newport (see p. 269). The fate of Pen-y-allt in all these troubles is unknown; it too may have been abandoned, or alternatively was retained as a modest outpost to guard the border of Cemais and the road north to Cardigan.

Location & access
Castell Pen-yr-allt lies on the edge of a wooded field behind Llantood farm, 4 km south-west of Cardigan and just off the A487 road to Fishguard (OS map ref: SS 157 421). Note that this site is not shown on the map on p.58. There is no right of way, but the site can be glimpsed from the public footpath that passes the church and farmyard and descends into to Cwm Ffrwd.

References
RCAHMW (1925); Davis (2000)

EASTINGTON, *RHOSCROWTHER*

Eastington Manor lies on the Milford Haven waterway beyond the near-deserted village of Rhoscrowther, an idyllic setting marred by the chimneys and tanks of an enormous oil refinery on the hillside nearby. The most obvious part of the site is an eighteenth-century mansion, but tucked on to the far end is the rugged stone shell of a medieval tower house. Eastington has a near-identical plan to Scotsborough mentioned above (and it was also built by the same family) but with one very important difference – the entire roof is surrounded with a battlemented parapet offering a more aggressive mode of defence. The ground floor is a gloomy vaulted room used for storage, with the principal residential chamber on the upper level. This is now reached by a large, external stone staircase, which is evidently an addition and possibly replaced a more easily defendable ladder-stair. The first-floor hall was a large and well-appointed chamber by medieval standards, and was provided with a fireplace, dressed stone windows and a garderobe in a small projecting turret. Unfortunately, the original roof has not survived, and the timbers are modern replacements. There are also marks of an attic floor and a blocked doorway beside the fireplace, although these features are probably alterations carried out when Eastington was refurbished in the eighteenth century. Beside the entrance a mural stairway leads up to the battlements, where an additional turret provided any observer with good views across the bay.

Cutaway reconstruction of Eastington Manor

Outside, the tower bears the very obvious scars of a demolished single-storey range. Experts still debate as to whether this was an addition or part of the original layout. The marks of the roofline and the stubby fragments of lateral walls are deeply embedded in the stonework, and two of the first-floor windows are shifted to the side, as if to purposely avoid the high roof. These details strongly suggest that Eastington was planned and built as a hall-and-tower combination, such as can be seen at a number of other late-medieval sites (such as Candleston in Glamorgan, p. 83). The long-destroyed Bonville's Court near Saundersfoot was a very similar building, as the drawings of Edward Lowry Barnwell indicate. Barnwell (1813–87) was a retired schoolteacher and antiquarian, and carried out a detailed survey of the old houses of Pembrokeshire in the 1860s. Of Eastington he wrote that the 'modern' house (i.e. the missing hall) had been removed a short time before his visit, so he does not include it in the drawing. Apart from the tower itself there are ruinous outbuildings, courtyards and walled gardens, so the whole site must have been far grander and extensive than it appears today.

The manor is associated with the Perrot family, a widespread and important local dynasty who were here from the at least the fourteenth century until the sixteenth century. The hall and tower would certainly have been built during their tenure, although the lack of any firm documentary evidence makes it impossible to pinpoint the date or the builder. Barnwell thought the tower could be early-fourteenth century on account of the surviving window detail, while the more recent 'Pevsner' guide suggests a date towards the end of the century. After the Per-

Eastington Manor as it stands today, missing the single-storey range

rots departed, Eastington was briefly held by the Philipps family of Picton Castle and in 1670 it was assessed for tax as a house of five hearths. As there is now only one fireplace in the tower the others must have been in the lost hall, or perhaps in adjoining buildings that have since disappeared.

Around the middle of the eighteenth century the Meares family were in occupation, and they improved the accommodation by adding the mansion to the upper end of the tower. Yet as early as 1769 a prospective purchaser wrote that the buildings were in a parlous state with leaking roofs and rotten timberwork. Repairs were carried out, but 40 years later the manor was again reported to be in decay, and by 1842 (when the estate was bought by John Mirehouse, who also owned nearby Angle) the house was deemed fit only to be let out to tenants. In the intervening years the Meares wing has been restored and is still occupied, but the tower is an echoing shell and some of the outbuildings and the adjoining walled gardens are now in a poor state of repair.

Location & access

Rhoscrowther village lies 6 km west of Pembroke off the B4320 road to Angle. A signposted turning off the road leads past the refinery to the little village. Beside the single row of houses there is a private track which heads down towards the sea where Eastington Manor house lies (OS map ref: SM 001 024). No public access, although the exterior can be seen from the road.

References

AC (1867–68); Smith (1988); Jones (1996); Pevsner (2004)

NEWHOUSE, *NARBERTH*

This neglected and poorly understood site lies deep in a tangled forest on the upper reaches of the Cleddau river, which in medieval times was a hunting preserve belonging to the Marcher lordship of Narberth. It has been suggested that the manor of Newhouse was established here by the Canaston family in the late thirteenth century, but more likely it originated as a hunting lodge belonging to the Mortimers of Wigmore, who had held the lordship of Narberth since 1247. The Mortimers were one of the major landowning dynasties in the Welsh Marches, and will often be encountered in later pages of this book. There is a document of 1623 that refers back to a dispute between Roger Mortimer III (d.1282) and Thomas Bek (bishop of St Davids 1280–93), in which the manor of *Newehous* is mentioned. More contemporary references are recorded in 1326 (where it appears as *Newhous*) and again in 1357 (as *Novadomus*). These names clearly imply that it was a fairly new foundation and not a relic of the original Anglo-Norman settlement of Pembroke. Lordship records from the 1360s also name the various *reeves* responsible for the day-to-day running of the manor.[2] By 1609 it had acquired a second title – *alias Red Castle*, and on John Speed's 1611 map of Pembrokeshire it is shown as Redcastle. Today it is usually known as Castell Coch, but this is considered to be a very late Welsh adaptation of the original English name.

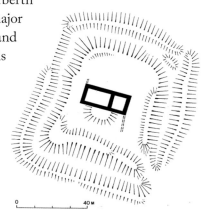

Site plan of Newhouse

The site lies on the edge of a stream valley a short distance away from the ruins of the old parish church, and comprises a rectangular platform surrounded with a ditch and an outer rampart. In the middle of the platform is a two-storey hall block, the only visible masonry still surviving above the dense undergrowth. Newhouse has been classed as a moated site or stronghouse, but these names are inaccurate and serve only to belittle its defensive capabilities. This was a substantial little fortification. The rock-cut ditches are over 4m deep and were never the shallow water-filled features normally associated with moated sites of manorial status. Around the edge of the platform is a rubble bank, apparently the remains of a demolished curtain wall, and a mound at the south-west corner could be the site of a flanking tower. A gatehouse probably occupied the opposite corner, but this side has been obscured by a later causeway built to provide easy access across the ditch.

A cutaway reconstruction of the hall block at Newhouse

The hall block remains largely intact apart from the missing battlements and east gable wall, but all the internal timberwork and partitions have decayed away. The ground floor was occupied by a long chamber entered from the courtyard through an arched door secured by two drawbars (the slots for holding the sliding timbers can still be seen). This level was lit only by small loopholes and was probably used for storage. Along the side walls are rows of square holes that once held the massive timbers supporting the first-floor hall. In one corner of the room there is a destroyed newel stair that rose to the hall and then on up to the wall-walk.

The main entrance to the first-floor hall was on the courtyard front and would have been reached by a timber stair (as suggested in the reconstruction drawing). However, this door lacks a drawbar or any other security features and so may be

Internal and external views of Newhouse today

a later insertion. There are other architectural oddities here too: there is no sign of an original fireplace and so the only way the room could have been heated was by a central hearth set on a stone pillar rising from the basement. This method of supporting a potentially hazardous fireplace on a wooden floor has been noted at a number of castles, and points towards an early date for the building.[3] There is no sign of any dressed stonework, and the windows may have been just basic unglazed openings. Even the smallest windows – which no one could ever have squeezed through – are fitted with drawbars for security. The doorways in the rear (north) wall are also puzzling because they lead nowhere. They also have drawbars and so were intended to be closed against anyone trying to break in, but it is not clear why the occupants should need *two* back doors. Perhaps they led into garderobe turrets at the back of the hall. In fact, the hall block may have undergone far more modifications than first appearances suggest, and clearance of the ivy followed by a detailed study of the stonework might clarify the building's development.

This is a much larger and more substantial structure than the Pembrokeshire tower houses and defensible dwellings previously noted, and significantly it lacks a vaulted undercroft. Another similar building survives at the Bishop's Palace at Lamphey, which has a rather forbidding appearance for an ecclesiastical residence and was probably built in the period 1260–80. It shares the beamed floor, battlemented parapet and projecting latrine turrets of Newhouse, but benefits from a wall fireplace and finely carved stone doors and windows. There are no dateable features remaining at Newhouse today, but the simple layout coupled with the lack of fireplaces and dressed stonework suggests it cannot be later than 1300.

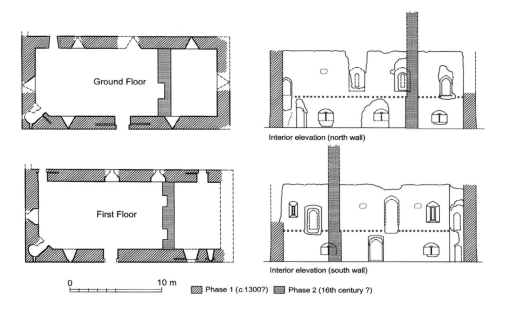

Ground Floor

First Floor

Interior elevation (north wall)

Interior elevation (south wall)

0   10 m

▨ Phase 1 (c.1300?)   ▨ Phase 2 (16th century ?)

Plans and elevations of Newhouse, which show the position of the later wall inserted probably in the mid 1500s when the castle was transformed into a more convenient residence

The basic arrangement of the medieval hall proved quite inadequate for the needs of later owners, and a cross-wall with multiple fireplaces was inserted into the hall, thereby reducing the length of the building by a third and dividing the interior up into smaller heated apartments on three floors. It appears that the eastern third was abandoned from this time on. Again, there is no direct evidence to date these changes, but they were probably carried out by the Barlows of Slebech, who acquired the manor around 1546. This powerful and acquisitive family hailed from East Anglia and made their mark on the locality during the reign of Henry VIII. William (d.1568) pursued an ecclesiastical life during the Protestant Reformation, becoming in turn bishop of St Asaph, St Davids and Chichester. His brother Roger (d.1553) led a far more adventurous existence as a seafarer, exploring the westerly trade routes and accompanying Sebastian Cabot on a voyage to the New World in 1526 (he is claimed to have been the first Englishman to set foot in Argentina). Along with his brother John, Roger Barlow purchased many of the former monastic lands in Pembrokeshire and established a branch of the family at Slebech just across the river.

Newhouse was leased out to another member of the Barlow family in 1657, but is thought to have been abandoned as a dwelling about 20 years later and gradually fell into ruin. Clearly the fortified hall formed only part of the site, for there is a fishpond, a walled garden and a little square moat (too small to have served a domestic purpose, but possibly for a dovecot or some other ornamental feature) – all now practically inaccessible in the dense undergrowth. To fully understand Newhouse, it will be necessary to strip away the weeds and bushes, undertake small-scale excavations to confirm what other buildings lie buried here, and carry out essential conservation work to preserve the upstanding fabric.

Location & access

Newhouse stands 4 km west of Narberth off the A4075 road from Canaston Bridge roundabout to Oakwood Leisure park. The ruin lies in private woodland bordering the Bluestone Holiday Village (OS map ref: SN 072 136). There is no public access at present, although footpaths do cross through Canaston Wood on the opposite side of the stream, offering a distant glimpse of the ruin.

References

AC (1868, 1922); DAT; Charles; Pevsner (2004)

OPPOSITE: The remarkable survival of the rib-vault in the basement of the south keep of Morlais Castle

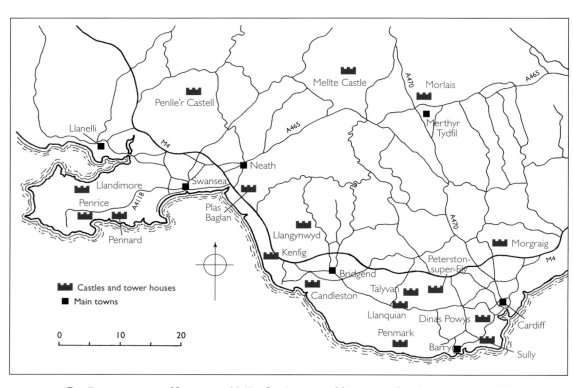

2

GLAMORGAN

Castles of the Vale

G LAMORGAN retains the largest number of castles in all the historic counties
of Wales (latest estimates stand at about 81 confirmed medieval sites) and
is furthermore blessed with an abundance of surviving medieval documents, collated by the Victorian engineer and historian G.T. Clark (1809–85). In addition,
the antiquarian gleanings of Rice Merrick (c.1520–87) provide a detailed picture
of Glamorgan in Elizabethan times. Merrick chronicled the Norman invasion
of the county and his account, wonderfully romantic and hopelessly inaccurate
though it is, still colours our view of the period. The story goes that the last Welsh
king of Morgannwg, Iestyn ap Gwrgant (d.c.1093), asked the Normans for help in
defeating a rival in battle, but once the conflict was over and Iestyn was victorious,
the mercenaries decided to stay on, ousted him, and divided his kingdom amongst
themselves. The 12 knights who had followed Robert Fitzhamon (d.1107) on this
escapade founded dynasties that still existed in Merrick's time.[1]

In reality, the Norman conquest of Morgannwg was a slower, more piecemeal
affair. The county is geographically split into two main regions: a low-lying coastal
plain (the *Bro*) extending from Cardiff to Port Talbot, and a larger, sparsely inhabited upland region of moors and deep winding valleys (the *Blaenau*). The Normans
were only interested in holding onto *Bro Morgannwg* for, as Merrick notes, the
Vale 'was always renowned as well for the fertility of the soil, and abundance of all
things serving to the necessity or pleasure of man, as also for the temperature and
wholesomeness of the air'. The first castle is believed to have been established at
Cardiff in 1081 by William the Conqueror, while on royal progress through south
Wales to meet with Rhys ap Tewdwr of Deheubarth. When Rhys was killed in
battle in 1093, the earl of Gloucester, Robert Fitzhamon, moved swiftly to secure
the prized lowland territory and create the new Norman lordship of Glamorgan
controlled from Cardiff. Robert of Gloucester (d.1147), illegitimate son of King

Henry I, acquired the lordship in 1113 through his marriage to Fitzhamon's daughter and oversaw further conquests as far west as the River Neath.

Once the defensive network of castles had been established through the Vale of Glamorgan, the growth of settlements was encouraged and villages with distinctly un-Welsh names sprang into existence (such as Bonvilston, Cosmeston, Cowbridge, Flemingston and Gileston). Monastic houses at Ewenny, Margam and Neath were also founded. The castles that kept this rich area firmly under Anglo-Norman control display a whole range of architectural styles from the earliest earthwork mounds through to state-of-the-art concentric fortresses and finally diminutive tower houses and defended farmsteads. Even after the feudal age had long passed, some castles remained in use and were adapted to the more sophisticated needs of aristocratic society, including Fonmon, Llandough, St Donats and St Fagans. While most of the major sites are looked after by Cadw, there exist many lesser-known castles that qualify for a place in this book. Four are looked at here, and the history of the Vale in medieval times is further touched upon in subsequent pages.

Pride of place among the forgotten castles of the Vale must be given to **Penmark**, the head of one of the largest and richest lordships in Glamorgan. Penmark was granted by Fitzhamon to Gilbert de Umfraville who appears to have built a ringwork on the edge of an escarpment, with a large outer bailey sweeping around to protect the more vulnerable southern flank, and enclosing as much as three acres of land along with the church. Natural erosion and deliberate infilling have now reduced

The rounded corner tower (left) and garderobe block added to the west wall at Penmark Castle

these formidable earthworks to a few insignificant hummocks. At some point the timber defences of the ringwork were replaced with a thick masonry wall of angular plan apparently lacking in flanking towers, and therefore probably of early date. In the thirteenth century a rounded tower and garderobe block were added to the west wall, and this is now the only upstanding part of the fabric. The overgrown masonry is in a poor state and show signs of recent collapse. A stony mound at the east end of the ward covers the remains of several rectangular buildings, but their plan and purpose will only be revealed by excavation. When the male line of the Umfravilles died out in the fourteenth century, Penmark was acquired by the St John family of nearby Fonmon, who appear to have neglected the castle in favour of their own ancestral stronghold. A small sketch of Penmark produced in 1622, suggests that the entrance was a simple gateway, and that there was a tower-like building within the courtyard, possibly a free-standing keep.

The very English sounding **Peterston-super-Ely** was home to the Le Sore family from the twelfth to the late fourteenth century. The name of Robert le Sore is mentioned in a document of *c.*1102 and he was probably granted this land, along with neighbouring St Fagans, by Fitzhamon. The story that Owain Glyndŵr captured the castle and beheaded Matthew le Sore is considered unlikely (even though his reputed skull was once displayed in the parish church), for the lordship had passed to the Butler family well before the rebellion started. By Leland's day the castle was 'all in ruin' and the most obvious relic is a chunk of masonry incorporated into a modern house beside the road. This seems to have formed part of a square tower on the north-west corner of the castle. A less obvious fragment of ivy-covered wall lies in the front lawn of the next house along, while in the rear garden there are traces of a thick-walled building (possibly a free-standing rectangular keep). These fragments are too slight to provide a convincing picture of the original appearance of Peterston castle. Jeston Homfray's charming 1828 lithograph shows that the remains have been fairly insignificant for a long time, although the village then comprised just a few thatched cottages beside the church. The large upstanding fragment of masonry shown in the foreground seems to have been part of the keep.

Homfray depicted **Talyvan** too, and this castle still retains the pastoral setting that Peterston has lost through urban growth. Unfortunately, the romantic image he presents of a hilltop fortress with gaping windows, no longer holds true, for in the intervening years the walls have fallen and the whole site is engulfed by trees. The castle was built by the St Quintin family who held this and the neighbouring Llanbleddian lordships from the beginning of the twelfth century. In 1233 John St Quintin was ousted from Talyvan by the adventurous knight Richard Siward (d.1248), who had joined forces with the rebel barons opposed to the policies of

Remains of early walling at Talyvan Castle (left),
and Jeston Homfray's lithograph of Talyvan (above)

Henry III. When peace was restored and the insurgents had crept back into royal favour, Richard should have returned the lordship, but instead held onto it, making the castle a favoured residence and seat for further exploits. The St Quintins had to make do with replacement lands in England. Siward may have been responsible for adding a large round keep in the fashionable style of the period, and replacing the ringwork palisade with a curtain wall, all of which is now very fragmentary.

Richard Siward did not enjoy his new-found privileges for long. In 1245 he was hauled before a court, accused of truce-breaking, murder and double-dealing with the Welsh. He was found guilty and outlawed. Siward was a far from innocent party in this affair, but there is also a strong hint of conspiracy among his powerful neighbours. He appealed to the king, but died before the case could be settled. Talyvan was seized by the ambitious earl of Gloucester, Richard de Clare (d.1262), who shortly afterwards established a new town at Cowbridge controlled from the older St Quintin stronghold of Llanbleddian.

Talyvan was no longer the centre of an independent lordship and declined in importance. By 1314 it was claimed to be worthless, but this must be an exaggeration since the castle was deemed a worthy target to attack in 1321 by rebels opposed to the hated and ambitious Hugh Despenser (d.1326), current incumbent of the lordship. Possibly it was repaired and continued to play a subsidiary role as a hunting lodge for an adjacent deer park, but by Leland's time it was 'in ruin'. Around 1700 a cottage was built up against the crumbling walls and the courtyard utilised as a garden and orchard. Many stones were said to have been taken away for building purposes in the nineteenth century, and the outer earthworks flattened by agricultural activity. Everything now lies in tangled ruin, and large-scale excavations would be needed to work out what actually stood on this hilltop.

Llanquian lies a few kilometres away from Talyvan and though small, is a particularly interesting site, for here can also be found traces of an abandoned church and settlement. The castle itself was a small ringwork set at the end of a ridge, not far from where the old Roman road crossed Stalling Down towards the town of Cowbridge. The earthworks are now very overgrown, but it is still possible to make out the foundations of a square masonry building on one side of the enclosure. The awkward way it aligns with the curving rampart strongly suggests it is an addi-

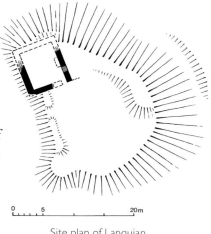

Site plan of Lanquian

tion, probably of the thirteenth century or later, though there are no distinguishing details left. The ground floor had a vaulted storeroom and the principal chamber was on the floor above. The plan and position suggest a keep-like structure, but the walls are far too thin to have had much defensive potential and so this is probably a very modest hall block. The surrounding rampart looks like an earthwork, but it probably conceals the remains of a stone wall. When the historian G.T. Clark was here in the 1870s more of the stonework seems to have survived, for he described

Reconstruction drawing of Llanquian

the castle as 'a shell of masonry, circular or nearly so, about 64 feet in diameter'. He observed a small projecting turret (perhaps for a garderobe, as suggested in the drawing) and considered that the hall-block was part of a gatehouse, although that seems less likely. A few early records link Llanquian to the Nerber family of Castleton, and the site is sometimes called Nerber Castle.

A few metres in front of the castle are the stony foundations of two medieval buildings and a boundary bank. These earthworks may be contemporary with the castle, or a later farmstead associated with a small settlement that existed here for many years. The ruinous outbuildings of the adjacent farm also incorporate what is thought to be the remains of a chapel dedicated to St James, which is mentioned in medieval documents.

This overview of the lesser-known castles of the Vale cannot conclude without a brief mention of several important sites that have now disappeared completely. John Leland saw the remains of towers at the hamlets of Wenvoe and Wrinstone. The Tudor farmhouses of St George and Castleton are built on the site of their medieval predecessors, possibly incorporating some vestiges in their thick walls. The vanished sites at Cadoxton, Cosmeston, Marcross and Rhoose may have been fortified manor houses rather than true castles. Perhaps the most regrettable loss was Marsh House at Aberthaw – not a castle at all, but a fortified warehouse dating from the early seventeenth century. The last remnant of this unique building was demolished in 1983.

Location & access
Penmark lies behind the church in the village just north of Cardiff Airport and sign-posted off the A4226 road to Llantwit Major (OS map ref: ST 058 689). There is no public access, but the remains can be seen from the churchyard. The remains at Peterstone too can be seen from the roadside and the village is signposted on a minor road accessed from either M4 Junction 34 or the A48 Cardiff to Cowbridge road (ST 084 764). Talyvan lies on private land 3.5 km north-east of Cowbridge, just off a minor road from Ysradowen to Welsh St Donats. A turning opposite Bwlch Gwyn Farm leads to the hilltop site (OS map ref: ST 021 772). Llanquian lies 2 km east of Cowbridge off the A48 by-pass. A public footpath starts from the service station and passes alongside Hollybush Farm and into the woods where the castle lies (ST 018 745).

References
Homfray (1828); AC (1872); all the castles of Glamorgan have been studied in great detail by RCAHMW (1991, 2000)

CANDLESTON CASTLE, *BRIDGEND*

Candleston lies in dense woodland on the edge of the Merthyr Mawr warren, a forlorn ruin almost overwhelmed by high dunes thrown up by changing climatic conditions in the later Middle Ages. Many coastal settlements in Glamorgan were obliterated by shifting sands (most famously the castle and town of Kenfig as described further on); but here at least the sand stopped short at the walls. Candleston is a fortified manor house rather than a true castle, and was intended to offer some security to the owners without the expense of major fortifications.

The tower house of Candleston Castle

When it was built in the early fourteenth century the creeping sands had yet to impact upon the area, and it stood on a low rocky headland overlooking fields and meadows rolling down to the sea. The Cantilupe family had been here from at least the thirteenth century, and the existing structure is thought to have been built by either Robert de Cantilupe (d.*c*.1320) or his grandson Nicholas, the last of his line. A facetted curtain wall was built around the tip of the headland to form a D-shaped enclosure, with a long range of domestic buildings set against the straight flank (see Figure **A** overleaf). Shortly after this first stage was completed, the small and compact tower house was built out from the hall to provide extra accommodation and give added protection to the adjacent gate (**B**). It had long been assumed that the tower was the original part of the castle, to which the other domestic buildings were added in less war-like times, but a survey by the RCAHMW proved, surprisingly, that it was the other way around. This tower contains a vaulted storeroom on the ground floor, with a residential chamber at first-floor level that connected with the adjacent hall. There was also a dark and basic attic room above. Each level is connected by straight stairs in the wall, which also provide access to the wall-walks.

Around 1500 the domestic range was considerably altered when the castle was in the ownership of Sir Mathew Cradock, an important figure in local events during the turbulent years of the late fifteenth century. The hall was reconstructed as a two-storey building with a large kitchen on the ground floor and a grand entrance lobby leading to the first-floor chamber (**C**). Enough dressed stonework survives to reveal that the work carried out was of exceptional quality. Another wing was added in the seventeenth century (**D**). At the beginning of the nineteenth century the building was thoroughly overhauled for Sir John Nicholl, who resided here in 1806–8 while his new house at nearby Merthyr Mawr was under construction. Fireplaces were added, windows enlarged, and a stable block was built against the tower. Candleston was subsequently occupied by tenant farmers and by 1900 it was

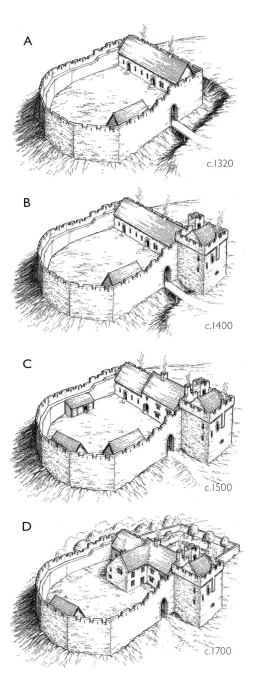

Stages in the development of Candleston, from its inception in the early 1300s down to 1700

derelict, though still had a roof. Thereafter it was left to fall into ruin and remained a vandalised shell behind barbed wire until Cadw undertook partial consolidation in 2008. The main structure has been cleaned up and made secure, but the curtain walls and outer buildings are still very overgrown. There is a very similar tower house just 3 km away at Tythegston Court, beside the A4196 to Porthcawl; however, this house has remained in occupation to the present day and has been modernised to such an extent that its exterior gives no hint of its medieval origins.

DINAS POWYS, *PENARTH*

Any description of Dinas Powys should start with untangling the myths that have grown up around this strange forgotten site, much like the weeds and brambles that now choke the towering walls. The castle was supposedly built by Iestyn ap Gwrgant, the last Welsh king of Morgannwg and was named in honour of his wife, a daughter of the ruler of Powys, hence its geographically inappropriate place-name ('citadel of Powys'). Iestyn's ill-advised alliance with the Normans led to his deposition and exile from the rich lands of the Vale, although, as previously recounted, the veracity of this Elizabethan history has long been discredited. What can be said with some certainty is that soon after Fitzhamon's invasion of Glamorgan in 1093 a lordship was established here and granted to one Roger de Somery. A castle was built on a naturally defensible ridge, and

Dinas Powys in 1986

at some stage in the twelfth century a rectangular keep was raised on the highest part of the site. Only a shapeless mound of rubble remains of this structure.

Adjoining the keep is an elongated enclosure with roughly-built walls constructed from limestone blocks hacked out of the adjacent slopes. The enclosure appears to be contemporary with the keep, since the scars of the bonding walls are clearly visible; however, the RCAHMW considers it to be a later addition and that the keep was partly rebuilt at the time. Since the remains are too ruinous to be sure at present, the argument will only be resolved by future excavation. The curtain wall has endured remarkably well and remains substantially intact, standing up to 6m high in places. There were two simple gateways on the south and east sides of the courtyard, protected by nothing other than wooden doors and drawbars. There must have been an outer ditch fronting the main gate at the south end, but it has been filled in; nor can anything be seen of a barbican noted by antiquarians. The buildings that once clustered the interior have vanished too, leaving only a few window openings and the scars of rooflines marked on the walls. The simple layout of the enclosure and feeble gateways suggest it was built before 1200 when more sophisticated castle designs began to appear.

The castle had an uneventful history apart from a brief siege (or an attempted one) in 1222, when the lord of Glamorgan took umbrage at the audacity of another Marcher lord occupying the castle during the minority of its rightful owner. Henry III had to intervene and order them to calm down and back off. There does not seem to have been any attempt to improve or upgrade the defences in subsequent years, but probably nothing was required. Dinas Powys was a relatively large castle for the time and offered ample accommodation for the owners, who in any case had estates elsewhere in England. When the last male de Somery died in 1321 the inheritance was split amongst the surviving heiresses. The castle was considered to be worthless in 1330 and was 'all in ruin' by Leland's time.

Neglect and undergrowth have left their mark and stone robbers have taken all the dressed blocks of limestone that graced its walls. Nevertheless, Dinas Powys is still a substantial structure and one of the most complete late twelfth-century masonry castles in Wales. The current state of neglect and indifference is shameful bearing in mind the extent of the remains and the close proximity to an urban centre. In 1981 a local charity acquired the site and undertook clearance work to transform it into a community amenity area. Unfortunately, work was halted when it became clear that the damage caused by the undergrowth would require costly and time-consuming specialist repairs. Public access was later stopped, and the site was subsequently sold. The vandalised fences no longer prevent unauthorised visits, but the impenetrable barrier of undergrowth is a sufficient deterrent at the present time.

Birds-eye view of Dinas Powys. The twelfth-century keep stands at the furthest and most secure point of the ridge. The appearance of the internal buildings is conjectural

Location & access

Dinas Powys is situated on a wooded hill just east of Dinas Powys village centre, 8 km south-west of Cardiff on the A4055 road to Barry (OS map ref: ST 154 716). There is no public access at present, although the overgrown ruins can be glimpsed through the trees in Lettons Way housing estate just off Mill Road.

References

RCAHMW (1991)

Kenfig Castle, *Pyle*

When John Leland travelled along the well-worn Roman road between Bridgend and Neath in the late-1530s, he saw 'a village on the east side of Kenfig, and a castle, both in ruins and almost choked and devoured with sands that the Severn Sea there cast up'. These besanded relics are still there today, more fragmentary perhaps and further obscured by the shifting dunes in the intervening 480-odd years since his day. Kenfig was not the only victim of climatic changes in the late Middle Ages, but it was the most notable – a fortified town and castle that had struggled for centuries against devastating Welsh raids, only to be overwhelmed by a creeping enemy no one could defeat.

A castle was established here in the early years of the twelfth century by Robert of Gloucester (d.1147) as part of a westward advance from the more securely held Norman territories in the Vale of Glamorgan. Kenfig was in an ideal position to control the main road and to guard the narrow coastal strip against Welsh raiders from the uplands. The first castle is thought to have been a ringwork positioned on the banks of the Cynffig river and would have been surrounded by deep ditches that could be flooded for added defence. The castle was located just upstream of an estuary where boats could dock and bring supplies even if the overland routes were under hostile control. The buildings and defences of the castle were built from wood, but in the centre of the courtyard stood a fine stone keep. This was a typically forbidding donjon of the period, with massively thick walls and pilaster buttresses on the outer facade, and contained a dark basement store with at least one upper living chamber. There would have been an external stairway to the first floor, and then another stair within the thick walls to give access to the upper levels and battlements. At a later date a garderobe turret was added to the rear of the tower. The keep was quite possibly part of the primary castle, rather than an addition as was so often the case. The earl built a far larger keep at Bristol, and a near-contemporary tower survives in a better state at Goodrich (Herefordshire), which would have closely resembled the one at Kenfig.

Earl Robert clearly intended Kenfig to be more than just a military foothold in a conquered territory, since he founded a settlement here as well. A document of *c.*1140 mentions a 'West Street' and a property 'outside the gate of the vill of Kenfig', and so a suburb had already sprung into existence by that time. The settlement lay to the south of the castle and was contained within an eight-acre enclosure protected by an earth rampart, wooden stockade and outer ditch. However, these defences failed to hold back the Welsh, and because the town was always in the forefront of an attack, it was razed to the ground on at least seven occasions between 1167 and 1316. The castle seems to have fared better (probably because the keep was so solidly built

A bird's-eye view of the town and castle of Kenfig as it might have looked around 1200

and could hold out longer). Even so, the wooden defences needed constant repair. There is a record of 24 ships bringing timber from Chepstow to make good the damage caused by an attack in 1185, and in 1232 the wooden defences are mentioned again. In fact, it is thought that the defences were not upgraded with masonry until after another attack as late as 1295. The ringwork palisade was replaced by a stone wall with a simple gatehouse, while one side of the keep had to be rebuilt, and its basement vaulted in stone. The leftover earth from the demolished rampart was used to level up the courtyard and bury the base of the keep, which later fooled antiquarians into thinking that the tower was standing on a motte.

The keep of Kenfig Castle today, semi-buried in sand dunes near the M4 motorway

The last recorded attack against Kenfig took place in 1321, but it was not angry Welshmen this time, rather a coalition of disaffected noblemen striking out at the greedy and unscrupulous Hugh Despenser, lord of Glamorgan and hated favourite of the pliable King Edward II. The rebels ransacked Hugh's castles across south Wales, specifically targeting the gates and doors to render them indefensible. The uprising was ultimately a failure; but although Despenser regained and repaired his castles (an extension to the outer gate may belong to this period) his downfall, along with that of his royal master, was not long delayed.

Thereafter, Kenfig was left in relative peace and continued to flourish. The town had long since grown beyond the cramped confines of the early defences and there was a suburb in the vicinity of St James's Church some 300m south of the castle. The dogged persistence of the townsfolk in the face of adversity was rewarded with the granting of borough status sometime in the fourteenth century, although the oldest surviving charter is dated 1397. Other documents list the privileges enjoyed by the residents, including the right to hold a fair twice a year, and to give any woman found guilty of spreading malicious gossip a turn in the ducking stool. The town had its own by-laws to ensure that each resident paved the road before their door, kept the High Street free of dirt, did not verbally abuse council members nor keep vagabonds or harlots in their homes. Like most medieval towns, Kenfig was divided up into a number of burgage plots, consisting of long narrow strips of land running back from the street with a house or shop at the front. The average number of burgages seems to have been around 144, and the population has been estimated at about 700 inhabitants.

An aerial view of Kenfig Burrows, showing the site of the castle (encircled)
and the outline of the town rampart (arrowed)

Kenfig was on track to becoming a major urban centre like the other nearby castle-towns of Bridgend, Neath and Swansea; however, by the end of the fourteenth century the number of occupied plots had dropped to 106. The Black Death probably contributed to this decline since towns nearest to ports were the worst affected by the plague, but the townsfolk would already have felt the first effects of the encroaching sands. Excavations carried out by the Kenfig Society in the 1990s revealed that the ploughed fields on the edge of the town had been periodically covered by blown sand as early as 1275. By 1316 a field known as *Conyger* (rabbit warren) had dropped in rental value due to inundation by the sea. Probably there had always been a thin strip of stable dunes along the shore, but a combination of strong Atlantic winds and tidal changes, caused more sand to be blown further inland. The townsfolk may even have made matters worse by cutting trees and allowing cattle to overgraze the meadows, thereby destroying the vegetation that had kept the dunes in check for so long.

A succession of bad storms during the fifteenth century caused widespread damage around the exposed coastline of Swansea Bay. At Kenfig the green meadows were replaced with an undulating waste of sand dunes, the estuary silted up and the river changed course. People drifted away to rebuild their lives on higher ground to the south and east, and in 1471 a new church at Pyle was completed using stones taken from the old church. The Elizabethan antiquarian Merrick described Kenfig as 'a borough town sometime of good account but long since decayed by overflowing of the sand'. He also repeated the old myth that the town was magically flooded overnight beneath the waters of nearby Kenfig Pool. In reality the lake is just the silted-up estuary of the old river. This was not quite the end of Kenfig though. In 1572 three plots were still occupied and one tenacious resident was living in a small cottage as late as 1665. Thereafter the sands engulfed whatever remained of the once-thriving town.

For such an important and richly-documented site, the surviving remains of Kenfig are pitiably few: some earthworks and inconspicuous foundations are all that remain of the town, while the castle was little more than a ragged arch on a mound until archaeologists from a local history society started digging here in 1924. They cleared away tons of sand to uncover the basement of the keep, part of the curtain wall and entrance passage, and discovered fragments of finely carved stonework that once adorned the tower. Unfortunately, nothing has been done to preserve the fabric since that time and the exposed walls are slowly crumbling away. At the time of writing the few remains are heavily shrouded in undergrowth and scrubby bushes, so that for much of the year the buildings are almost completely hidden from sight. The fate of Kenfig is a salutary lesson in the changes nature can inflict on a seemingly unalterable landscape.

Location & access

Kenfig Castle is located on the Kenfig Burrows Nature Reserve between Port Talbot and Porthcawl (M4 junction 37) approximately 1 km north-west of Mawdlam Church (OS map ref: SS 801 827). Access is freely accessible by several paths. From Mawdlam Church head across the dunes in a north-westerly direction, keeping the M4 embankment on your right, until you reach some disused railway sidings. The castle is not immediately conspicuous, but lies close to the railway. There is a shorter walk from the B4283 Pyle to Margam via the M4 underpass.

References

Brut; RCAHMW (1991). There is an interesting website on this and similar deserted villages at www.abandonedcommunities.co.uk. See also www.kenfigsociety.org

Landimore Castle, *Gower*

The Normans seized the peninsula of Gower from the Welsh around 1106 and, except for a few interruptions in the early thirteenth century, succeeded in creating a thoroughly anglicised lordship (as the many English sounding place-names testify). For its relative size, Gower is a land blessed with an abundance of castles. Major strongholds like Swansea and Oystermouth protected the eastern approaches, while its hinterland was guarded by the likes of Penmaen, Pennard (p. 113), Oxwich and Penrice (p. 116). The manor of Landimore on the north coast was valued at a knight's fee and would have had a castle too (one is specifically mentioned in 1353); but it would not have been the ruin beside the village, which now has the alternative name of Bovehill Castle. This is clearly a late-medieval structure and shows no sign of occupying the site of an older fortification; in fact, there is a tradition that the original settlement was located elsewhere and was abandoned due to coastal flooding.

The so-called castle comprises a rectangular walled courtyard set on the edge of an escarpment overlooking the salt marshes. Various buildings line the inner walls while at the southern end of the courtyard stood a large cross-wing, undoubtedly the great hall. There was an additional courtyard beyond the hall containing another domestic range, which has a set of garderobes discharging down the slope. All the walls are now ragged ruins, but the layout can still be traced, except towards

The remains of the great hall of Landimore 'castle'

the north end where modern buildings obscure the plan. This is where the gateway must have been positioned. As none of the buildings show any obvious signs of fortification Landimore might be considered an undefended manor house; but in the field to the west, where the land rises gently and an enemy might be expected to strike, there was an additional outer courtyard defined by a thick stone wall with small corner towers. This wall is far more ruinous than all the other buildings and may have been deliberately robbed away, but it indicates that Landimore was once more strongly protected than it now appears. It should be classed as a fortified manor or stronghouse, rather than a true castle.

There is no documentary evidence to pinpoint the construction date or the builder, but a likely candidate was Sir Hugh Johnys (d.1485), a distinguished soldier knighted in the Holy Land in 1441, and a staunch supporter of the duke of Norfolk (then lord of Swansea and Gower). In 1451 the duke granted the manor to Sir Hugh, and it may be supposed that the castle was built by him as a suitable residence within his newly-acquired land. After his death the property was acquired by Sir Rhys ap Thomas (d.1525), a prominent Welshman who had been instrumental in helping Henry Tudor seize the throne from Richard III in 1485. Rhys was an enthusiastic collector and restorer of castles, and he certainly undertook building work at nearby Weobley (a splendid little fortified manor in the care of Cadw located just a short distance away), but it is not known if anything was done to Landimore. The generally poor state of the remains together with antiquarian evidence suggest it had been abandoned as a residence at a fairly early date and was left to fall into ruin.

Location & access

Landimore Castle lies on the northern edge of the Gower Peninsula, best reached off M4 junction 47 and then follow signs to Gower, via the B4295 through Penclawdd. Just past Llanrhidian village take the right fork (signposted to Weobley and Llanmadoc) and after 2.5 km turn right to Landimore. The village is beside the sea, but the castle is up on the hill (OS map ref: SS 465 933). The site is on private land, but the exterior is visible from a public footpath that passes through Bovehill Farm.

References

RCAHMW (2000)

Llangynwyd Castle, *Maesteg*

The village of Llangynwyd lies in the heart of the south Wales coalfield, an area that has endured heavy industrialisation for over 150 years, which has left a familiar image of narrow winding valleys strewn with terraced housing and grey-black mounds of colliery waste. Yet a visit to Llangynwyd will come as a surprise to anyone expecting to see such a distinctive landscape. There is only a church, a pub and a few scattered houses here, in fact a typical rural settlement one might find almost anywhere in the Welsh or English countryside. Even the surrounding basin of farmland is uncharacteristic of the geography that has defined the Glamorgan uplands. Probably it was this factor that led Earl Robert of Gloucester to establish an enclave here after founding nearby Kenfig. The surrounding area was known as *Tir Iarll*, (the Earl's Land) and a castle would certainly have been needed here to defend against the hostile Welsh neighbours, although the first mention of one occurs as late as 1246. This early castle was a large ringwork set at the end of a steep-sided ridge in the valley below the old church. The wooden stockade surrounding the courtyard was later replaced with a rough stone wall.

Contemporary documents provide further details of the next appearance of the castle, for on 13 July 1257, Llywelyn ap Gruffudd attacked 'Llangunith and burnt the castle of the lord earl, killing 24 of the earl's men'. The Welsh also destroyed 80 houses in the lordship. Some repairs must have been carried out, for in 1262 the castle was taken over by Humphrey de Bohun (d.1298), earl of Hereford, and garrisoned with 28 men and 8 horses during the minority of the rightful owner, the earl of Gloucester, Gilbert de Clare (d.1295). As soon as Gilbert came of age, his first priority was to ensure that his castles were up to scratch and capable of withstanding another attack. Llangynwyd was rebuilt and given a twin-towered gatehouse of the type still standing proud at Gilbert's main stronghold of Caerphilly. The entrance passage lay between two D-shaped flanking towers, and was protected by arrow loops, two wooden gates and two portcullises. The rest of the defences consist of the patched-up wall and a small half-round tower jutting out from the north flank. The foundations of several internal buildings can be seen, but even so, accommodation within the courtyard must have been very cramped. Rock-cut ditches protected the castle on all

Stony mounds define the remains of the gatehouse at Llangynwyd Castle

Aerial view of Llangynwyd Castle, showing the large outer bailey (foreground)
with the remains of the inner ward obscured by trees at the top

sides except the east, where the steep slopes proved adequate, and the approach to
the main gate was strengthened by a semi-circular barbican. In the field in front
of the gate are the worn-down ramparts of a large outer bailey, which some have
suggested might be the remains of an Iron Age fort.

Llangynwyd fell to the Welsh during a widespread uprising in 1294–95 when the
de Clare properties in south Wales were targeted. It appears no more in the records
thereafter and was perhaps so severely damaged that it was given up as a lost cause
and not restored. The uplands were left in peace, the parish church was rebuilt on
a grander scale, the simple timber homes of the upland farmers were replaced with
more durable stone houses and the forgotten castle crumbled into decay, little more
than a handy quarry for building materials. The finely-dressed blocks of Sutton
limestone imported here by Gilbert's workmen from the quarries at Ogmore-by-
Sea, now adorn the adjacent farm buildings. Other pieces have been placed in the
church for safe-keeping. The castle mound had become so neglected and overgrown
that its true purpose was not revealed until excavations started in 1906. Since then
the site has become overgrown once more and the exposed stonework crumbles at
an alarming rate. Llangynwyd needs to be re-excavated and properly conserved
before the few visible features have gone for good.

Interpretative reconstruction of how Llangynwyd Castle may have appeared following its rebuilding in the late thirteenth century

Location & access

Llangynwyd lies about 8 km north-west of Bridgend off M4 Junction 36. Follow the A40632 to Maesteg until you reach the modern village of Llangynwyd, then take the signposted left turn uphill to 'Llan'. At the village follow the road around the churchyard and over the crossroads, passing the Cornerhouse on the right, and descend to the valley. Just past a sharp bend, and up the hill, and the large farmstead on the left marks the site of the castle (OS map ref: SS 853 887). The castle lies on private land and is not accessible to the public. Permission to visit may be obtained from Castle Farm.

References

Brut; RCAHMW (1991)

Mellte Castle, *Ystradfellte*

This very remote and little-known site lies over the border from Glamorgan on the edge of the Brecon Beacons National Park. The builders exploited the natural protection offered by the confluence of two fast-flowing streams, and erected a castle using the local red sandstone, hence its alternative name of Castell Coch ('Red Castle'). However, the use of poor-quality earthy mortar has not helped its longevity, and the walls have since collapsed into heaps of moss-covered stones. Nevertheless, the basic plan can still be traced and consists of a walled courtyard of pentagonal plan with a rounded tower at the southernmost point, and a simple gateway at the north-east corner. In the middle of the courtyard a great mound of rubble marks the remains of a rectangular building – either a keep or a first-floor hall, measuring about 19m by 11m. The approach to the castle from the north is protected by a large outer bailey with a massive rampart and ditch. It is tempting to see this as a two-phase site: the large earthwork enclosure coming first, followed by the more compact inner masonry fort.

There is hardly any historical reference to this site other than the appearance of *Stratmelthin* in a list of properties belonging to the lord of Brecon, William de Braose (d.1230). Clearly this is an English clerk's attempt to master the tongue-twisting Welsh place-name Ystradfellte, and presumably the castle was built by that powerful Anglo-Norman family to secure the frontiers of their lordship. The rectangular keep would hint at a twelfth-century date for construction, but the round tower suggests it was thirteenth. However, the relatively small size of the castle and its location make it unconvincing as a strategic military outpost, and it was probably a hunting lodge occupied periodically by the lords, whilst their retinue encamped in the bailey. The vast expanse of mountains, moors and wooded valleys that now forms part of the National Park was once a jealously guarded hunting preserve.

There is a possibility is that the stone castle was built by Llywelyn ap Gruffudd around 1260 when most of Breconshire came under his sway. It certainly looks like the sort of small and relatively simple castles that the Welsh were building at this time, but there are no deep ditches that form such characteristic features of other Welsh castles, making an Anglo-Norman origin more likely. During the great dispute between the warring earls of Gloucester and Hereford (see p. 106) one of the hearings was convened at Ystradfellte in 1291. Presumably the castle was the site of that meeting, but historical references to the later history of the building are lost. If Castell Coch was a hunting lodge then it may have remained in some use to the lords of Brecon until the estate became Crown property in 1521.

Reconstruction of how Mellte Castle may have appeared when completed

Location & access

Ystradfellte can be reached from either the A465 at Glyn-neath, or from the A4059 Hirwaun to Brecon road. At the little village take the road north to Sennybridge for about 2 km, and then turn right down into the valley. The castle site can be seen in the trees upstream from the bridge (OS map ref: SN 935 145). The site lies on private land, but is visible from the road and footpath along the right-hand branch of the river.

References

Brycheiniog (1968–69)

Morgraig Castle, *Caerphilly*

When this peculiar little fortress was rediscovered at the dawn of the twentieth century, learned opinion considered it likely to have been a native castle, but more recently academics have favoured an English origin, thus sparking off a fierce controversy that far outweighs the actual remains of the castle and its historical insignificance. There are no records or documents that might shed any light on the matter, and excavations in 1903–5 only proved that it was an unfinished thirteenth-century castle. Was Morgraig therefore an English outpost guarding against incursions from the bleak hill country, or an ambitious Welsh border stronghold marking the limits of native territory? Despite all the pros and cons of the respective arguments, that question will probably never be resolved. Before summarising all the relevant issues, it is necessary to put the castle in its geographic and historical context.

Morgraig is situated at the southernmost point of the upland territory of Senghenydd, a long narrow strip of bleak moors and winding valleys extending from the Cefn Onn ridge near Cardiff to the borders of Breconshire beyond Merthyr Tydfil. Anyone stationed on this part of the ridge could keep the whole of the Cardiff plain and Severn estuary under observation, although (significantly) the view north to the uplands is more restricted. Ever since the earl of Gloucester invaded the old kingdom of Morgannwg at the end of the eleventh century, these uplands had been left in Welsh hands, the native rulers acknowledging the nominal overlordship of their Norman masters at Cardiff. With the arrival of the de Clare family in the thirteenth century things began to change. Richard de Clare would not tolerate this back door threat and set about bringing the semi-independent territories under direct English control. By the time the earl died in 1262 only Senghenydd was left in Welsh hands and was held by Gruffudd ap Rhys, an acknowledged vassal of Prince Llywelyn ap Gruffudd.

In 1267 the new earl of Gloucester and Glamorgan, Gilbert de Clare 'The Red Earl' (so named from the colour of his hair, or perhaps on account of his fiery temperament) set about completing his father's work. Senghenydd was invaded and the unfortunate Gruffudd was

A view across the castle courtyard

captured, disappearing for life into an Irish prison. The following year Gilbert de Clare began to build a monumental state-of-the-art fortress at Caerphilly, a blatant threat to Welsh authority that Llywelyn could not ignore. Hastening south, the prince found himself embroiled in protracted negotiations with the Red Earl before opting for the simple approach and burning the unfinished structure to the

A bird's-eye view of Morgraig as it might have looked in the late thirteenth century, had the building scheme been carried through to completion

ground. Although he was defending the rights of his incarcerated vassal, Llywelyn was undoubtedly more concerned about the loss of Welsh territory. His dominions now extended beyond Brecon, and Senghenydd offered a strategic foothold within English dominated Glamorgan. In the meantime, the stalemate between Gilbert and Llywelyn continued. After several months of tedious wrangling Gilbert broke the truce, sneaked back into his unfinished castle and resumed building. By 1271 Caerphilly was substantially complete and Llywelyn was forced to withdraw from the area.

With these facts in mind, it is clear that Morgraig would not have been started after 1268 (since the building of Caerphilly rendered it obsolete), and from the style and details it is unlikely to have been constructed much before the middle of the thirteenth century. Its subsequent history is as obscure as its origin. The derelict shell was probably used in 1316 when Gruffudd's son Llywelyn Bren rose in revolt. The rebels gained control of the ridge and fortified it against frontal attack, but they were defeated when the English army outflanked them. Thereafter the site was abandoned and must have been buried in rubble from an early date, for the abundance of dressed stone found by the excavators suggests it was not heavily robbed, as might be expected. Only a series of stony earthworks could be seen before the Cardiff Naturalists Society began digging in 1903, and so no one really knew what was here. The intact ground plan of a well-preserved thirteenth-century fortress was soon laid bare, comprising a five-sided enclosure with towers jutting out from each angle. One of the towers is a lop-sided rectangular keep measuring about 19m by 14m, while the other four are elongated D-shaped structures. One of these was a kitchen since the ground-floor chamber contained an oven and at least one fireplace.

The castle was evidently unfinished since no roofing materials were found, there was no wear on the dressed stones, and there was little evidence for any internal buildings. The walls stop at roughly the same height across the site and it seems that only the ground-floor chambers were completed. However, work on the upper levels must have been started since the excavators discovered stone fragments of newel steps; and since there are no structural staircases here (access to the first floors of the towers was apparently by external wooden stairs), the stones could only have been intended for the unbuilt top floors. From what we know of medieval construction practices this would imply that the builders had only been working on the castle for one, or at most two, seasons; then they simply downed tools and left.

And so too did the archaeologists once the site was exposed. No effort was made to preserve the ruins, and the pristine walls that they found, standing up to 4m high with intact door and window openings, were left to look after themselves. Most of the dressed stone discovered on site has since disappeared and the walls are still surrounded by the spoil heaps from the century-old excavations. On a return visit in the spring of 2021, the whole site could hardly be seen, so heavy has been the growth of brambles and bushes since the photographs here were taken.

Part of the outer walls of Morgraig

The excavators had few doubts that it was Welsh castle, for the English simply didn't build things like Morgraig. The rectangular keep was considered old fashioned by the mid thirteenth century (though it still enjoyed a certain vogue among the Welsh), and the other towers are similar to the native apsidal keeps at Castell y Bere, Carndochan and Ewloe; however, their integration with the defensive perimeter is far more characteristic of English castles. For instance, the same basic arrangement is present at Beeston (Cheshire), Bolingbroke (Lincs), Clifford (see p. 179), Grosmont, Holt, and Whittington (Shropshire); and yet, significantly, Morgraig is quite unlike any of the other de Clare castles in Glamorgan. Even their nearby hilltop fortresses of Llantrisant and Castell Coch feature run-of-the-mill round towers. Many of the finer details are badly thought out for an English castle – all the walls are roughly built from locally quarried millstone grit, a more intractable material than pennant sandstone obtainable only a short distance further north; and, as already noted, access to the upper floors was clumsily arranged. There was no provision for any garderobes in the towers (in fact there seems to be only one latrine in the whole castle), and there was no gatehouse, just a feeble archway. The absence of ditches is another surprising feature for a military base.

All of these oddities could be explained as typically idiosyncratic Welsh work, which might have seemed less peculiar had the scheme been carried through to completion. If Morgraig was located in Gwynedd or Powys, then no doubts would ever have arisen over its origin. However, when compared to the few known Welsh masonry castles in upland Glamorgan and Gwent (such as Castell Meredydd p. 131 and Plas Baglan p. 124), Morgraig is a remarkably ambitious structure and one that the petty ruler of an impoverished upland tract would never have had the resources to build. It is also unlikely that Richard de Clare would have allowed such works to proceed unchallenged so close to his main base at Cardiff. After reviewing all the evidence, the RCAHMW returned a verdict of 'Not Welsh' in their detailed study of the Glamorganshire castles. The smoking gun was the presence of dressed stone from quarries at Ogmore-by-Sea, presumably off-limits to the Welsh builders.

This balanced interpretation should have been the last word on the origin of Morgraig, but instead the official view only served to heat up the arguments. There seems to be a very strong hint of nationalistic pride in wanting this castle to be seen as a native bastion of resistance against the invading English. My own opinion is unfortunately rather equivocal: I do not believe that Gruffudd ap Rhys had the manpower or money to build such a fortification – but with the backing of Prince Llywelyn then Morgraig *would* have been a feasible undertaking. Llywelyn seems to have been involved in localised castle building among his vassals elsewhere at this time (see Castell Du, p. 178) and was desperate to keep Senghenydd in native control. The brief lull following the death of Earl Richard in 1262 would be a likely time for Gruffudd to begin building this castle under Llywelyn's aegis in order to secure the southern border of his lands; indeed, it may have been this provocative act which sealed his fate and brought the works to an abrupt end once Gilbert came to power. Further archaeological work is unlikely to resolve this mystery, and at this point in time it is far more desirable that a programme of essential conservation work should be carried out, to halt the wretched decline of this major medieval site.

Location & access
Morgraig Castle lies north of Cardiff beside the A469 Thornhill road to Caerphilly, in the woods uphill of the Traveller's Rest public house (OS map ref: ST 160 843). The site lies on private land, but a gate provides access from the pub car park and the castle can be reached by a short walk up the ridge.

References
TCNS (1905); RCAHMW (2000). For further information on the Morgraig controversy see www.stcenydd.org.uk

Morlais Castle, *Merthyr Tydfil*

Morlais was one of the largest and strongest castles in Wales, and an ambitious symbol of English might set in a remote, mountainous area on the edge of the Brecon Beacons. It was built towards the end of the thirteenth century by the most powerful warlord in south Wales, Gilbert de Clare (d.1295), earl of Gloucester and lord of Glamorgan. Gilbert's greatest achievement in the field of military architecture was his vast fortress of Caerphilly, one of the most complete examples of a concentric castle in Britain. At Caerphilly we can appreciate the scope of the Red Earl's ambitions and the scale of what was attempted at Morlais; but while Caerphilly has been restored, the moats reflooded, the ruined towers rebuilt, very little has been done to preserve Morlais. It was in ruins before the end of the medieval period and John Leland dismissed the remains with a brusque comment. When Samuel and Nathaniel Buck sketched Morlais in 1741, they depicted a heap of shattered walls with a few doors and windows visible – a shapeless pile nevertheless impressive in its ruin. During the first half of the nineteenth century antiquarians and amateur archaeologists poked about the remains and pronounced on the history and architecture of the castle (some theories more fanciful than others) but many of the features then in existence have since crumbled away. Yet Morlais still manages to hide one remarkable secret from all but the most observant of passers-by.

An aerial view of the crumbling hilltop remains of the once-mighty Morlais Castle

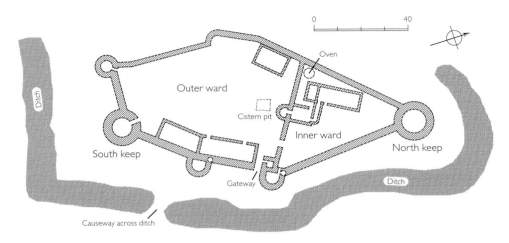

An interpretive plan of the masonry remains of Morlais Castle in c.1294

What caused this powerful castle to fall into such neglect? To answer that question and to explore the origins of the castle, we must continue with the history of the de Clare family outlined in the previous entry.[2] During the power struggle with Llywelyn ap Gruffudd in 1268, Gilbert asserted his authority in Senghenydd by building Caerphilly castle; but even with Llywelyn's downfall the flames of rebellion flickered for some years to come. In 1287 there was an uprising in West Wales and Gilbert led a huge army of foot soldiers and woodcutters northwards to clear the mountain road to Brecon and ensure an effective line of communication. On the way he diverted manpower to begin a new stronghold at the furthermost point of his dominions, overlooking the deep rocky gorge of the river Taff that had formed the ancient boundary between Glamorgan and Breconshire. But this rapid advance provoked the anger of Humphrey de Bohun (d.1298), earl of Hereford and lord of Brecon, who claimed that the land was his. He was mistaken in this, but the building of a huge castle on his doorstep was an affront too blatant to ignore.

In June 1289 royal officials attempted to ease the situation by forbidding Gilbert to continue with the construction work, noting that the earl had 'begun to erect a castle in the foresaid land to Humphrey's disinheritance, and that [Gilbert] keeps ... an immense number of armed men there'. The castle is not named, but it is certainly Morlais. Gilbert chose to ignore the warnings and carry on building. Early in 1290 the two earls were summoned to a hearing, but Gilbert refused to turn up. He was overly confident in the knowledge that his exalted position would soon be even greater, for a long-arranged marriage with the king's daughter was finally going ahead. They were married on April 1290 – but pride, as the saying goes, comes before a fall.

An interpretative reconstruction showing how the castle might have looked in c.1294.
The main defences and rock-cut ditch were massed on the side most vulnerable to attack

The quarrel had already escalated into open violence and Gilbert's retainers carried out armed raids into Brecon, killing some of Humphrey's men and seizing livestock. By the laws of the March these two warlords could rule virtually unopposed within their own domains, but King Edward was in no mood to deal leniently with over-mighty subjects while the Welsh were still a potential threat. Because Humphrey had asked for the king's help in the matter, Edward could legitimately meddle in Marcher law and he decided to clip the wings of his subordinates. At first de Bohun abided by the king's command to hold back, but after further raids he too was provoked into armed response against de Clare. Hearings were convened in 1291 to settle the matter but Gilbert still refused to appear, and it was only the arrival of the king himself at Abergavenny that made further procrastination unwise. The two lords were found guilty and summoned to appear at Westminster the following January for sentencing. There they were imprisoned, fined and had their estates confiscated for a short time. Gilbert was obviously the more culpable and received a heavier fine.

To add to his woes, there was another Welsh uprising in 1294 and his estates in south Wales were targeted by Morgan ap Maredudd of Machen, a local ruler he had dispossessed some years before (see p. 131). Both Morlais and Caerphilly were attacked by the rebels, although the great strength of the latter prevented much damage apart from the destruction of the fledgling town. As a final insult, the rebels eventually submitted to the King rather than the earl. Morgan claimed he had struck out against Gilbert's harsh rule rather than openly rebel against the Crown, and this clever move saved his neck and allowed Edward to get another dig at the humbled earl. Morgan was taken into the king's favour and, like so many of his countrymen, later served as a soldier in the French wars. King Edward visited Morlais in June 1295 while on route to Brecon, but we have no idea of the state the castle at that time.

Gilbert died a few months later at the age of 53 and was laid to rest at Tewkesbury Abbey, the family mausoleum of the earls of Gloucester. His estates were administered by his widow Joan until her death in 1307. His son and heir (another Gilbert) did not enjoy the vast inheritance for long; a typically brave and enthusiastic warrior, the young Gilbert was one of many unfortunate knights slaughtered at Bannockburn in 1314. The male line of this once-great family came to an end, and the estates were carved up among the surviving heiresses.

Morlais castle therefore had a very short life. It was begun about 1288 and disappears from the records after 1295. There is a lingering tradition that it was never finished, but the evidence of the Buck drawing and the vast heaps of rubble strewn about the site reveal that something major once stood here. The limestone rock on which the castle is situated would have provided an abundant supply of building materials without having to source from further afield and, since the greater part of Caerphilly was built in just four years, the likelihood remains that Morlais was substantially complete by the time the Welsh attacked in the autumn of 1294.

It is assumed that the castle was so badly damaged in the war that it was abandoned as a lost cause – but this is merely a supposition based on the absence of any documentary evidence. It is not impossible that the castle was repaired and continued in use for some years afterwards, for the Clares were immensely rich and had invested a huge amount of money and manpower into their lordship castles. But what must have been a decisive factor in its rapid neglect was the remoteness of the site – this bleak windswept ridge some 380m above sea level would hardly have encouraged the development of a settlement that would bring some measure of economic value to the area. The only town to develop hereabouts was Merthyr Tydfil, and that was due to the growth of the iron industry in the late eighteenth century. Morlais was, first and foremost, a border stronghold and therefore could not have existed beyond its military *raison d'être*.

Despite the centuries of decay, it is easy to recover the basic ground plan of the castle, which is particularly obvious from the air. The heaps of rubble and scree define an impressively large enclosure laid out on the headland like a beached ship. Massive round towers mark the bow and stern, lesser ones guard the vulnerable flanks, and access from the north and east was blocked by sheer-sided ditches cut through the bedrock. Indeed, these ditches are a particularly imposing feature of the site and in places are 15m wide and over 5m deep. The remaining sides of the castle were protected by steep rocky slopes, but modern quarrying has transformed these natural defences into precipitous cliffs. On the southern side of the hill there are traces of worn-down rubble ramparts that could have formed a lightly defended outer bailey contemporary with the castle, but perhaps are more likely to be the remains of an Iron Age hillfort.

The entrance into the castle was an arched gate beside one of the flanking towers, which seems to be a very insignificant structure compared to the great gatehouses that were being built at this time, and which feature prominently at Gilbert's other castles. There are footings of a square inner tower, so perhaps the gate was more strongly defended than it now appears; but even so, could it have been this inadequate entrance that enabled the Welsh to overrun the castle? There are signs of another simple gate or postern, half-buried in the rubble of the southern curtain wall.

The graceful rib-vaulting in the basement of the south keep (see also the chapter frontispiece)

Within the spacious courtyard can be seen the foundations of several rectangular buildings and a yawning chasm that was dug as a well or cistern to store water. The furthest point of the castle is crowned by a massive round tower measuring 11m in diameter with 4m-thick walls. Presumably, this was the hulking ruin shown in the Buck brothers' drawing and which came crashing down during a storm at the beginning of the nineteenth century. Only the basement level now remains, but the drawing shows one or two upper floors, possibly with some kind of porch or forebuilding in front. Another similar round tower stood at the opposite end of the courtyard, jutting forward to meet any attacker face-on. A great mound of rubble masks the remains of this second keep, but an arched doorway in one side leads down into an octagonal basement chamber, roofed over with a rib-vault springing from a central pillar. When considering the parlous state of the rest of the castle the survival of this room is truly remarkable, and the quality of the carved stonework reflects what else may have been lost at this shattered site.

Location & access

Morlais Castle lies 3 km north of Merthyr Tydfil off the A465 Heads of the Valleys road at Gurnos. Take the turning off the A465 to Pant Estate. Ignore the sign for Morlais Castle Golf Club, but continue over the crossroads along Pontmorlais road passing Rabart's showroom, and along a narrow lane that starts to descend into the valley. There is a lay-by on the left at the start of the disused Morlais quarries, with a gate giving access to the open hillside. A longer path can be followed around the quarries from the Brecon Mountain Railway station, on the road beyond the golf club (OS map ref: SO 049 097). The site lies on private land, but is accessible by several paths around the quarries.

References
RCAHMW (2000)

PENLLE'R CASTELL, *AMMANFORD*

Perhaps the oddest thing about this peculiar site is its location – on an upland ridge far from any habitation or settlement, a remote outpost seemingly guarding nothing but an expanse of windswept moorland. Only the mountain road from Swansea to Ammanford crosses this bleak landscape and provides access for modern travellers, but even so, the castle is easy to miss as it lies just below the crest of the hill. The view to the south is blocked by rising ground, but from west to east the castle

Aerial view of the isolated and windswept moorland site of Penlle'r Castell

oversees a superb panorama across the Amman and Loughor valleys to the ridge of the Black Mountain and beyond. The name says it all – Penlle'r Castell – 'the high place of the castle'; but what is the origin of this strange earthwork and why was it built in the middle of nowhere?

There are no documents or records that unequivocally provide the answer to this, and the earliest known reference to the site is a brief comment ('Lle'r Castell now in utter ruin') by the Elizabethan antiquarian Rice Merrick around 1585. Since the Welsh word *castell* does not always signify a fortification of medieval date, puzzled antiquarians once thought it was an Iron Age or Roman fort. The superficial resemblance to a motte-and-bailey led others to the more reasoned conclusion that it was a medieval work, and that its unusual shape and location pointed to a Welsh origin. However, further research has plausibly identified Penlle'r Castell as an English fort established here around the middle of the thirteenth century during a border dispute between Rhys Fychan of Deheubarth and the lord of Gower, William de Braose VI (d.1291). According to one record, in 1252 Rhys attacked and burnt William's newly built castle in Gower (*Novum Castrum de Gower*), and this is believed to be that site.

Gower is today renowned as the idyllic coastal peninsula stretching west from Swansea, but in medieval times the lordship extended far inland, and included a sparsely-inhabited upland region abutting Welsh territories. Until the middle

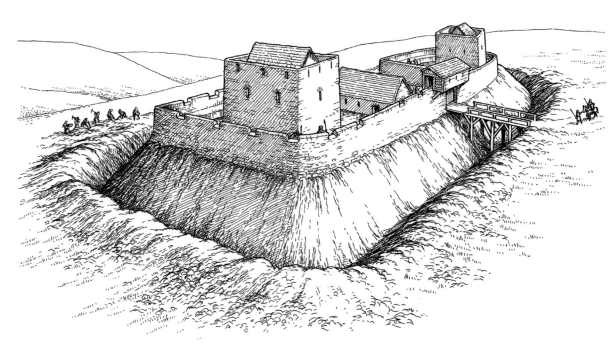

Reconstruction drawing showing how Penlle'r Castell may have looked in the thirteenth century

of the thirteenth century the river Amman formed the northern limits of the lordship, but friction between the Welsh and English kept pushing the boundary back towards Swansea, so that by 1252 King Henry III was forced to intervene and settle the conflict by legal means. The border was eventually fixed at a line just north of the castle (where it acts as the county boundary to this day), but the dispute still rumbled on for years and ownership of this barren waste caused so much strife that the area became known as 'Stryveland'.

This is the historical context in which Penlle'r Castell was built. On the mountainside overlooking the contested territory, the builders marked out a bullet-shaped area and surrounded it with a deep ditch, using the spoil to create a flattened platform rising only slightly above the level of the moor. The remaining rubble was dumped around the outer rim of the ditch to form an irregular (and apparently unfinished) counterscarp bank. The upper end of the platform is almost cut through by a separate ditch and forms a sort of *faux* motte, on which can be seen the foundations of a rectangular tower. The remainder of the platform is very uneven and bears the outlines of collapsed walls and another tower, all built from drystone and consequently very ruined. Clearly, the castle was raised as quickly and cheaply as possible to meet an imminent threat, and the restricted southerly view was considered less important than the northward vista (the direction from which any attack might be expected). The location therefore makes sense if Penlle'r Castell was intended as a short-lived military base to reinforce English authority in this contested corner of the lordship. It could only ever have been such, for no settlement would have been feasible here. By the beginning of the fourteenth century the need for such a remote and inadequate outpost was long past and the castle would have been abandoned, perhaps even demolished, to render it unusable by an enemy.

Location & access

Penlle'r Castell lies about 5 km south-east of Ammanford on the highest point of the mountain road to Morriston. This road starts from the town centre via a roundabout on the A474 (signposted to Bettws and Garnswllt), or from Pontamman just east of the town (and marked by a green sign to Bettws Mountain viewpoint). Keep driving uphill past the wind farm and onto the open moorland until you reach the highest part of the hill (limited parking on the verge). Walk across the moors for about 200m in an easterly direction to get to the site. The mountain road can also be followed from its southerly end from Morriston Hospital (M4 junctions 45 or 46), following signs to Felindre and Craig Cefn Parc (OS map ref: SN 665 096). The site lies on open moorland and is freely accessible.

References

RCAHMW (2000)

Pennard Castle, *Gower*

The gatehouse of Pennard Castle

Not a great deal remains of this little castle, but the spectacular coastal setting more than justifies the trek needed to reach it. It lies on the edge of an extensive area of sand dunes overlooking a river valley winding its way down to Threecliff Bay. From the valley below, the castle looks fairly complete, the ragged battlemented wall dramatically silhouetted against the skyline; but from above the parlous state of the ruin is all too obvious – most of the walls have fallen, the courtyard is open to the wind-blown sands, and the gaping gateway has been clumsily patched-up with concrete to prevent further collapse.

Pennard was a twelfth-century ring-work castle founded by the Norman invaders of Gower sometime after 1106. The early defences were revealed by excavations in 1960 when a stone-built hall in the courtyard was unearthed. There is another ringwork castle on the opposite side of the bay at Penmaen Burrows, and this is worth a visit as it shows how Pennard would have looked before it was given a masonry upgrade. This too, has been excavated, and also had a simple stone hall with a thatched roof. Penmaen seems to have

Aerial view of Pennard Castle

been abandoned at an early date, but Pennard remained in use for much longer and sometime in the late thirteenth century (almost certainly after the threat of Welsh attack had receded) the castle was rebuilt in stone, by either William de Braose VI (d.1291) or his son and heir William VII (d.1326).

The ringwork rampart was overlain by a crude curtain wall, pockmarked with scaffolding holes, and so flimsy that there was no proper wall-walk, just a timber platform supported on cantilevered beams. The rough and simple limestone circuit was broken only by a tiny round tower and a garderobe turret, but to guard the approach the builders constructed a twin-towered gatehouse. Even so, it was a very modest version of the more imposing structures that had been built at Caer-philly, Neath and elsewhere. It had a portcullis and guardrooms on either side of the entrance passage, and there was probably a drawbridge over the silted-up outer ditch. The first floor seems to have been one large residential chamber for the constable. There were probably timber-framed buildings ranged against the inner wall of the courtyard, and in the centre stood the hall left over from the ringwork days. An additional room was later built jutting out on the very end of the cliff, probably to increase the meagre accommodation on offer. And that is all there is to Pennard – a little doll's house built by the lords of Gower with minimum imagination and expense.

There was a village here too, but only the foundations of the church can now be seen in the middle of a golf course. A gradual encroachment of sand in the later medieval period signalled the end for Pennard, as it had for Kenfig and several other coastal communities in south Wales. By 1535 the Vicar complained that the church and houses were 'utterly and clearly destroyed … by the drifting sands of

Reconstruction drawing of how Pennard may have looked around 1300,
with the twelfth-century hall standing in the courtyard

the sea', and in 1650 the castle was said to be 'desolate and ruinous … scarcely there remains one whole wall'. A slight exaggeration perhaps, for in 1741 the Buck brothers published an engraving of the castle that shows the site much as it appears today.

Location & access
Pennard Castle lies on the south coast of Gower just south of Parkmill village on the A4118 road from Swansea city centre. There are several ways to get to the site, either by following the path from the village green and along the valley towards the beach, or by a careful walk across the golf course from Southgate hamlet, which is reached off the B4436. The site is freely accessible at any time.

References
RCAHMW (1991)

PENRICE CASTLE, *GOWER*

This is arguably the most substantial 'forgotten' castle in Wales – a spacious and ivy-covered ruin mouldering away in a quiet part of the Gower peninsula. Penrice may not be as large as Morlais or Llangybi (p. 147), but the walls still stand up to battlement level and the defensive perimeter is comparatively intact. The continued survival of the castle is a testament to the original builders who utilised the rugged local limestone to create a plain, but very durable fortress. Penrice has never been accessible to the public and there are no immediate plans for it to be so, for it lies within the private grounds of a Georgian mansion. A public footpath crosses the estate and offers an external view of the walls, and it is possible to catch a glimpse from the main road. The lack of consolidation work and the absence of proper access are regrettable, for Penrice is a major historic building on a peninsula already rich in ancient monuments and archaeological sites.

The castle originated in the aftermath of the Norman takeover of Gower in 1106, when King Henry 1 allowed Henry de Beaumont, earl of Warwick, to establish a lordship centred on a new castle and town at Swansea. There is a tradition that de Beaumont himself built the first castle at Penrice, but this evidence is now discredited, and it is more likely that it was founded in subsequent years as the peninsula was carved up amongst his followers. The Penres family probably settled here at an early date and established a castle, church and village in the typical Norman

An aerial view of the impressive remains of Penrice Castle

Internal view of the round keep (left), and the outer facade of the triple gatehouse (right)

fashion. The overgrown ramparts of the original ringwork can still be seen behind the village today. The seizure of Gower did not pass unchallenged and the main castles were frequently attacked by the Welsh. In 1215 Rhys Gryg of Deheubarth gained supremacy over the region and forcibly evicted all the English settlers from the land. The bloodshed and hardship inflicted upon the civilians by that act has gone unrecorded in the chronicles of the time, but it did not lead to a permanent Welsh victory and Gower was to remain one of the most anglicised parts of the country. By the time the Penres family had regained their lands, the old timber castles were out of date and more efficient masonry defences were needed to repulse attack. Rather than rebuild the existing castle in stone, they decided to relocate to a new site on a rocky promontory across the valley.

The first phase of the stone castle was probably completed by 1250 and comprised an irregular enclosure wall studded with round buttresses, and linked to a circular keep on the highest part of the site. This is one of the castle's many odd features. It is a modestly-sized keep of the type then in vogue throughout the Marches, containing a basic ground-floor store with one upper room reached by an external stair; but while this chamber has windows and a garderobe, it lacks a fireplace, so if it was intended to be the main apartment then a portable brazier must have been used for heating. There was also no mural stair to get to the roof, and so the only way to reach the battlements would have been by a ladder and trapdoor. Possibly the builders never completed the keep to its intended height. Additional accommodation may have been provided by a long building set against the east curtain wall, but the remains are incomplete and do not display any obvious signs of domestic usage. It is usually considered to have been a barn.

The rear of the triple-towered gatehouse, as seen from the courtyard

Cutaway view through the gatehouse. The larger inner tower contained guardrooms and the portcullis mechanism, while the two outward-facing towers contained small living rooms on the upper levels

This large (but very basic) structure served as the home of the Penres family until about 1270 when a series of new works were carried out to improve the castle. The threat of Prince Llywelyn's rise to power would have occasioned the need for Robert de Penres to set about upgrading the defences. A new gatehouse was built to replace whatever had stood before and, once again, the Penrice builders opted to create a strikingly odd and unique structure. Most gatehouses of the period consist of two elongated towers flanking the entrance passage, but here there are three – two set forward of the gate and a third spanning the passage at the rear. Access into the castle was controlled by a portcullis and wooden doors in the rear tower. The towers are square in plan with rounded external corners, and contain two upper floors of small living rooms with fireplaces, garderobes and windows. There was no glass, just wooden shutters which could be secured with drawbars. The interior walls in places are still covered with plaster. As with the keep, there seems to have been no proper stair within the gatehouse, so access to the upper floors and battlements must have been by ladder.

The next improvement to the castle was the building of a hall block adjoining the keep and, since this work involved the demolition of part of the curtain wall, it would likely have been carried out after Llywelyn's downfall and when the threat of Welsh attack was reduced. Unfortunately, this block is now the most ruined part of the castle and the internal layout is unclear. There was a ground-level storeroom with a hall on the floor above, and a square tower jutting into the outer ditch. Shortly afterwards a second tower was added at an awkward angle, and this contains fairly comfortable apartments with fireplaces and garderobes on the two upper floors, so very likely functioned as the solar or private chamber of the owners. In order to bring the battlements of the keep up to the same level as the hall block, the tower was raised by another storey (although the extra room thus created was a useless dark void accessible only by ladder from the chamber beneath). Even more bizarrely, a curving porch or chemise was added to the keep to give extra defence for the entrance, but since it only surrounds part of the tower, it could hardly have been very effective. All of these additions resulted in a self-contained residential block of haphazard plan, perhaps intended to be defensible even if the rest of the courtyard had been overrun by an enemy.

This phase of building was possibly carried out by Robert's successor, William de Penres, who briefly held the castle at the end of the thirteenth century. In 1284 Edward 1 granted William a seven-year respite from knightly service, perhaps as a concession to the financial burden of castle building. The de Penres family were relatively insignificant landowners and a castle of this size must have been a severe drain on their limited resources. Many of the oddities and imperfections in

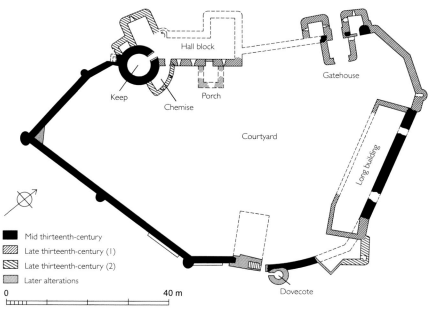

Keep

Chemise

Porch

Hall block

Gatehouse

Courtyard

Long building

Dovecote

■ Mid thirteenth-century

▨ Late thirteenth-century (1)

▨ Late thirteenth-century (2)

▨ Later alterations

0   40 m

Reconstruction drawing and plan of Penrice Castle, showing how it might have looked
in the late thirteenth century

the design can be accounted for by the lack of funds and the inexperience of local builders. Yet, as previously noted, the strength of the mortar and durability of the local limestone has ensured that Penrice has survived relatively well, while other more finely-constructed castles have not been so lucky.

From 1304 until at least 1341, the castle was the favoured residence of another member of the family to bear the name Robert. He was a loyal servant to the Crown and was made keeper of the royal fortress of Haverfordwest as a reward for his services. Yet he was also accused of stealing some of Edward II's treasure left in his care during the closing years of that monarch's troubled reign. Although Robert was cleared of the charge in 1331, the recent discovery of a rare jewelled brooch at his nearby manor of Oxwich suggests he may not have been an innocent bystander in the affair. After his death the castle passed to his brother Richard (d.1356) who built up the family fortunes by marrying the de Camville heiress and acquiring their large coastal fortress of Llansteffan in Carmarthenshire. His son, yet another Robert, was a somewhat disreputable character who apparently neglected the upkeep of his castles, so that by 1367 they were said to be ruinous. Edward III was then at war with France and expected every good knight to do their patriotic duty and ensure their castles were properly fortified in the event of an attack. Robert was ordered, on pain of forfeiture, to get Penrice and Llansteffan in working order, and the king sent a commissioner to ensure that the necessary works had been carried out. Another impending French attack in 1377 prompted a further royal warning, but in the summer of that year Robert's estates were seized by the Crown when he was convicted of having 'feloniously killed' (i.e. murdered) Joan, daughter of William ap Llywelyn of Llansteffan seven years previously.[3]

After a hiatus of 14 years his son regained the Penrice estate on payment of a large fine, but within a short time he was dead, and the castle passed to a cousin, John de Penres. During the Glyndŵr rebellion, Gower was in Welsh control from 1403 until 1408, and the unfortunate John spent some years in captivity. He was released, but died without an heir in 1410, and so the property was conveyed by Isabella de Penres to her husband, Hugh Mansel. The Mansels were another Gower family of no more than local significance until their fortunes rose in the sixteenth century. Sir Rice Mansel (1487–1559) rebuilt Oxwich Castle as a large mansion and acquired the former monastic lands at Margam, where another grand house arose. Their Gower estates were leased out to tenants and at Penrice a farmhouse was built below the abandoned castle. The only remaining evidence of the Mansel tenure is a circular stone dovecot adjoining the curtain wall, mentioned in a document of 1534. By that time the only real value the castle had was to keep pigeons as a handy source of meat and eggs, and several of the derelict towers were fitted out with stone nesting boxes.

At some point in the next two centuries the outer front of the hall block was demolished. This must have been the result of deliberate action rather than natural decay, since the rest of the circuit is so well preserved. The most likely time for this to have happened is during the Civil War in the seventeenth century, when many reused fortresses were crippled by artillery bombardment, but it is not certain that Penrice ever played a role in that conflict. Perhaps it was rendered indefensible as a precautionary measure. By the time the Buck brothers published their engraving in 1741 the castle looked very much as it does today.

A short time after their visit, the Mansel estates passed by marriage to the Talbot family of Lacock in Wiltshire. The secluded rural surroundings of Penrice found favour with Thomas Mansel Talbot (1747–1813), who commissioned the architect Anthony Keck (1726–97) to build a neoclassical villa here in 1773. The landscaped gardens and lily ponds were laid out by a student of Capability Brown and the old castle was pressed into service as an ornamental feature. The walls were repaired, and a walkway made around the southern battlements so that the owners could enjoy the vistas over the park to the sparkling expanse of Oxwich Bay. No self-respecting landowner of the time could be without a picturesque gothic ruin and Thomas was fortunate to have a real one in his grounds, but even this wasn't enough. He added a castellated lodge by the gates, which still makes quite an eye-catching feature on the main road. Keck's modest villa was greatly extended in Victorian times, but the fickle tastes of the aristocracy changed again, and Penrice was abandoned in favour of a vast gothic pile at Margam. In 1910 the estate passed to the Methuen-Campbells, descendants of the last Talbot heiress, who own the house to this day.

Location & access
Penrice Castle is located within the grounds of Penrice Castle House, Gower. From Swansea city centre follow the signs westward to Gower and Port Eynon via the A4118. About 5 km beyond the village of Parkmill there is a sharp left turn to Oxwich bay where a castellated lodge marks the entrance to the estate; but carry on along the main road and take the next left to Penrice village, where there is a car park down in the valley (OS map ref: SS 497 886). The castle stands on private land with no public access, but it is visible from the public footpath that starts from the car park and crosses the estate to the lodge.

References
AC (1961); RCAHMW (2000)

PLAS BAGLAN, *PORT TALBOT*

There is an enduring tradition that the Norman invaders of Glamorgan allowed the descendants of Iestyn ap Gwrgant to retain possession of some of their ancestral lands, and that a castle was built at Aberafan from which they ruled the truncated territory. There is no doubt that Iestyn's grandson Morgan ap Caradog (d.1208) controlled this strip of mostly upland territory, but it was through brute force rather than Norman generosity. The Welsh dynasty of Afan proved to be a persistent menace to the Anglo-Norman settlers of the Vale: castles, churches and monastic properties were frequently raided, truces periodically made and broken.

When Gerald of Wales passed through Afan in 1188 his party was accompanied across the hazardous estuary of the River Neath by Morgan 'the leading man of those parts'. What he does not mention is that Morgan had recently built a castle on a crag above the river to control the crossing. The site of this lofty fortress was destroyed a few years ago when the M4 viaduct was constructed. At least two other castles were built by the Welsh to secure this area: a small motte on the slopes of Mynydd Dinas, and the larger fortification of Plas Baglan opposite the early medieval site of St Baglan's church. The latter was probably the main stronghold

Reconstruction drawing showing the possible original appearance of Plas Baglan

and control centre of the belligerent lords of Afan. The site now appears to be nothing more than a tree-covered platform on a ridge between two streams, but a few glimpses of masonry suggest that there is a substantial little castle buried here. The remains outline a rectangular hall or keep measuring approximately 17m by 10m with a walled forecourt at the front and a broad outer ditch. The ditch has been largely filled in, so that the site does not appear as strong as it would once have been. A few dressed stones have been vaguely dated to the twelfth or thirteenth century, but only excavation would provide more information about the site.

After many years of violence towards their neighbours the Welsh lords of Afan bowed to the inevitable and threw in their lot with the victorious English, even adopting the curious surname 'De Avene'. By the beginning of the fourteenth century, Morgan's great-grandson Lleision de Avene had established his seat at Aberafan (the castle was flattened for housing in the 1890s). The growth of a borough was encouraged by the grant of a charter to the townsfolk, and another charter of rights was signed by John de Avene in 1350. Sometime before 1373 the last of the family line exchanged the territory with the chief lord of Glamorgan for lands in England. Ownership of Plas Baglan had in the meantime been granted to Lleision's brother Rhys, and it was used by this branch of the family and their descendants for many years as a manor house, rather than a fortress. By the fifteenth century Plas Baglan was renowned as a cultural centre for Welsh bards and minstrels and appears to have remained in occupation until the early seventeenth century, when it was abandoned for a new house close by. By the end of the century this one-time stronghold of native independence and cultural aspiration was a decaying shell, and stones from the site were later used to build a nearby farmhouse which now, like the castle itself, is just a tangled ruin.

Location & access
Plas Baglan lies on the hillside above Baglan church, Port Talbot (M4 junction 41a). From the A4211 road follow the signposted path at the back of the houses on Small-wood Road, and up over the hill to Cwm Afan. After passing through a gate beside a ruined farm the castle earthworks can be glimpsed at the bottom of the field on the left (OS map ref: SS 736 923). The site is on private farmland, but just visible from a public footpath.

References
RCAHMW (1991); Davis (2007)

Sully Castle, *Barry*

For hundreds of years the ivy-covered walls of Sully castle had been left to moulder in peace, hardly noted by antiquarians and archaeologists until housing developers started eyeing up the potential of the site in the 1960s. Lying between the expanding suburbs of Barry and Cardiff, the coastal village of Sully had become an ideal haven for wealthy commuters. This is not the only rural village in Wales to swell up almost overnight and consume its own green mantle (and it certainly won't be the last), but was the destruction of Sully castle really necessary to provide upmarket homes? Admittedly, there was not a great deal to see here – no towering walls and battlements, just short, low stretches of crumbling masonry defining a roughly rectangular enclosure beside the parish church; and it could be argued that excavation provided more information than could ever have been gleaned from just studying the stonework; however, the fact remains that another piece of heritage was swept away and replaced by houses that could have been built on any available piece of land.

Excavations were carried out here in Victorian times when G.T. Clark discovered the foundations of a stone keep, but more detailed work was undertaken by archaeologists between 1963 and 1969 in advance of redevelopment. The evidence recovered pointed to a surprisingly complex site that had first been occupied in prehistoric times. Around the beginning of the twelfth century a castle was established on the hilltop next to St John's church probably by a founder-member of the Sully family, although the name does not appear in records until the end of the century. This first castle was a very large ringwork enclosing a number of stone buildings and a massive rectangular keep. Only the lowest courses of masonry survived, but the remains indicated a substantial building measuring around 20m by 10m, with a projecting garderobe turret. The 5m-thick east wall probably contained the entrance lobby and stairway leading to the upper floors. This keep was positioned on or close to the ringwork bank and probably overlooked the gateway for added security. A very similar layout was adopted at the surviving twelfth-century castles of Bridgend and Coity further west (both in the care of Cadw).

This Norman stronghold remained in use until the end of the thirteenth century when the whole site was redesigned and extended beyond the earthwork defences. A curtain wall was built to enclose a pentagonal courtyard, which had two feeble towers at the north and west corners and a simple gateway. The great keep now occupied a central position within a courtyard and formed part of a residential complex of buildings. The new works clearly reflected a bias towards domesticity rather than defence, for by 1300 the Welsh threat had receded and the castle's location deep within the Vale of Glamorgan rendered it secure. The archaeologists

In the early twelfth century Sully Castle comprised a substantial stone keep
and much simpler masonry buildings within the courtyard

By 1300 the castle had been extended and rebuilt,
with the keep forming a central building within the courtyard

concluded that the site became uninhabited sometime in the early fourteenth century, possibly after the last member of the family, Raymond de Sully, died in 1317. The estate later passed to the chief lord of Glamorgan and was administered from a new manor house at Middleton nearby. A reference in 1349 to 'a certain messuage [property or holding] enclosed by a stone wall, with a garden ... [and a] stone dovecot' may relate to the castle, suggesting that it was still being utilised, if not occupied at the time. In subsequent years the slow decay was hastened by local people helping themselves to the abundant rubble to construct their houses.

Location & access
Sully Castle stood behind the church in Sully village, 3 km east of Barry on the B4267 to Penarth. The churchyard wall is said to incorporate the last vestiges of the castle (OS map ref: ST 152 683).

References
RCAHMW (1991)

OPPOSITE: The surviving south-east corner tower at Llanfair Discoed

3 MONMOUTHSHIRE

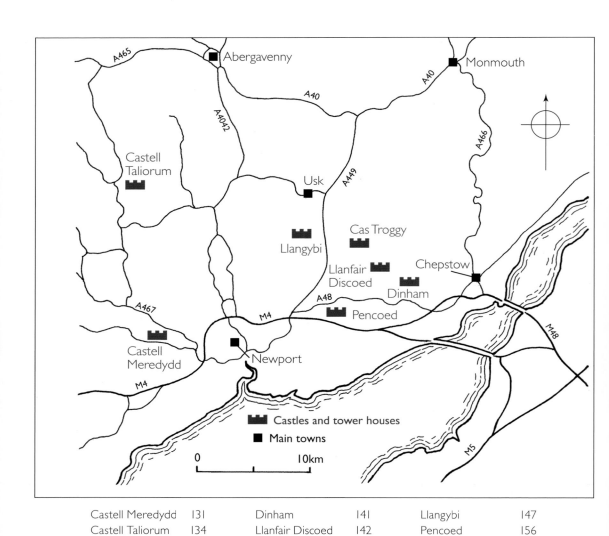

3

MONMOUTHSHIRE

CASTELL MEREDYDD, *MACHEN*

THIS fragmentary Welsh castle lay within the cantref of Gwynllŵg, a narrow strip of land squeezed in between Glamorganshire to the west and Monmouthshire to the east. Like many of the early land divisions in this part of south Wales, it comprised a fertile low-lying coastal plain backed by more sparsely populated upland valleys. Norman incursions into this region had taken place soon after William fitz Osbern, earl of Hereford, had established advance bases at Chepstow and Monmouth around 1068. Under the leadership of his son and successor, the Normans advanced as far west as the River Usk and reached some kind of agreement with the native ruler of the area, Caradog ap Gruffudd (d.1081). Caradog was using Norman mercenaries against his enemies in 1072, but when he was later killed in battle the Normans took advantage of the power vacuum and moved further west, building a major castle at Cardiff and possibly another at Caerleon. Both are massive mottes utilising pre-existing Roman fortifications. Several smaller castles were later built to control the lowland portion of Gwynllŵg as well, while the less accessible uplands were left in nominal Welsh control.

The descendants of Caradog were successful enough to make their mark on the politics of the region, and control of Caerleon castle was often ceded to them (albeit reluctantly). Machen was presumably a back-up base used by the native rulers when their hold on Caerleon was disputed by the Normans. It was located in the foothills of the Rhymney valley, close enough to exert some influence on the coastal plain and yet offering a retreat and escape route into the more secure uplands. The building of Machen castle can be ascribed to either Hywel ap Iorwerth (d.*c*.1217) or his son Morgan ap Hywel (d.1248).

The castle had certainly been in existence for some time before 1236 when it made its first appearance in contemporary documents. The *Brut y Tywysogion* records that Gilbert Marshal (d.1241), earl of Pembroke and lord of Usk, ousted Morgan from Caerleon and seized Machen. He then fortified it against a Welsh

How Castell Meredydd may have appeared after rebuilding work in 1236

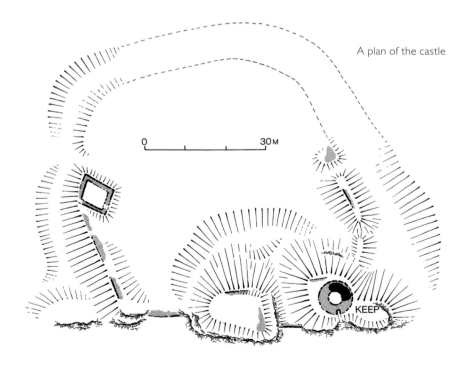

A plan of the castle

0   30 M

KEEP

counterattack, but as this belligerent action took place during a period of truce between Llywelyn the Great and King Henry III, Marshal was forced to relinquish the castle to its rightful owner. Morgan must have been pleased to have had his family stronghold upgraded at someone else's expense. When he died in 1248 Morgan was still in possession of Caerleon and had outlived the Marshal dynasty that

A surviving remnant of the round keep

had caused him so much strife. Lacking a direct heir, the territory passed to his relative Maredudd ap Gruffudd, and in turn to his son, Morgan ap Maredudd.

The lordships of Usk and Glamorgan were by then under the control of the powerful de Clare family, who made it their business to stamp out any native strongholds in their territories. Gilbert de Clare invaded upland Gwynllŵg around 1270 and seized the castle, which then passed into his ownership.[1] However, in 1294–95 there was a general Welsh uprising against the English occupation and the southern insurgents were led by Morgan ap Maredudd, who had his own axe to grind. Gilbert's castles were specifically targeted; Caerphilly was attacked, Llangynwyd and Morlais damaged beyond repair, and perhaps Machen too, suffered from the rebels' anger. It was listed among the possessions of the last de Clare who died in 1314, but such an insignificant little castle could hardly have been of much value and would surely have been left to decay at an early date.

The few surviving remains represent a very odd and typically unique Welsh castle, set on a rocky escarpment above the Rhymney valley. The outcrop has been quarried to form two motte-like mounds of roughly equal height. On the eastern summit there was a modest round keep within a walled enclosure, while the other knoll had either a building or a small courtyard (the remains are too slight to be sure). There is much loose stonework scattered about the site and the surviving masonry has suffered from erosion and tree root damage. Enough remains to indicate that the keep had an external diameter of about 8m with at least one upper residential chamber, since a garderobe drain can be seen discharging over the cliff edge.

The escarpment provided sufficient protection for the southern flank, while the more vulnerable northern approach was defended by a walled bailey with a broad outer ditch. This was the 'great fortification around' the castle specifically referred to in the chronicles as having been built by Gilbert Marshal in 1236. The other structures were presumably already in existence. Most of the courtyard has long been occupied by a cottage garden and any early features seem to have been obliterated. There are the foundations of a small rectangular building on the west side, which may be associated with the gateway, although the thin walls suggest it could be a relatively modern structure. The whole site is now very overgrown, and excavation is needed to establish the full layout; but a far more desirable course of action would be to clear away the trees and consolidate the few remains of this strange Welsh castle.

Location & access
Castell Meredydd lies 8 km east of Caerphilly on the A468 road to Newport. Pass through Machen village and after a bend in the road there is a left turning (marked 'Hanson Quarry'). Follow this under the railway bridge, then continue on foot (public right of way) up the hillside to where the castle site will be seen in the trees behind the first house (OS map ref: ST 225 887). The remains are on private land and there is no public access, but they are visible from the path.

References
Brut; BBCS (1979); Bradney (ed.1993); GCH (2008)

CASTELL TALIORUM, *LLANHILLETH*

On a mountaintop overlooking the former mining valley of Abertillery stands the redundant church of St Illtyd, accompanied in its isolation by a few houses and the prominent motte of a Welsh or Norman castle. Far less obvious than either the mound or the church is a scatter of stones in a hummocky field behind the pub, which marks the site of Castell Taliorum. The site makes no appearance in early documents[2] although the inconspicuous earthworks had long been known to antiquarians. In 1801 William Coxe described the site as 'a small tumulus and circular entrenchment ... [with] vestiges of subterraneous walls faced with hewn stone'. However, it was not until excavations took place in 1924–25 that the site was identified as a medieval castle. The partial foundations of two freestanding towers were uncovered. One was a substantial round keep having an external diameter of about 18m, and retaining the base of a central pillar to support the upper floors. Just 7m away stood a slightly larger tower of a unique cruciform plan. Very few dressed stones were recovered from the round keep, but a large number were found in the cruciform tower, including pieces of a newel stair and round-headed doorway, and window frames from the vanished upper floors. The only dateable finds were some late-Roman coins, fourteenth- or fifteenth-century pottery, and various pieces of refuse from the seventeenth century onwards. No sign of an enclosing curtain wall was revealed in the limited excavation trenches. After two seasons the dig was concluded and since that time no further exploratory work has been carried out. The site thus remains a puzzle.

The possible appearance of the unique cruciform tower of Castell Taliorum

Was it a Welsh castle? The peculiar shape, arrangement and location of the towers would suggest so; but the archaeologists believed that the dressed stones were imported from the Forest of Dean, which makes a native origin less likely, and the sheer abundance and quality of the ashlar points to a wealthy aristocrat rather than an impoverished upland princeling. It has been suggested that the towers were built by Gilbert de Clare while suppressing the independent rulers of Gwynllŵg around 1270. The circular keep is very similar to the ones he built at Castell Coch and Morlais, yet the round arches of the cruciform tower are characteristically Norman and imply an origin no later than the beginning of the thirteenth century. Furthermore, Llanhilleth is not in Gilbert's territory at all, but in the neighbouring lordship of Abergavenny.

Why were the two towers built so close together, yet had no connecting curtain walls? Quite possibly they are not contemporary and relate to separate phases of occupation. From these meagre clues, a plausible scenario might be offered: (1) around 1200 the lords of Abergavenny established a fortified settlement on the mountaintop next to the existing church, and built a cruciform stone keep within an earthwork enclosure. (2) Much later in the thirteenth century, perhaps around 1300 or so, construction work began on the round tower as an upgrade to the existing defences, or even as the first stage in a planned new castle – but the lack of ashlar implies that this second phase was never completed.

An alternative theory is that the whole site is an ornate fourteenth-century hunting lodge. Such a late date might explain the cruciform keep, since many oddly-shaped towers appeared in the later Middle Ages, and the antiquated round arches might have been used purely for decorative effect. But this is all conjecture; answers to the mystery may only be obtained by a more thorough and meticulous excavation than that carried out in the 1920s.

CAS TROGGY, *NEWCHURCH*

In summer, the most that can be seen of this neglected site is an overgrown copse in a field, and even when the undergrowth has died back in winter the view is not much better; the few wall fragments are so wreathed in mature trees that it is hard to see where the roots begin and the masonry ends. The centuries of neglect and complete lack of consolidation work has brought this small fortress to a deplorable state. Much of the structure lies buried metres deep in its own rubble. This was a sizeable building in its day, sporting the advanced, luxurious details that typify late-medieval castle architecture, yet it served merely as a hunting lodge for the wealthy lords of Chepstow.

The odd place-name is thought to derive from the Troggy brook which breaks out beside the ruin, and in medieval records it appears as 'Tarogi' or 'Toroggy'. In Thomas Churchyard's rambling poem, 'The Worthiness of Wales' (1587), there is a brief mention of this site: 'Castle Stroge doth yet remain three mile from Usk, but the Castle is almost clean down'. Some 50 years earlier, Leland commented on the 'very notable ruins' to be seen here. Clearly it had long been ruinous and appears never to have played a role in the history of the region.

A few scant records link the origin of Cas Troggy to one of the richest and most powerful men in the late-thirteenth century – Roger Bigod (d.1306), fifth earl of Norfolk and Lord Marshal of England. Roger was the last of a dynasty that had held sway in East Anglia since the time of William the Conqueror. The already sizeable Bigod estates were increased with the acquisition of the lordship of Chepstow in 1245. When the Earl Roger succeeded to the title in 1270, he took a great interest in his Welsh properties and transformed the old Norman

The crumbling and overgrown remains of Cas Troggy (left)
with the massive arched entrance to the garderobe pit (right)

stronghold of Chepstow into a palatial residence worthy of his standing. He carried out building work at his other estates in England, and practically financed the wholesale reconstruction of Tintern Abbey, thereby leaving to posterity one of the grandest monastic sites in Britain.

Not surprisingly, these costly schemes helped to plunge the earl into debt, and by the end of the century Roger's financial problems were as bad as his relationship with the king. In a celebrated encounter at Parliament in 1297 Roger refused to fight in France on the king's behalf, considering it to be outside his feudal obligations; 'By God earl you shall either go or hang' roared the king, to which Roger replied 'by God O king, I shall neither go nor hang'. This heated exchange seems to have involved a deliberate pun on his surname. Roger stood his ground against the formidable Edward I, but by 1302 the earl was an elderly widower with no direct heirs and, rather than allow his hated brother to claim the estate on his death, he made everything over to the king in return for an annuity. In the few years left to him, Roger embarked on another building spree at the monastic grange of *Plateland*, which he acquired from the monks of Tintern. Expense accounts for the year 1303–4 mention the 'New Castle' and a 'Master William the Mason', and so he had lost no time in starting work, despite his dwindling bank balance.

Two years later Roger died, and the inventory of his estates mentions 'a certain tower newly built which is worth nothing after its maintenance per annum'. Royal accounts for 1308–10 record wages paid to a keeper, but the lack of subsequent entries suggests that the castle might have been neglected and abandoned thereafter. Since it was located in a marshy hollow of negligible defensive strength and of little strategic value, the castle's real purpose was to provide quality accommodation for the earl and his aristocratic guests while hunting in the surrounding forest of Wentwood.

This vast expanse of upland heath and oak woodlands stretched between the Usk and the Wye, and in ancient times separated the region in two – Gwent Uwchcoed and Gwent Iscoed (literally, 'above' and 'below' the woods). From the sixteenth century onwards, gradual enclosure reduced the area to its present extent of about 1,000 acres, although it is still the largest ancient woodland remaining in Wales. A number of small castles had been established along the edge of the forest in order to control the resources of the area, and include Dinham, Llanfair and Pencoed (all three discussed further on). Wentwood was a jealously-guarded hunting preserve where the rights and laws of the Forest were laid down in statutes that lasted well beyond the medieval period.

The fortunate survival of a survey dated 1271 lists the owners of neighbouring estates who held certain liberties within the forest. These included *housbote* (the right to gather wood to repair and maintain a house), *heybote* (collecting underwood to repair fences and hedges) and *pannage* (allowing swine to feed on acorns and beechmast in the autumn). Those who were caught poaching game, stealing beehives, robbing hawks nests or cutting down trees without authorisation, faced a swift and severe punishment. A court met twice a year at an ancient copse of trees known as the Forester's Oaks, and any convicted thief would be strung up from the study branches. Tenants had to pay a yearly rent to the lord and provide an annual meal for the forest ranger in order to retain their rights. A record of 1664 states that on one occasion a Mr Lawrence of Wilcrick provided a meal comprising boiled beef, leg of pork, double rib of roast beef, roast goose, a loaf of bread and four gallons of ale. Presumably this feast was for several officers, rather than one gluttonous ranger. The forest is still a nature reserve today, cared for by the Woodland Trust and the Forestry Commission, although most of the great oaks have been replaced by conifers.

Cas Troggy overlooks the Usk valley on the northern side of the Forest, and if the undergrowth allows, then it is possible to make out a rectangular enclosure bounded by a boggy ditch and an earthen rampart (doubtless concealing the remains of a collapsed wall). Within the courtyard are several terraces and foundations indicating the position of vanished buildings. The most obvious part of the site is a tree-covered mass of rubble and masonry, representing the remains of a substantial two-storey hall block capped at either end by large towers. The hall itself is now very ruined and only the outer wall is still upstanding, in which can be seen the ragged openings of two windows, a central fireplace and a newel stair.

How Cas Troggy might have looked after the hall block was finished

The towers, however, are in a much worse state and it is difficult to confirm their original shape. They were certainly octagonal or multangular on the inside, and the few surviving fragments and antiquarian plans suggest that they may have been so on the outside as well (as suggested in the reconstruction drawing). If so, they would have contrasted with the more traditional rounded plan of Earl Roger's buildings at Chepstow, and also Gilbert de Clare's contemporary work at Llangybi Castle not far away; but multangular towers had appeared before – most notably at Caernarfon and Denbigh in the 1280s, and Stokesay (Shropshire) around 1290 – and they achieved a certain vogue as the fourteenth century progressed. Quite probably Earl Roger wanted something a bit fanciful for his country seat.

Earl Roger Bigod's round tower at Chepstow (left) and a multangular tower at Caernarfon (right). The towers at Cas Troggy could have resembled either of these late thirteenth-century examples

Whatever their shape, these massive towers would have contained a basement store and at least two upper floors of high-quality accommodation, with stairs, fireplaces and ample garderobes. The eastern tower retains an enormous vaulted cesspit with an arched entrance so large that it could have accommodated a cart for workers to shovel out the muck. That such a dangerously vulnerable opening should be built at all, says much about the attitude to defence at this time and the growing importance of domestic comfort over military needs.

The hall block may not have been intended to stand alone and probably represents the first stage of an ambitious, unfinished scheme in which further ranges and towers would have been added.[3] The proximity of the Troggy spring makes it probable that the outer ditch was flooded, the intention being to provide a 'feature' for approaching visitors, who would have been greeted with the towered profile of the castle reflected in the still water. Yet while the moat is impressively broad and deep on the southern flank, it is absent on the remaining sides, which suggests it was never dug out as intended. Furthermore, the east tower (on the right in the drawing) awkwardly juts far out beyond the line of the courtyard. This implies that the relatively insignificant courtyard buildings are the remains of an older structure (perhaps the monastic manor) which would have been swept away as Earl Roger's work progressed, had death not intervened and brought the project to an abrupt halt.

Location & access

The ruin of Cas Troggy lies approximately 5 km north-west of Llanfair Discoed, which is signposted off the A48 at Caerwent. Follow the road through Llanfair village and up into Wentwood Forest. After the woods are cleared and the road begins to descend towards the Usk valley, take the next right turn (signposted to Shirenewton). Just past the first house, the overgrown castle site can be seen in a field on the left (OS map ref: ST 414 953). The remains lie on private land, but are visible from the roadside and from a signposted footpath which crosses the adjoining field.

References

Morgan & Wakeman (1863); GCH (2008); For detailed information on the castle and Roger Bigod's works, see R. Turner & A. Johnson, Chepstow castle, its history and buildings (Logaston Press 2006)

DINHAM, *CAERWENT*

Long before Roger Bigod's masons began work on Cas Troggy, numerous manors on the fringes of Wentwood had already been provided with small castles for defence. A few, like Penhow, Pencoed and Llanfair, remained in use for many years and underwent considerable extensions and rebuilding; Dinham was an unlucky one, abandoned long before the medieval period had passed and now little more than a chaotic jumble of rubble in dense woodland. The site consists of a rather weakly-defended escarpment overlooking a little valley winding down from the hilltop village of Shirenewton. Scattered about are several stony earthworks and ruined foundations, the most obvious being a small rectangular building set within a walled enclosure of roughly oval plan. At the western end of the site, one wall survives of a square building (or tower) that has largely collapsed down the slope. The abundant rubble clearly indicates that *something* once stood here, but the layout is rather confusing and none of the walls appear to be thick enough for defensive purposes.

The few known historical facts about Dinham were collated by Octavius Morgan and Thomas Wakeman in their book, *Notes on the ecclesiastical*

Some of the remnant walling at Dinham

remains at Runston, Sudbrook, Dinham and Llanbedr (1856). Dinham was one of three *hardwicks* (farmsteads belonging to herdsmen) recorded in the Domesday survey of 1086. In 1128 it is again mentioned in connection with disputes over the ownership of church lands, and in the 1271 Survey of Wentwood, Adam Walens de Dynam is mentioned as holding rights in the forest. Further genealogical information has less relevance here, but it is significant that the authors, too, were puzzled by the remains. They noted that the site was known locally as 'the old church', implying that it was not a castle at all but an ecclesiastical building – perhaps the forerunner to a later church that once stood at nearby Dinham farm.

Records do suggest there was a castle at Dinham in medieval times, but was it an insignificant earthwork here in the valley, or at another site nearby? Are the remains in the wood those of a church, or a manor house with nominal defences? An archaeological evaluation of the site has recently been carried out and the suggestion has been mooted that the remains are those of a demolished medieval castle with a later church built on top.[4] Only an excavation should reveal what lies buried here and solve the mystery of Dinham.

Location & access
Dinham is situated in the Golden Valley approximately 1.5 km south of Shirenewton village, which lies just off the B4235 road from Chepstow to Usk (OS map ref: ST 481 924). The site is on private land and there is no access, although a public footpath passes through the valley below. The path starts on Red House Lane below the church, just opposite Newton house.

References
Morgan and Wakeman (1863)

LLANFAIR DISCOED, CAERWENT
Not far away is another neglected castle that once guarded the upland hunting preserve of Wentwood, but unlike the scanty remains of Dinham, a substantial amount of Llanfair Discoed Castle still survives. It is, however, in a very poor state, with mature trees sprouting from the walls and the interior wreathed in nettles and brambles. No attempt has been made to consolidate the masonry and a private house occupies the grounds.

The south front and south-east tower at Llanfair Discoed

The place-name means 'the church of St Mary below the woods' – a reference to the great forest that played such an important role in the history of this area. In Domesday, Llanfair appears as *'Lamecare'*, one of the three hardwicks established in the eastern reaches of the lordship of Chepstow by 1086. The estate was valued at a knight's fee, and so was probably defended by a castle, although the only documentary reference to one occurs much later. The historian Sir Joseph Bradney collated some information relating to Llanfair and provided a detailed genealogy of the twelfth-century owners of the manor, starting with Payn fitz John (d.1137) of Painscastle. The Fitzpaynes were in possession of Llanfair until the end of the thirteenth century, by which time most of the primary masonry castle must have been constructed. Robert Fitzpayne and his 'house' at Llanfair is mentioned in the 1271 Survey of Wentwood.

The family line continued into the fourteenth century, but for some unclear reason, by about 1290, the castle had passed into the ownership of Ralph de Monthermer (d.1325), erstwhile earl of Gloucester during the minority of the de Clare heir. Monthermer (who presumably came from Monthermé in the Champagne region of France) rose from obscure origins to a position of some standing by secretly marrying Joan of Acre, daughter of Edward 1 and widow to the Red Earl, Gilbert de Clare. Surprisingly for the time, this seems to have been a genuine

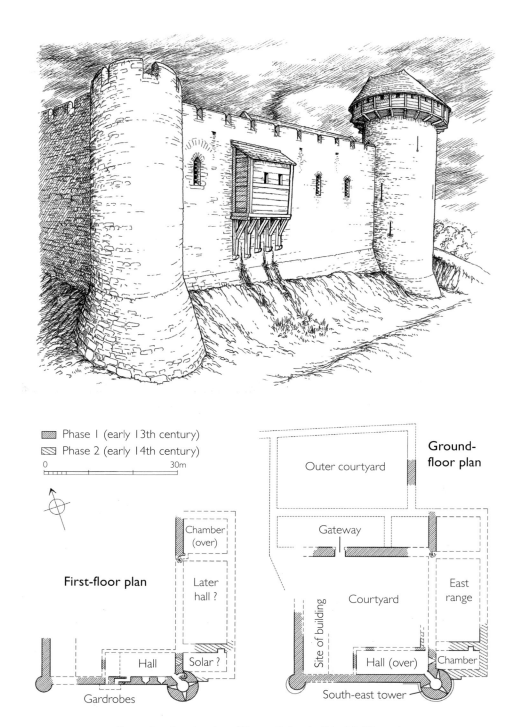

Reconstruction drawing of the south front of Llanfair Discoed,
with first- and ground-floor plans of the surviving masonry remains

First-floor plan

Phase 1 (early 13th century)
Phase 2 (early 14th century)

0   30m

Chamber
(over)

Later
hall ?

Hall   Solar ?

Gardrobes

Ground-
floor plan

Outer courtyard

Gateway

Site of building

Courtyard

East
range

Hall (over)   Chamber

South-east tower

love match rather than just ladder-climbing. When the king found out about his daughter's clandestine marriage to a mere squire, he flew into a rage, confiscated her property and imprisoned Ralph in Bristol castle. Joan bravely faced up to her father and begged for his release, saying that it was no disgrace when a great earl married a lowly girl, therefore why should a great woman not marry a promising young man? Several noblemen added their pleas for clemency and the king was swayed to release Ralph, who was thereafter allowed to hold the late earl's titles until Joan died in 1307. The estates then reverted to the young Gilbert de Clare, and Ralph was ennobled with the title of Baron Monthermer. Both lords later fought in the royal army against the Scots, but while Gilbert died in the mêlée at Bannockburn, Ralph was captured alive and later released.

Llanfair Discoed remained with the Monthermers for the duration of their short-lived dynasty. Ralph's sons Edward and Thomas both died in 1340 and the estate passed to Thomas's daughter Margaret, who conveyed it by marriage to John Montacute, earl of Salisbury (d.1390). It is hardly conceivable that a small castle in the increasingly settled Welsh countryside should thereafter be considered of much importance to such a powerful family. Ownership passed through various members of the Montacute-Salisbury line until the estates were seized by the Crown in 1541 when the elderly Countess Margaret, having incurred the suspicions of the tyrannical Henry VIII, was savagely executed. Llanfair was granted in succession to a number of local magnates before ending up with the Kemeys of Cefn Mably (whose descendants still own the property to this day). In 1635 Rhys Kemeys built a large house down in the village, and so by that date the castle was probably considered unsuitable for occupation. It is not known if it played any role in the Civil War, but since substantial parts of the walls are missing, there may have been some punitive or preventative slighting. Antiquarian drawings depict a ruinous structure much as it appears today, with only the south curtain wall and corner tower dominating the view. In 1801 William Coxe published his *Historical Tour of Monmouthshire*, noting that the overgrown site was used as a kitchen garden by the occupants of an adjoining cottage. A modern house was built within the outer bailey in the 1970s.

A survey of the castle reveals that it consists of two clearly-defined parts: a rectangular masonry stronghold overlooking the church and village, and behind it a large earthwork enclosure guarding the western flank. The latter is presumably an outer bailey, but since it stands slightly higher than the rest of the castle, it is tempting to consider that it may actually be the primary castle here, consisting of a large ringwork. There are slight remains of a small round tower on the rampart (which in some published accounts is claimed to be part of a gatehouse) but the thin, ragged walls prompt the suspicion that it is a later structure, possibly the remains of a dovecot. Excavation would be needed to clarify the date and function of this outer enclosure, but as it is now occupied by the house and gardens then the archaeological potential is not very promising.

The best-preserved section of the castle is the southern front, which is defined by a straight length of curtain wall with a rounded bastion on the west angle and a cylindrical tower on the corresponding east corner. This tower survives up to battlement level (indeed it is amazingly intact considering the state of the remainder). There are three floors, each under 3m in diameter and provided with plain arrow slits covering practically every approach. There are no fireplaces or garderobes within the tower and so it was intended purely for military needs. The top floor seems to be a later addition, and it was provided with holes for an external timber hourd around the battlements. The hall adjoined this tower and occupied the first floor above a dark basement. Perhaps the most surprising feature here is the odd arrangement of the garderobes, which were reached by a mural passage from the hall and were housed in a timber lean-to structure jutting out from the castle and supported on stone brackets (this type of feature survives intact at Stokesay Castle in Shropshire). Such an arrangement hardly makes much military sense and would have been a particularly vulnerable target during a siege; and yet it appears to be original and not an alteration of less war-like days.

Stone robbers have been particularly busy at Llanfair and one of the few dateable pieces of ashlar remaining is a fragment of an arrow slit with a square oillet (opening) at its base. This detail also appears at Caerleon, Chepstow and Usk castles and is believed to date from the first quarter of the thirteenth century. The round tower bears a marked similarity to one of the towers at Usk, and which was raised by William Marshal between 1210 and 1220. On this analogy the likely builder of Llanfair was Roger Fitzpayne (d.1239). The simple details and unsophisticated design accord well with an early thirteenth-century date, and we might envisage a four-square enclosure with round towers on the corners.

Regrettably the rest of the castle is not as complete or informative as the southern side. There is no sign of a gatehouse and the complex of rectangular buildings and courtyards only serve to confuse, rather than clarify, the plan. The castle was evidently extended beyond the confines of the early circuit, and the large east range was built out into the ditch to increase the accommodation. Although appearing to be more of a domestic character, these additions have walls thick enough to withstand most siege machines, and therefore must have been built when attack was still a possibility. There is the suggestion of a square tower at the northern end of the range, served by a spiral staircase. The tenure of the Monthermers would be a likely period for these additional works. Clearly a fuller understanding of the history and evolution of this castle will only be unravelled by geophysical survey and excavation, followed by essential conservation work to preserve the fabric from further decay.

Location & access

The village of Llanfair lies about 2.5 km north-west of Caerwent and is signposted off the A48 Chepstow to Newport Road. Pass through the village and the castle site will be seen in the trees behind the church (OS map ref: ST 446 924). The site is on private land and no access is allowed. Parts of the ruins can be seen from the churchyard.

References

Morgan & Wakeman (1863); Bradney (1932); Pevsner (2000)

Llangybi Castle, *Usk*

One of the largest and grandest medieval fortifications in Wales, Llangybi is now one of least well-known. Long-hidden by dense forestry, it comes as a shock to stray from the footpath and see towering walls shrouded in trees and creepers, like some forgotten jungle ruin. Some of the encroaching undergrowth was cut back for small-scale excavations carried out by *Time Team* in 2009, but Llangybi is still an overgrown and unconsolidated ruin with no official public access. The decay and subsequent neglect of this castle is due to a combination of factors, but its location within the private grounds of a country house (a situation comparable to Penrice) is the main reason. The house has long gone, but the ruin is still owned by a descendant of the family that has lived here since the sixteenth century. Apart from a few brief antiquarian accounts, the first proper study of the building was carried out by David Cathcart King and Clifford Perks in 1956. Their survey has since been augmented by a re-examination of the structural and documentary evidence by Stephen Priestley and Rick Turner in 2003, and the following account is based on these sources.[5]

The vegetation-covered walls of Llangybi

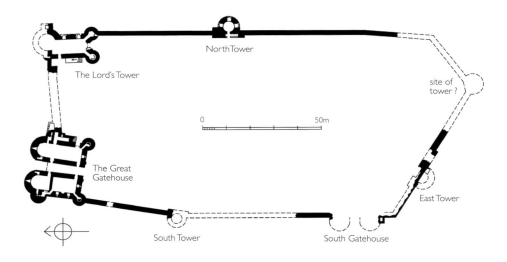

Plan of Llangybi Castle

The history of the castle begins with the building of a Norman ringwork nearby to control the lands lying between the main strongholds of Usk and Caerleon. Throughout the medieval period this was known as the manor of Tregrug, but to avoid confusion, the modern place-name will be used here. Usk was extensively rebuilt by the powerful Marshal dynasty in the early thirteenth century, but there does not seem to have been any interest shown in Llangybi until the lordship passed to another influential castle-building family, the Clares. Much of their history has already been touched upon in previous entries. At some point in the 1280s, the Red Earl, Gilbert de Clare, granted Llangybi to his disreputable and spendthrift brother Bogo, who often stayed here prior his death in 1294.[6] The earl himself died in 1295, and his widow Joan and her second husband, Ralph de Monthermer, controlled the lordship before the young heir, Gilbert, succeeded to his inheritance in 1307.

At some point the Norman ringwork was abandoned in favour of a new site on the adjacent hilltop, although when that happened is uncertain. In 1262 only 12 soldiers were required to garrison the castle, so it must still have been the old ringwork (it would have taken a lot more than a dozen men to adequately guard the big hilltop site). Therefore, the changeover of sites must have occurred sometime after that date. Building accounts for the lordship of Usk mention various towers and buildings being repaired due to war damage between 1301 and 1306 (presumably the result of Madog's uprising a few years earlier). These accounts refer to a hall, stable, kitchen and bakehouse, but provide no clue as to where they stood.

Reconstruction drawing based on the plan of the castle opposite

Priestley and Turner believed that it was the Red Earl's son and heir Gilbert who ordered the construction of the big hilltop castle, soon after coming into his money in 1307. However, the results of the *Time Team* investigation indicated that the western facade, with its enormous gatehouse, was a secondary phase of development to an earlier structure. Therefore, it is likely that the initial phase of the hilltop castle was built by the Red Earl himself, sometime after 1262 and before 1294 (when it was damaged in Madog's revolt). It is just possible that Bogo de Clare had a hand in the process, but it seems more likely that this indolent man would have lavished his income on personal luxuries rather than stone and mortar.

It is possible that young Gilbert ordered parts of the castle to be reconstructed soon after 1307, but his unexpectedly early death at Bannockburn in 1314 would have brought these works to a temporary halt. His widow Matilda was allowed to hold the lordship in dower right, and pushed ahead with the scheme, for surviving documents provide us with clear evidence of major building work proceeding at this time. Accounts dated 1315–16 refer to a gate and portcullis; in 1319–20 a 'little hall' and stable are mentioned and, significantly, a substantial tower was under construction, which was finally roofed with 2,000 tiles in 1321.

Reconstruction of the Lord's Tower seen from the north. It is here assumed that the battlements were topped with ornamental heads (as at Chepstow – see photo on p. 140).

By that time Matilda was dead, and the vast Clare inheritance had been split between Gilbert's three surviving sisters. The lordship of Usk passed to Elizabeth and her husband Roger Damory, and one of their first acts was to strengthen Llangybi with timber defence works – they were evidently expecting trouble. The accounts mention hourds and *targes* (literally 'shields', perhaps a type of shutter or flap attached to the battlements to provide extra cover for the defenders). At that time the country was nominally ruled by King Edward II, but the real power behind the throne was the ruthless and grasping Hugh Despenser, who had acquired the lordship of Glamorgan through his marriage to another of Gilbert's sisters. The sudden acquisition of the Gloucester estates pushed the ambitious Hugh into the limelight and onto a path that ultimately led to disaster. Hugh inveigled himself into the confidence of the weak and pliable king and, with the help of his equally pushy father, built up a power-base using whatever unscrupulous means possible.

The rapid rise of Hugh Despenser created many enemies amongst the aristocracy, including Damory who was ousted from his own favoured position with the king. Finally, in 1321 Damory and a group of Marcher lords rose in rebellion against the new favourite, sacked his castles and forced the king to concede to his banishment. But the setback was only temporary and in 1322 Despenser turned the tables on his enemies. Royalist opposition was crushed at the battle of Boroughbridge. Damory was condemned as a traitor but died of his wounds before the sentence could be carried out. Elizabeth and her children were imprisoned, and she was coerced into handing over Usk. With such blatant abuses of power going on, there were few people who shed any tears for Despenser's eventual downfall and savage execution in 1326 – least of all Elizabeth, who regained her rightful inheritance with the accession of King Edward III. Although her favourite residence was Usk, she often stayed at Llangybi with her household during the summer months and commissioned additional residential buildings there in 1341–42. The castle makes fewer subsequent appearances in the records and it is safe to assume that all the main works had been carried out long before she died in 1360.

The immense fortification that the Clares built on the hill was a fairly simple enclosure of roughly rectangular plan, with at least three rounded flanking towers and two gateways. But in scale and detail it is truly remarkable; the courtyard alone encompasses almost three acres, making it one of the largest single enclosure medieval castles in Britain. The flanking towers are now poorly preserved; so too is the south gate, which seems to have been a typical twin-towered structure of the type the Clares built at Llangynwyd and Caerphilly.

However, this pales into insignificance when compared to the monumental buildings on the western front of the castle. Principal among these is the Great Gatehouse, a hugely ambitious structure with a host of features that make it doubtful it served a military purpose alone. Anyone entering the castle would have approached along a raised ramp crossing the outer ditch. The entrance was rather weakly defended by a set of wooden doors and at least one portcullis, although the passage had a raised wooden floor that could have been fitted with trapdoors to hinder any attacker.[7] The two elongated D-shaped towers on either side of the entry passage would normally contain basic guardrooms, but here they are well-appointed domestic chambers with stairs, fireplaces and ample garderobes. In fact, the quality of the sanitary arrangements here is most surprising given the norm in medieval castles. There was a large cesspit on the south side of the gatehouse with stone arches to support multiple privies at different levels of the building. One chamber even has a carved stone washbasin beside the seat for necessary ablutions. The disappearance of the upper floors is most regrettable. Gatehouses of this period usually had a chamber at first-floor level above the entrance passage, containing the drawbridge and portcullis mechanism. There would be smaller rooms for the garrison, perhaps even a small chapel, with a larger residential apartment on the top floor for the constable and his family. However, given the ambitions of the builder, we cannot be sure how elaborate the upper levels were.[8]

From the gatehouse a spacious walkway along the top of the western curtain wall led to another surprising feature, a keep-like structure now known as the Lord's Tower. The building has an unusual asymmetrical plan (conjoined round and rectangular blocks) with flanking turrets of varying shape. One contains garderobes, another a spiral stair, while the third seems to have been an elaborately decorated closet or oriel. In places the finely-dressed stonework looks as sharp as it did when it was carved seven centuries ago. The ground-floor entrance to the tower was defended with a portcullis to bar access from the courtyard. Few details survive to indicate the layout of the upper level, and it is not certain if there were any further floors above. The Lord's Tower may be plausibly identified with the building roofed in 1320–21.

There is nothing quite like this elsewhere in Wales. During the later Middle Ages bizarrely-shaped towers appeared in England, probably inspired by examples from the Continent, and include Caesar's Tower (at Warwick Castle), Dudley, Nunney, Pontefract and Warkworth. Tower houses of the Scottish borders display a similar mishmash of round and square plans, although these date from a much later period. If any building inspired the design of the Lord's Tower then it may have been Marten's Tower at Chepstow, which had been built by Roger Bigod around 1290. This massive three-storied residential keep incorporates some of the elements noted at Llangybi, particularly the portcullis-barred entrance and the flanking turrets, yet it retains a more traditional D-shaped plan.

There appears to be a very strong decorative element to Llangybi, as if it were really a grand house dressed up like a castle; and perhaps it was, for the Clares didn't need another stronghold midway between the older fortresses of Usk and Caerleon. Priestley and Turner consider that this huge edifice was a showpiece hunting lodge and rural retreat for one of the richest families in medieval England. Perhaps it is significant that the Great Gatehouse and Lord's Tower are not positioned on the flank most exposed to attack, but instead overlook

Finely-dressed stonework at Llangybi: a door and portcullis groove (left), and a vaulted ceiling (right)

the deer park stretching away to the west. There was also a rabbit warren here and fishponds in the valley below. Anyone crossing the park would hardly fail to be impressed by the gleaming whitewashed walls of the elaborate western facade, which would have crowned the summit of the hill like the ornate castles depicted in contemporary illuminated manuscripts. The broad walkway between the Lord's Tower and Great Gatehouse seems to have functioned as a viewing platform for the residents – it even has its own garderobe for anyone taken short while perusing the view!

A strategic military base it may not have been, but it would be wrong to conclude that Llangybi was merely a 'pleasure palace' for the elite. Strong defences were still essential for a nobleman's residence in the barely quiescent Welsh Marches, and the young Gilbert may have embarked on this costly scheme to show off his ambitions and to live up to his father's castle-building reputation. Gilbert also rebuilt Llanbleddian castle near Cowbridge around the same time and, although built on a smaller scale, this shares certain similarities and might even be considered a dry run for Llangybi. As for the lingering belief that Llangybi was left unfinished at Gilbert's untimely death, the existence of all the building accounts spread over a 25-year period should quash that supposition.[9] In any case, Countess Elizabeth would hardly have spent so much time here if the place was a builder's yard.

After Elizabeth died in 1360 Llangybi was probably neglected, but it was not completely abandoned since modest sums were paid to caretakers to look after the buildings. The estate passed to her granddaughter and down through the Mortimer line by marriage. Whether the castle was ever used in the Glyndŵr rebellion is uncertain. Usk was prepared for the worse when the revolt spread south in

1402, and in the following year Newport and Abergavenny were besieged; but there are no records of any involvement of Llangybi. It must have been garrisoned as a precaution, for it seems unthinkable that this great edifice had decayed in the intervening years to such an extent that it was incapable of defence. Yet the absence of the castle from the lists of Mortimer assets in 1398 and 1424 might be taken as evidence that it had indeed, deteriorated irretrievably. The lordship became Crown property in 1461 when the Mortimer heir Edward, earl of March, became King Edward IV.

John Leland was here around 1539 but he does not comment on the condition of the castle; in fact, the lack of any specific reference to this huge structure prompts the suspicion that he never saw the castle up close. In 1555 Roger Williams of Usk purchased the estate and either refurbished some existing buildings or constructed a new house here before his death in 1585. The evidence for this supposition is provided by the Elizabethan poet Thomas Churchyard, whose long prose poem 'The Worthiness of Wales' (1587) contains many references to the local castles; 'Upon a mighty hill Langibby stands, a castle once of state: where well you may the country view at will, and where there is some buildings new of late'. This implies that something notable had happened to the castle in recent years. The historian Sir Joseph Bradney did not believe Williams occupied the old castle, and that his dwelling was on the same site as the later mansion at the foot of the hill; but during the Civil War Sir Trevor Williams (d.1692) garrisoned Llangybi for the king with 60 men, and in 1645 the place was described as 'strong and inhabited and fortified'. The *Time Team* excavations indicated that both gatehouses were being used at this period to get inside the castle, which means that the circuit of walls must still have been intact. The outer ditch appears to have been substantially modified and additional earthworks constructed to serve as artillery bastions during the war.

Oliver Cromwell distrusted Williams immensely (and with good reason, for he had changed sides twice) and ordered his arrest in 1648: 'he is a man … full of craft and subtlety, has a house, Langebie, well stored with arms and very strong … if you seize his person, disarm his house'. This must surely be a reference to the old castle. Presumably there was a Tudor building standing in the vast courtyard – a similar arrangement to Montgomery, Pencoed and St Fagans. Unfortunately, no internal buildings can be seen today, and no convincing trace was revealed by the excavations. The courtyard has suffered considerable damage from ploughing and tree root growth over the years, and it must be supposed that the foundations of what were probably timber-framed buildings, have been thoroughly obliterated.

The state of the ruin visible today suggests that Cromwell's orders to disarm the 'house' were carried out with gusto. The systematic demolition was exacerbated by stone-robbing for the construction of a new mansion at the foot of the hill once Williams had been restored to his lands. It is significant that the worst-preserved sections of the castle are along the eastern side facing the mansion, where it would have been easiest to cart the stonework away. All the outlying earthworks have been filled in on this side too. New gardens were laid out to suit the refined sensibilities of the time, and trees were planted in a splendid avenue stretching down to the river 1.6 km away. The old castle became a picturesque ruin in the deer park and the Norman ringwork was utilised for quite a different purpose (it is still known as the 'Bowling Green' today). But the fate of many country estates befell Llangybi and, after years of declining fortunes and neglect, the derelict mansion was demolished in 1951. Only the stable block and a few ruined outbuildings remain today.

However, one other relic of the castle may be preserved in an old building down by the Usk road. Tregrug Barn dates from the seventeenth century and has recently been converted into a private dwelling, but it has reused roof timbers taken from a high-status late-medieval building. The arched trusses would have supported a panelled or plastered ceiling above a grand chamber, measuring at least 18.6m by 5.6m. It is thought this roof was brought from the castle and, if so, may have formed part of the Tudor buildings dismantled after the chaos of the Civil War.

Location & access
Llangybi castle stands within the grounds of Llangybi Castle estate, 1 km north-west of Llangybi village on the road between Usk and Caerleon. A whitewashed lodge marks the beginning of a public footpath along the drive and up through the wooded hillside on which the castle stands (OS map ref: ST 364 974). The overgrown ruin is not accessible, though a public footpath passes close by.

References
Fox & Raglan (1951); AC (1952, 2003); GCH (2008); Knight & Johnson (2008); Time Team excavation report is available on the Wessex Archaeology website

PENCOED CASTLE, *LLANMARTIN*

Although called a castle, what survives at Pencoed today is actually the shell of a vast Tudor mansion dressed up with turrets and battlements to reflect its feudal past. A small portion of medieval fabric does remain, so there is some justification for including it here. This is one of the major casualties of the changing fortunes of the country house during the last century, a massive building still substantially intact and offering potential for rescue and reuse, but teetering on the edge of irredeemable decay.

The documented early history of Pencoed is meagre. It was another of the fortified manors established in the vicinity of Wentwood Forest, and was associated with a local family, the de la Mores. Richard de la More's 'house at Pencoyde' is mentioned in the 1271 Survey of Wentwood, but only some truncated curtain walls and a small round tower survive of this. The tower occupies the south-west corner of a rectangular enclosure and has three floors with a corbelled parapet. The square-headed dressed stone windows are later insertions. The few details can only broadly hint at a thirteenth- or fourteenth-century date. The formidable-looking gatehouse contains a vaulted ground-floor passageway and two upper chambers with stairs and privies housed in polygonal flanking turrets. This was once thought to be medieval, but is now considered to be a Tudor addition when mock-military features were all the rage. Similar gatehouses survive at the inhabited mansions of Moynes Court and St Pierre not far away. Probably the original castle was a simple square enclosure with corner towers and an outer moat, a layout reflected by the arrangement of the later buildings that now dominate the site.

The transformation from medieval castle to Tudor mansion began in the 1480s when Thomas Morgan (d.1510) was rewarded by Henry Tudor for his services on the battlefield of Bosworth Field. Thomas was not the only local magnate to benefit from the accession of a monarch of Welsh descent. He was knighted in 1495 and undertook the rebuilding of Pencoed to reflect his newfound wealth and status. Only part of the north range survives of his work, but probably more of the earlier buildings were absorbed into the ongoing reconstruction by his descendants. The main part of the house is a stunning three-storied range containing vast kitchens, a central hall and a tower-like chamber block. The abundance of apartments, fireplaces, stairways, windows and privies clearly reveals what mattered most to the Tudor gentry, and the few remaining medieval military features were retained just for show. Surrounding the house there were extensive gardens, ponds and outbuildings.

Ownership of Pencoed subsequently changed hands with alarming frequency, and by the end of the eighteenth century it was little more than a tenanted farm. When the antiquarian William Coxe paid a visit around 1800 it was semi-ruinous,

The crumbling remains of the Tudor gatehouse (top), and the medieval corner tower (bottom), with the Tudor mansion in the background

with broken windows and sagging roofs. Another century of neglect passed before a valiant rescue effort was undertaken by David Alfred Thomas, Viscount Rhondda, who acquired the estate and used some of his vast wealth accrued from the coal industry to restore the ailing house. The architect G.H. Kitchen drew up the plans and began work, notably adding huge new windows to the hall and a very fine timber ceiling to the Great Chamber. Far less praiseworthy was his transformation of the roof-scape, replacing the original high-pitched dormers and tiled gables with flat lead roofs and fake battlements.

However, the rescue came too late. The year was 1914 and within a short space of time a devastating World War was to transform the social order of Britain forever. The work was halted, and Viscount Rhondda died in 1918. His wife resumed the restoration the following year and employed another architect, Eric Francis, to continue with the scheme. Francis also built an attractive Arts and Crafts house beside the great hall, but this second phase of restoration also ended prematurely, and the estate was eventually sold in 1931. The unfinished buildings were left to moulder, and at one time were ignominiously used to house chickens. Further schemes have been mooted to restore Pencoed to life – by converting it into a 200-bed luxury hotel with golf-course, or into offices or upmarket flats. The most ambitious project (and the one that raised the most hackles) was for it to be restored as part of a £750 million 'Legend Court' Disney-style theme park. All the schemes have so far fallen flat, the sheer size of the undertaking being a most daunting challenge for any entrepreneur. In September 2020 the site was sold for over £1 million, with planning permission to restore the castle, convert the outbuildings to offices and erect a dozen new dwellings on site. Any proposed development will no doubt be watched keenly by officials and local residents in the months to come.

Location & access
Pencoed Castle lies just off the A48 Newport to Chepstow road, approximately 5 km east of M4 junction 24. Take the turning off the A48 south to Llandevaud, pass through the village and at a sharp bend continue straight on along a narrow lane leading up to the castle (OS map ref: ST 406 895). There is no access to the derelict building, but the exterior can be seen from the lane and from a public footpath that starts in Llandevaud and crosses the fields at the rear of the property.

References
Coxe (1801); Pevsner (2000); Tree & Baker (2008)

OPPOSITE: The shell of Urishay Castle, incorporating medieval and later fabric

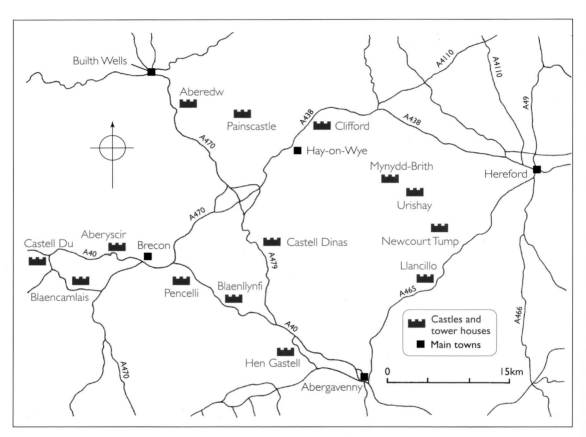

4

Mid Wales and the
Southern Marches

Aberedw castles, *Builth Wells*

THE patchwork of native territories between the Wye and Severn rivers in mid Wales was bitterly contested by the ruling princes and Norman interlopers during the twelfth and thirteenth centuries. Documentary evidence for the foundation of the numerous small castles that exist in this region is scarce, but it is known that a Normandy family, the Tosnys, were active here in the late eleventh century. Later members of the dynasty launched a protracted legal case to gain possession of the surrounding lordship of Elfael, and so perhaps the original castle at Aberedw was their foundation. It was built close to St Cewydd's church on the edge of an unassailable river gorge that provided an effective defence against

Aerial view of the site of the first castle at Aberedw

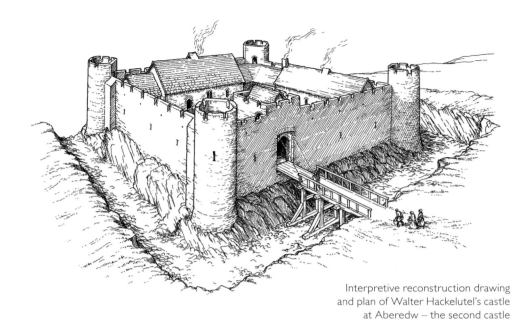

Interpretive reconstruction drawing
and plan of Walter Hackelutel's castle
at Aberedw – the second castle

attack. A rock-cut ditch surrounded the motte on the landward approach, but there does not seem to have been a bailey. This modest grassy mound may look like a typical earthwork castle, but recent erosion has revealed a core of layered shale, suggesting it was stone built from the start, perhaps with a masonry tower on the summit. If so, then it would have resembled Castell Prysor in Gwynedd (see p. 249) and might instead have been a Welsh foundation when the territory was back under native control.

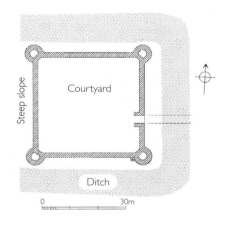

Aberedw only achieved historical prominence in the mysterious events that clouded the last days of Llywelyn ap Gruffudd. As the war against King Edward struggled on through the winter of 1282, Llywelyn left his secure, mountainous territory of Gwynedd and headed south to rally support among his followers. The prince did not enjoy the trust of all his allies and there was a scheme afoot to depose or assassinate him (one chronicle has a tantalising reference to a group meeting in the belfry of Bangor Cathedral to plot his betrayal). This statement has given rise to a rich crop of conspiracy theories, the most popular being that

Llywelyn was separated from his main force and lured to Aberedw, ostensibly to discuss terms with some Marcher lords who were planning to change sides. The prince and his attendants were captured and murdered upon arrival; while another version of the tale has Llywelyn fleeing to the hill opposite the castle and sheltering in a small cave (still to be seen amongst the rocks), before rejoining the main army the following day.

The few reliable accounts of the events of 11 December 1282 suggest that a battle took place near a river crossing and ended in a rout; Llywelyn and a small group of men were hunted down, and the prince was speared as he tried to escape. Llywelyn's mangled body was taken to the Cistercian abbey of Cwm-hir for burial, while the severed head was sent in triumph to King Edward. The fateful skirmish may have taken place at Aberedw, although the spot favoured by tradition is Cilmery west of Builth, where a modern memorial to the fallen prince now stands.

The dust of battle had hardly settled before the Marcher lords moved in to consolidate their gains. Edmund Mortimer (d.1304) evicted the Welsh tenant and gave the land to one of his knights, Walter Hackelutel, who straightaway began work on a new castle a short distance away from the old motte. In November of 1284 King Edward confirmed what was, in effect, retrospective planning permission: 'Mortimer has granted by his charter to Walter ... all the lands in Elfael ... and Walter has commenced to build a castle there, to which the king has given his willing consent; the king grants that Walter may complete the castle thus begun and may hold it when so built without trouble from the king or his heirs'. The trouble, when it came, was from a different source. By 1293 Ralph Tosny was clamouring for the return of his alleged ancestral lands, and instigated court proceedings against Walter. He eventually lost the case and Hakelutel retained Aberedw until his death in 1315. However, afterwards the lordship passed along with the Tosny estates to the Beauchamp earls of Warwick.

It is unlikely that these powerful aristocrats, with so many estates elsewhere, should have cared for this small fortress, and it is hardly surprising that by the end of the fourteenth century it was said to be worthless. In truth, the castle built by Walter was a very inadequate structure for the time – just a small square enclosure with rounded towers on the corners, a textbook example of a thirteenth-century stronghold but on the scale of a toy fort. The walls are too thin, the towers too small, and there was no strong gatehouse. Only a deep, rock-cut ditch around the landward approach adequately served to hold off any attacker. Walter had financial problems raising this meagre structure, for in October 1285 the king relieved him of a debt of £57 owed to a Jewish moneylender for building expenses. Interestingly, the entry in the accounts states that the money was needed for 'erecting a house in the Welsh

Marches and afterwards crenellating it by the king's license for the security of those parts'. The wording suggests that Walter's castle was actually a fortified dwelling rather than a strategic military stronghold, and this is confirmed by the rather modest remains.

The crumbling walls of the second castle

The tree-covered enclosure lies behind the village and backs onto a steep slope above the river Wye. Hardly any trace of internal buildings remains, and so much of the castle is now buried in its own rubble that only future excavations will reveal the complete layout. Vestiges of the entrance passage can be seen within the east curtain wall, but the apparent causeway across the ditch is almost certainly the result of later infilling (the ditch would originally have been spanned by a timber ramp with a drawbridge). The south-east corner tower is the only one of the four to remain fairly intact and it is still possible to make out the curving face of the inner room, which measured barely 3m in diameter. This cramped chamber was evidently intended for residential accommodation since there is an adjoining garderobe shaft serving the vanished upper level. Presumably the other corner towers were similarly equipped.

The visible stonework of Walter's castle is now in a wretched state and continues to crumble due to the flaky nature of the local stone and growing tree roots. In the nineteenth century the Cambrian Railway was driven through the slope below the castle and the steep cutting undermined some of the walls (though it has not completely destroyed the west side as some accounts in print suggest). This site needs to be excavated and properly conserved before erosion and neglect combine to wipe away the few visible remains for good.

Location & access
Aberedw village lies on the B4567 in the Wye valley, approximately 5 km south-east of Builth Wells (OS map ref: SO 074 473). Both castles are on private land but crossed by public footpaths. The motte can be reached from the back of the churchyard; Walter's castle by a poorly-marked path that runs from the main road along the old railway embankment at the entrance to the village.

References
Radnor (1951); AW (1994); Remfry (1996)

Aberyscir, *Brecon*

This unremarkable castle mound is one of the many relics of the Norman invasion of the Welsh kingdom of Brycheiniog in the late eleventh century and has made hardly a mark on recorded history; nevertheless, it is essential to understand what happened here nine centuries ago in order to put the more substantial castles described in the following pages in their proper historical perspective.

Soon after the Battle of Hastings, William the Conqueror rewarded one of his chief supporters, William fitz Osbern, with the earldom of Hereford. Fitz Osbern ordered further inroads into Welsh territory and had secured most of lowland Gwent before his death in 1071. His son Roger continued his father's work but became embroiled in a failed rebellion in 1075 and was stripped of his lands and title. The king then chose to partition Roger's forfeited earldom among lesser lords rather than repeat the risk of having so much territory under the control of one man. The more notable beneficiaries were Ralph de Mortimer, Walter de Clare, Philip de Braose and Walter de Lacy, and the dynasties they founded shaped the politics of the Welsh Marches for the next two centuries.

Another of King William's followers was Bernard de Neufmarché, a relatively obscure knight from Normandy who may not have participated in the initial invasion of 1066, but subsequently received estates on the borders of Herefordshire. With a band of loyal knights, he began to move into the native territory of Brycheiniog in the 1080s and completed the conquest initiated by the earl of Hereford. Rhys ap Tewdwr of Deheubarth who, only a few years earlier, had been acknowledged as ruler of south-west Wales by King William, put up a strong resistance, but at Easter 1093 he was killed in battle. This was a crushing blow to native independence, for it not only allowed the transformation of Brycheiniog into the Norman lordship of Brecon, but also opened the way for a widespread advance in other parts of the country. Bernard's followers erected lesser fortifications at strategic locations to secure their own allotted lands and act as buffer zones to his main base at Brecon. They followed the course of the Usk and

A thin fragment of a circular tower overlying the curtain wall, which might, therefore, be a later feature

other river valleys winding deep into the countryside, and left the bleaker, less accessible uplands under nominal Welsh control.

This method of colonisation was repeated throughout the coming years, as indeed it had been by earlier invaders. The Romans had established one of their military bases on the hill beside the confluence of the Usk and Yscir rivers, and the ruined walls must have been plainly visible to the Normans in their westwards progress. The founder of Aberyscir castle is variously claimed to be Bernard fitz Unspac or Hugh Surdwal, but whoever it was chose not to utilise the existing Roman fort, but opted instead for a smaller and more easily defendable promontory between the confluence. Another deciding factor may have been the pre-existence here of a church dedicated to St Cynidr, which was later given a dual dedication to St Mary.

The end of the ridge beyond the church was scarped into an oval motte measuring about 40m by 50m with an outer ditch. There was probably a bailey, but all traces have been obliterated by the later buildings of Aberyscir Court. Along the river frontage there is a 20m length of masonry, standing barely 2m high, which is all that remains of a curtain wall or shell-keep that once surrounded the summit of the motte. The adjacent Roman fort would have provided abundant building materials for replacing the initial timber buildings with stone, which presumably took place sometime in the twelfth or thirteenth century. There is also a solitary fragment of a round tower here, but it is very thin and overlies the curtain wall, so it is likely to be a later addition, and could just be part of a folly associated with the adjacent Court. All other stonework has been robbed away and if it were not for these few meagre remains then Aberyscir would probably be classed as just another modest earthwork motte. It is interesting to think that other similar sites in Wales may retain unsuspected masonry hidden beneath the turf.

Location & access

Aberyscir castle is located 4.5 km west of Brecon along the A40 towards Sennybridge on the north bank of the Usk. Turn off at Aberbran and take the next right back towards Brecon to where a T-junction sign marks the way to Aberyscir church (OS map ref: SO 001 296). The site is on private land and there is public access to the church only. The tree-covered mound can just be seen from the graveyard and also from the A40 across the valley.

References

Brycheiniog (1961); Remfry (1999)

BLAENCAMLAIS, *SENNYBRIDGE*

An obscure entry in a medieval chronicle refers to a 'new castle beyond Brecon' destroyed by English forces under the command of Prince Edward in 1265. The castle was apparently the work of Llywelyn ap Gruffudd when his authority had spread beyond Gwynedd, and most of Breconshire was subject to his rule. The location of this lost castle has puzzled historians, but a good contender was the large mound at the head of the Camlais valley, west of Brecon. From a distance the mound is quite a prominent object on the skyline. It superficially looks like a large motte encircled with a ditch and massive counterscarp bank; but the cratered summit is ringed with jagged masonry forming the base of a round keep with an internal diameter of 6.8m and walls about 3m thick. The foundations appear to extend down to the natural bedrock and so the mound is just rubble heaped around the base of the keep, and not the remains of a reused Norman motte as has been suggested. There is no sign of a bailey or any ancillary buildings, and so it seems that the castle was nothing more than a lone tower on the edge of the moors.

The visual evidence does suggest a typically modest Welsh fortress, and the castle student D.J. Cathcart King at first believed that this was Llywelyn's lost castle of 1265; however, the subsequent discovery of a manuscript in the National Library of Wales put paid to that: a 1358 deed records a settlement of land in this area and mentions a *Castrum de Gamleys* founded by Humphrey de Bohun, earl of Hereford. There were at least eight family members with that name, but Brecon was only acquired around 1241 when Humphrey v (d.1265) married an heiress of the de Braose family, so the search can be narrowed down. Round keeps like this are generally ascribed to the early thirteenth century, so Humphrey v would be the most plausible candidate. However, Cathcart King thought it more likely that the builder was Humphrey vi (d.1298) who came of age in 1270 but would

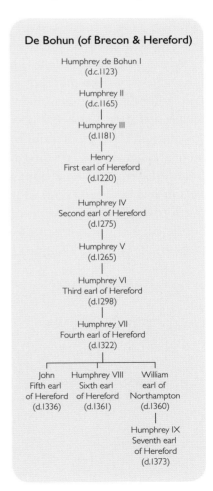

De Bohun (of Brecon & Hereford)

Humphrey de Bohun I
(d.c.1123)
|
Humphrey II
(d.c.1165)
|
Humphrey III
(d.1181)
|
Henry
First earl of Hereford
(d.1220)
|
Humphrey IV
Second earl of Hereford
(d.1275)
|
Humphrey V
(d.1265)
|
Humphrey VI
Third earl of Hereford
(d.1298)
|
Humphrey VII
Fourth earl of Hereford
(d.1322)

John
Fifth earl
of Hereford
(d.1336)

Humphrey VIII
Sixth earl
of Hereford
(d.1361)

William
earl of
Northampton
(d.1360)
|
Humphrey IX
Seventh earl
of Hereford
(d.1373)

Aerial view of the surviving castle mound (left) and reconstruction of the round keep (right)

only have had the chance to start work on the castle after Llywelyn had been forced to withdraw from Breconshire following his defeat in 1277.

Would such an archaic-looking castle have been built at the end of the thirteenth century when more advanced types of fortifications were commonly used? An earlier date may seem more probable on stylistic grounds, but large round towers and detached keeps were still being built at this time. Gilbert de Clare had them at Castell Coch and Morlais, and even the king's normally adventurous architects constructed them at Builth, Flint and Hawarden. Blaencamlais could feasibly have been intended as a precaution after de Bohun's rebellious Welsh tenants had quietened down. It seems unlikely that this minor outpost remained in effective military use for very long before being abandoned, though its location on the edge of the vast expanse of the Fforest Fawr preserve may have made it occasionally useful as a hunting lodge.

Location & access
From Sennybridge village on the A40, take the A4067 signposted to Swansea and after 1 km fork left for Merthyr Tydfil (A4215). Continue along this road for about 3 km, ignore the first signposted turn to Cwm Camlais, but take the next left at the crossroads. After 1.5 km the road levels out beside a pond, and the castle mound will be seen in the fields on the left (OS map ref: SN 956 261). There is no public access, although the mound is visible from the road and from a public footpath further along the road.

References
Brycheiniog (1965, 1984–5)

BLAENLLYNFI, *BWLCH*

The parlous state of Blaenllynfi castle today is not due to savage Welsh raids or devastating bombardment from Parliamentarian cannons, but simply the result of shoddy workmanship. The prominent stumps of masonry that rise above the overgrown earthworks are merely buttresses built to shore up the crumbling defences – and these have lasted far better than the walls they were meant to support. There is only one short length of upstanding curtain wall remaining here today, and as it survives up to wall-walk height it gives the only clue to the former scale of this remote and little understood site.

The castle guarded a hill pass from the Usk valley to Llangorse and Talgarth. The location may have been ideal for that purpose although the defensive position was very poor, for it lay within a marshy hollow overlooked by higher ground. Therefore, the stream was dammed to form a wide and deep moat to keep attackers away from the main structure. This took the form of a roughly rectangular enclosure with two small round towers and three larger square towers. The entrance seems to have been a simple gateway at the north corner, and within the courtyard there were a number of domestic buildings ranged against the inner walls. Because the masons chose the cheaper option of using clay instead of mortar, the walls began to crumble at an

Aerial view of the tree-clad site of Blaenllynfi Castle

How the decaying castle might have looked in the early fourteenth century

alarmingly early date and required constant repair. One corner tower even collapsed (or was knocked down) and the breach in the wall was simply blocked off. Evidently the owners had only enough cash and enthusiasm to make do and mend.

The origin of Blaenllynfi must be traced back to the aforementioned invasion of Brycheiniog by Bernard de Neufmarché in 1093, although whether a castle was built here at such an early date is unlikely, for the surviving earthworks do not look typically Norman. Bernard died around 1125 and Brecon passed to his daughter Sybil, the wife of Miles Fitzwalter, earl of Hereford. Miles was succeeded in turn by four sons, who had all died by 1165 so the inheritance was then split between Miles's three daughters and their husbands – Humphrey de Bohun II, Herbert Fitzherbert, and William de Braose II. It was William who ended up with the rich prize of Brecon and Abergavenny. There is a certain amount of confusion as to what happened afterwards. Some historians believe that Herbert carved out an independent lordship with Blaenllynfi as its caput, and a subsidiary fortress at Castell Dinas (see below); while others think it was still part of William's inheritance until 1208.

The de Braose family were among the most important Marcher dynasties in Wales. William de Braose I (d.1096) arrived from Briouze in Normandy and was given lands in Sussex by the Conqueror. During the next reign, his son Philip (d.c.1134) seized on the Welsh territories of Builth and Radnor. Philip's son was William de Braose II who, as mentioned above, laid claim through his wife to a share of the Hereford estates, including Brecon. His heir, William III (d.1211), earned a justified reputation for treachery that was bad even by the standards of the day. His most notorious act was to slaughter unarmed Welsh guests at a Christmas feast at Abergavenny castle in 1175. William's downfall came after picking a quarrel with King John, a man as ruthless and double-dealing as himself. In 1208 William's lands were seized, and he fled to die in impoverished exile. His wife and son were not so lucky; they were caught and starved to death in a royal dungeon.

The demise of William de Braose sent shock-waves through Marcher society. The lords realised that the king could turn on anyone, and John's already precarious reputation tumbled headlong. Although the family later regained most of their lands under John's heir, King Henry III, they were never as powerful as before.[1] On William's fall, the lordship of Blaenllynfi was granted to the king's current favourite, Peter Fitzherbert (d.1235) – though, as noted above, it is possible he merely recovered what had formerly been in his father's possession. Peter may have set about building (or rebuilding) the castle in stone to strengthen his hold on the territory.

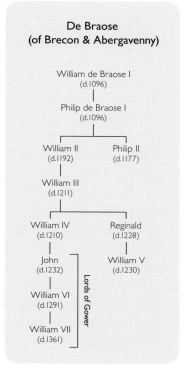

De Braose
(of Brecon & Abergavenny)

William de Braose I
(d.1096)
|
Philip de Braose I
(d.1096)
|
William II   Philip II
(d.1192)   (d.1177)
|
William III
(d.1211)
|
William IV   Reginald
(d.1210)   (d.1228)
| |
John   William V
(d.1232)   (d.1230)
|
William VI   *Lords of Gower*
(d.1291)
|
William VII
(d.1361)

One of the medieval buttresses built to support the crumbling walls

The earliest documentary reference to the castle occurs in 1215 when it was captured by a Welsh army led by Giles de Braose, Bishop of Hereford and younger son of the unfortunate William. Giles died in the same year, and his brother

Reginald (d.1228) continued the struggle to recover the family inheritance. He allied himself with the Welsh and stubbornly refused to compromise with the other Marcher lords, adding his name to the Magna Carta in defiance of King John. With the help of Llywelyn the Great (an alliance strengthened by a politic marriage to the prince's daughter Gwladys Du), Reginald was in a position of some power in the Welsh Marches. However, when Henry III was crowned, Reginald came to terms with the king and was received back into royal favour. Blaenllynfi was then returned to Peter Fitzherbert.

This rapprochement inevitably caused a rift between Reginald and his father-in-law, and in retaliation Llywelyn devastated a number of castles in Breconshire in 1233, including Blaenllynfi and Castell Dinas. The subsequent lords of Blaenllynfi, Reynold Fitzpeter and his son John, were a bad lot (John was even accused of torturing and hanging a clerk without trial). Continuous financial troubles forced them to sell off their assets to the Crown, and the subsequent owners were more concerned with gathering revenues from the lordship than ensuring the upkeep of the castle. Surveys were carried out in 1330 and 1337, and paint a very bleak picture of a building well past its prime and desperately in need of costly repairs. Certain rooms and towers were said to be in decay; others on the point of collapse or already fallen. One survey lists all the items of value within the castle, including such medieval bric-a-brac as two brass pots, four trestle tables, a portable altar and a pair of worn-out cartwheels!

In 1354 the lordship passed to another powerful Marcher family, the Mortimers of Wigmore and through them, via the duke of York, it became Crown property in 1461. There may have been an attempt to establish a borough here, for when the Tudor antiquary Leland passed through Blaenllynfi he noted 'a very fair castle now decaying, and … a borough town, now also in decay'. What may be the remains of that abortive venture can be seen as faint earthworks in the adjacent fields, while the old watermill and silted up millpond still survive below the castle mound. By the time the topographers Samuel and Nathaniel Buck sketched Blaenllynfi in 1741 the site looked much as it does today, although they did notice the tall fragment of a tower that has since fallen.

From the 1960s onwards the landowner was allowed to carry out minor excavations under strict guidelines, and some of the internal walls and buildings were uncovered. Conservation work in the 1990s helped to preserve these meagre remains, but in 2020 a long-term programme of re-excavation and conservation was started as a collaboration between Cadw and the current owner, so that hopefully more of the layout of this buried fortress will soon be revealed.

CASTELL DINAS, *TALGARTH*

The term 'hermit crab castle' perfectly describes sites which rely on pre-existing fortifications to bolster their own defences, much like the aforementioned crustacean uses a discarded shell. In Wales the castles of Cardiff, Caerwent and Loughor are all built within Roman forts, and further afield in England there are excellent examples at Brough, Brougham (both in Cumbria), Pevensey (Sussex) and Portchester (Hampshire). Here at Castell Dinas it was a massive Iron Age hillfort that the Normans utilised as they conquered their way through Wales. The site was admirably chosen by Celts and Normans alike – a steep-sided hill standing within a gap in the Black Mountains, so that traffic passing between the Wye and Usk valleys could be observed and controlled. Appropriately enough,

The scant masonry remains of Castell Dinas (left) and the hilltop site, high in the mountains (right)

An aerial view of the site from roughly the same angle as the plan opposite, the most prominent features being the central keep and the cross-ditch separating the main castle from the outer bailey

the site was known in medieval times as Bwlchyddinas ('the pass of the citadel') a name that is still occasionally used today. At over 450m above sea level, this is the highest situated castle in England and Wales, and that fact reveals the reason for its ultimate decline. Despite the admirable natural advantages of the site, this breezy peak is not the most pleasant of places to live, and once the military demands had passed, then Castell Dinas was quickly abandoned to the wind and the rain.

From the elevated viewpoints on either side of the hill the full defensive advantages of the site can be appreciated. Worn-down banks and ditches dug over 2,000 years ago, wind their sinuous way around the slopes. In medieval times the fort was strengthened by recutting the ditches and building rough masonry walls and towers around the summit, and although the stonework has crumbled into heaps of rubble, the overall plan is still discernable. At the northern point of the hill the multiple ramparts form a convoluted pathway up to the main entrance, which retains the only piece of the masonry castle to stand above the turf. Part of a square gate-tower with an arched opening can be seen, now almost blocked to the top with rubble, and which indicates how much of the structure still remains buried below ground.

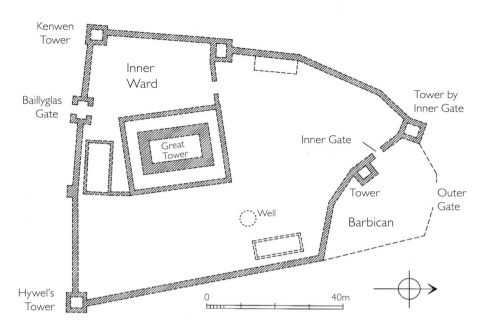

Kenwen Tower

Inner Ward

Baillyglas Gate

Tower by Inner Gate

Great Tower

Inner Gate

Tower

Outer Gate

Well

Barbican

Hywel's Tower

0   40m

Interpretive plan of the masonry remains of the castle

Very little is known about the early history of the site, and it makes few appearances in the native chronicles. As explained in the previous entry, Castell Dinas belonged to the lordship of Blaenllynfi, but there is some uncertainty as to when that territory was created. It may have been after 1165 (when the inheritance of the earl of Hereford was partitioned among his three daughters and their husbands), or around 1208 (when King John dispossessed William de Braose and gave the land to Peter Fitzherbert instead). Either time would be propitious to have a strong masonry castle on the mountain to secure the northwards route and guard the boundaries of the new lordship. Since the castle has a relatively simple layout and lacks any obvious thirteenth-century military features (such as round towers and substantial gatehouses), then a date around 1200 or earlier seems logical. It has been claimed that it was built by William fitz Osbern as part of an advance into Welsh territory in the 1070s, but it seems unlikely that a large and costly masonry castle would have been built so far into enemy territory at such an early date.[2]

It was certainly standing here in the autumn of 1233, when Llywelyn the Great invaded Breconshire and reportedly destroyed Blaenllynfi, Castell Dinas and Pencelli. The chroniclers must have exaggerated the severity of the attack, for the garrison was back in occupation before the year was out, suggesting that comparatively little needed to be done other than essential repairs.

How the inner ward might have looked in the twelfth century seen from the outer bailey, showing the Great Tower in the background and the Baillyglas Gate in the middle

However, the situation was very different when the lordship passed to the Crown in the fourteenth century. By that time the castle seems to have been in a very neglected state and a survey was carried out to ascertain what remedial work was needed. When the inspectors arrived on the mountain in January 1337, they saw the 'outer gate with a mantlet [a defensive wall or barbican] ... so weak and ruinous that they must be newly built'. The terms 'weak and ruinous' recur frequently in the report. A series of towers along the walls are mentioned and named (Hywel's Tower, Kenwen Tower, Watch Tower), including the Great Tower, which is now marked by the huge heap of rubble in the middle of the courtyard. This dominating structure doubtless contained several residential chambers over a basement store, and would have formed the main accommodation at the castle. It was roofed in lead and was enclosed by a narrow, walled courtyard for extra protection. Defects were noted in the roof and internal timberwork. Alongside the tower can be seen the foundations of a rectangular building, probably the main hall. The inspectors considered that all the repairs would amount to £65, though this was a very low sum compared to their estimate of £451 to patch up Blaenllynfi.

The area enclosed by the masonry defences amounts to about a third of the actual hilltop, and the remaining part lay to the south beyond a shallow cross-ditch. The open field was accessed through the Baillyglas Gate (a hybrid name meaning simply the 'green enclosure'). This area was probably used to pen livestock, for the inspectors noted an abundance of cattle here. Interestingly, during the war of 1277–78 the unscrupulous constable had taken advantage of the unsettled conditions to steal cattle belonging to Llanthony Priory just over the mountains. He was even accused of pushing a monk off his horse and stealing that as well! Although of lesser importance, this outer enclosure could not have been left undefended and there must have been a surrounding wall, if not a fence or impenetrable thorn hedge to keep the animals safe. There also appears to have been a secondary entrance into the castle at the south-west corner of the hillfort. Aerial views clearly show the outlines of a number of structures here, though they appear to be much slighter than the rest of the buildings on the hill and may belong to the late period when the castle was valued more as a cattle ranch than as a military fortress.

The end of Castell Dinas is as mysterious as its beginning. It seems to have remained in use throughout the fourteenth century, and is thought to have been provisioned against attack during the Glyndŵr rebellion. In fact, the best clue to the ultimate fate of this remote fortress is provided by John Leland, in an unusually loquacious entry for that most succinct of antiquarians: 'Dinas Castle stands a good mile from Blaen Llynfi upon a top of a notable hill. It is now ruinous almost to the hard ground. There be manifest tokens of three wards walled about … The people of Dinas did burn Dinas Castle that Owain Glyndŵr should not keep it for his fortress'. Whether Leland actually climbed to the top, or relied on local knowledge for his information is unclear, but the tradition that the castle was demolished as a precautionary measure during the great rebellion is a plausible fate.

Location & access
Dinas Hill lies in the Black Mountains about 4 km south-west of Talgarth, and is located prominently, close to the A479 road to Abergavenny (OS map ref: SO 178 301). The castle is freely accessible as the hill forms part of Tir Gofal managed historic landscape scheme. There is a signposted footpath from the car park of The Castle public house, and another via the farm track at Pengenffordd crossroads.

References
Brut; Brycheiniog (volume X and XXXI)

Castell Du, *Sennybridge*

Only a fragment of a D-shaped tower survives of this little-known castle, which is set on a hilltop at the back of a bungalow overlooking the confluence of the rivers Senni and Usk. The tower measures about 8m in diameter and jutted out from the southern side of the castle, though it is now almost completely obscured with ivy and undergrowth. There are fallen blocks of masonry scattered about and many loose stones have been used to build garden features. On the west side of the hill stands a Second World War pillbox, but this too is now just another ruined and overgrown monument to past conflicts. Nothing else remains, and any discussion on the form and extent of this castle would inevitably be conjectural. Even excavation is unlikely to help, since any buried archaeological features have probably been obliterated by the modern houses.

A fragment of a D-shaped tower is all that remains of Castell Du

When John Leland passed this way around 1539, he saw a 'ruined little pile on Usk strongly built as a lodge', which suggests there was a still a substantial structure here at the time, and that its use as a hunting lodge was still remembered locally. The only earlier reference to the place is in a letter written here in 1271 during a dispute between Llywelyn ap Gruffudd and a local Welshman, Einion Sais. Einion was here to swear allegiance to the prince and give hostages as surety for his loyalty. Evidently, he was a reluctant vassal and quickly changed sides when King Edward moved against the Welsh in 1277.

Was Castell Du Einion's own castle, or that of his overlord, Llywelyn? David Cathcart King alluded to this enigmatic little ruin in two papers and concluded that it was probably the castle reportedly built by Llywelyn in the 1260s when Breconshire was under his control (see the previous entry on Blaencamlais). Although Llywelyn's castle was supposedly destroyed in 1265, it must have been rebuilt for Einion to be occupying it in 1271 as a base for Welsh resistance in the area – unless we presume that they were two quite separate sites. To add to the confusion the Breconshire antiquarian Theophilus Jones stated that Einion also had a castle beside Penpont church 3 km to the east, but that the remains had long been destroyed.[3] If this statement can be believed, then there might have been *three* Welsh castles in this area.

CLIFFORD, *HAY-ON-WYE*

Clifford was a first-generation castle built in the wake of the Norman invasion, and its founder was one of the most powerful and richest men to have benefited from the bloodbath at Hastings. William fitz Osbern, lord of Breteuil in Normandy, was a cousin of the king and a member of his close circle of loyal and enthusiastic supporters. According to the *Battle Abbey Chronicle*, it was fitz Osbern who turned a bad omen into a good sign when the would-be Conqueror disembarked from his ship in 1066, and promptly fell flat on his face; 'Lo! He hath embraced England with both his hands, and sealed it to his posterity with his own blood,' he cried to the discomforted soldiers. William was amply rewarded in the aftermath of the battle and received many of the estates that had formerly belonged to King Harold. By 1067 he had also been entrusted with the earldom of Hereford, and departed west to secure the border against Welsh raids. He spent the next few years enforcing his authority on the region with a paradoxical mix of violence and conciliation. The contemporary chronicler Orderic Vitalis described this freebooter as 'the first and greatest oppressor of the English [who] harshly supported a huge following which caused the ruin and wretched death of many'. The kingdom of Gwent was quickly pacified, and the first Marcher lordships were established.

Fitz Osbern rebuilt the pre-Conquest sites of Ewyas Harold and Hereford (both founded by Norman mercenaries during the reign of Edward the Confessor) and established his own border strongholds at Chepstow, Monmouth, Clifford and Wigmore. Most of this work was carried out by his followers and feudal tenants, for William was often away fighting on the King's behalf or mopping up pockets of resistance in other parts of the country. He returned to the Continent on two occasions, but was killed in battle in Flanders in 1071, and the earldom passed to his son Roger of Breuteil. Roger, though, did not inherit his father's good fortune:

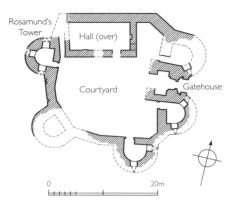

Aerial view of Clifford Castle and plan showing the extent of the surviving masonry

just four years later he became involved in a failed rebellion and was stripped of all his possessions, spending the next 16 years in prison. King William decided not to entrust such a huge legacy to any one person in future, so the territory was split up and partitioned among more loyal warriors who continued with the process of transforming Welsh lands into Marcher lordships.

Clifford was therefore one of the earliest castles in the area and, like Wigmore and other first-generation strongholds, was built on a massive scale. A promontory overlooking a ford on the River Wye was scarped into a huge motte, standing between 10m and 17m high, with a summit diameter of about 30m, and protected by deep ditches cut across the spine of the ridge. Only the top 3–4m seem to be man-made, and the rest of the mound is natural. The remainder of the site was protected by steep slopes (which were made even steeper along the riverside when a railway was cut through in the nineteenth century). In front of the mound lay a large bailey of almost 2 acres, guarding the level approach along the ridge from the east, and which may at first have sheltered a small town. Bailey and motte are now linked by an earthen causeway, but it is conceivable that this is a later feature, and that the original access across the deep ditch was along a ramped timber bridge. There is claimed to be a third bailey behind the mound, but this triangular piece of land is perhaps more likely to be the tip of the ridge that was left isolated when the ditch was dug.

By the time Domesday Book was compiled, Clifford Castle was in the hands of fitz Osbern's brother-in-law, Ralph Tosny (d.1102), and there was a small settlement here comprising 16 burgages. The castle was doubtless intended to be the centre of an important lordship. A Cluniac priory was founded here and there was a deer park nearby – though curiously it was not the compact settlement that one might expect, for both the parish church and priory lie some distance away from the castle. Ultimately, competition from nearby Hay stifled the urban venture and Clifford remained a village to the present day.

By 1140 Walter fitz Richard (d.1190) had married into the Tosny family and became tenant-in-chief of the lordship. He was the first to adopt the Clifford place-name as a suffix. The family received a step up on the social ladder (albeit in a rather ignoble way), when Walter's beautiful daughter, Rosamund Clifford, attracted the roving eye of Henry II. For some years the 'fair Rosamund' was the king's mistress, secreted within a maze in the gardens of Woodstock Palace in Oxfordshire, far from the prying eyes of his formidable wife, Eleanor of Aquitaine. But the queen eventually got wind of the affair and found her way through the maze, confronted Rosamund, and forced her to take poison – or at least it is claimed in the romantic fables that were later woven around the affair. In reality, it seems that Rosamund retired to a nunnery once Henry's affections had moved on, and died there in 1176 aged just thirty. The west tower of Clifford Castle is named after her, even though she was long dead by the time it was built.

Excavations carried out here in the 1920s revealed traces of stone foundations on the summit of the motte and, more recently, substantial postholes have been found of an eleventh-century wooden structure, presumably the central keep. However, the ruins that now survive belong to a later phase of the castle's history when the mound was reshaped and crowned with a remarkable little fortress. This has been described as a shell-keep, but perhaps an 'inner ward' might be a more appropriate term to use, for this is not just an enclosing wall (as at Cardiff and Kilpeck for instance), but a compact polygonal enclosure bristling with half-round towers projecting down the sides of the mound. There are five towers, two of which are set on either side of the entrance passage into the courtyard, which was defended by wooden gates and a portcullis. The towers appear to have been two-storied structures with a store or guardroom on the ground floor, and a residential chamber on the first floor, as some had been provided with garderobes. A first-floor chamber block lay up against the more secure side overlooking the river. There is no sign of any stairwells, so the upper rooms must have been reached by wooden stairs from the courtyard. All the buildings have been reduced almost to ground level apart from the so-called Rosamund's Tower and sections of the adjoining curtain wall.

It has been pointed out that the layout of this inner ward bears considerable similarity to the Tosny ancestral base at Conches-en-Ouche in Normandy, and therefore a twelfth-century date has been proposed. However, certain architectural details suggest that it was more likely to have been built in one phase during the

Aerial view of the castle site, showing the motte (right) and the large bailey (left)

early thirteenth century. There are some similarities to the royal castle at Montgomery (begun in 1223), but the closest comparison is Grosmont on the far side of the Black Mountains, which dates to around 1219–32.[4] Both castles were instigated by Hubert de Burgh (d.1243) chief advisor to the young King Henry III, and one of the most innovative castle builders of the period. If this dating is correct, then the man responsible for the inner ward would have been Walter Clifford III, who succeeded to the lordship in 1221. Building a castle, as has been noted before, was a very costly business, and it may be significant that by the early 1230s Walter was in debt to a Jewish moneylender to the tune of £666 (a very substantial sum at the time).[5] However, we cannot be certain that the loan was indeed for construction work – let alone for Clifford – since Walter had other important castles that might have needed upgrading.

The only other visible masonry consists of a short length of wall linking the motte to the bailey, and the excavated foundations of an outer gateway. This consists of a long narrow passage with two rounded turrets at the front, but its position right in the middle of the bailey implies that the large enclosure was planned to be subdivided. Archaeologists are unsure whether the work was ever completed, for there is little convincing evidence of any other walls or towers under the earthen

A suggested reconstruction of the early thirteenth-century inner ward

ramparts, so it may be that the full scheme of refortification was never carried out.

In 1233 Walter Clifford joined a coalition of barons angry at the king's blatant favouritism and financial mismanagement. The rebellion was short-lived, and in August the castle was besieged and surrendered to royalist forces. Walter submitted to the king and had some of his lands relinquished, but had to wait until the following spring for the return of his castles. In all likelihood the towers had already been raised by the time of the attack (though it is not inconceivable that it was built afterwards as part of a programme of refurbishment). Walter stayed on Henry's good side for the rest of the reign, though like other Marcher lords he was stubbornly protective of his rights and opposed to any regal meddling in his own affairs. The chronicler Matthew Paris recorded an episode in 1249 when a messenger sent by the king was beaten up by Clifford's men and forced to eat the letters, wax seal and all! Such culinary punishments, it seems, were often meted out to the bearers of unwelcome news. In the event, Walter again threw himself on the king's mercy and chose a stiff fine rather than a court appearance for misconduct.

When Walter died without a male heir, the lordship passed via heiresses and marriages to a succession of owners, including the Mortimers of Wigmore. The generally held view is that the residential use of the castle declined during the fourteenth century as the new owners had extensive estates elsewhere. There are records of some repairs being carried out, and during the Glyndŵr rebellion temporary custody was granted to a neighbouring lord whose own castle had been destroyed by the rebels. For this reason, it must still have been relatively intact and capable of withstanding a siege at the time. But its days as an important seat of the nobility were over, and by the eighteenth century the castle was of value only to antiquarians and landscape artists. A house was built within the bailey in the 1920s and some excavations took place, but the ruins continued to deteriorate and eventually ended up on the *Heritage at Risk Register*. Fortunately, in 2017–18 the crumbling walls were treated to much needed consolidation work by Historic England, including the removal of undergrowth and ivy so that much more of the structure can now be seen. Further work is still needed though, to uncover more of the buried walls, so that the architecture and history of this important Marcher stronghold can be better understood.

Location & access
The castle stands in the village of Clifford, 4 km north-east of Hay-on-Wye via the B4350, just off the A438 from Hereford to Brecon. The castle is private property, but the owners permit access on certain days of the year (see website for details).

References
RCHME; Cliffordcastle.org; Historic England research report No.69 (2018)

HEN GASTELL, *LLANGATTOCK*

The meagre remains of this castle can easily be missed even though it lies just a few feet from a country lane, for the mound is only fully revealed once the winter months have stripped away the leaves from the covering screen of trees. Although it superficially resembles a small motte with a marshy ditch fed by natural springs, the abundance of tumbled stonework reveals that the mound is, in fact, the collapsed remains of a small and compact masonry fortification. The outlines of a rectangular hall or keep, measuring approximately 23m by 15m can be traced on the south side of the mound, while the northern flank overlooking the valley is enclosed with a narrow walled courtyard. Presumably the access was on this side too – probably just a simple gate reached over the ditch via a wooden bridge.

This is very similar to the Welsh castle of Plas Baglan, but this should not necessarily be taken as evidence of a native origin. In fact, this is one of those sites that has slipped through the records without leaving a trace. No documents chronicle the history or owners of Hen Gastell, and there are no dressed stones in the rubble to helpfully indicate a particular period of construction. The rectangular layout might suggest a twelfth-century origin, and the proximity to Abergavenny and Crickhowell would indicate it was also an Anglo-Norman foundation. However, the site is not a naturally strong one for an early castle and this may instead be a fortified house, built by someone of less prominent social standing at any time between the thirteenth and fifteenth centuries. The simple truth is that we know little about this obscure ruin and unless some documentation comes to light or the excavator's trowel unearths some clinching evidence, then the history of Hen Gastell will remain lost in the realms of conjecture.

Location & access
The remains of Hen Gastell lie in a field on the hillside, 2 km south of Llangattock village, just off the A40 at Crickhowell. Follow the signs to Llangattock and continue through the village on the main road (Hillside Road) passing over the canal, and along a narrow country lane for about 1 km. After the second sharp bend, the tree-covered castle site will be seen on the downhill (left) side of the road (OS map ref: SO 213 166). The site lies on private farmland, but is easily visible from the roadside.

References
Brycheiniog (1968–69)

LLANCILLO, *PONTRILAS*

The place-name is evidently of Welsh origin, but thanks to the territorial appropriations of the Norman conquerors, the border has shifted and Llancillo now belongs in England. There is no village here, only a castle mound, a redundant church and a seventeenth-century house, all tucked away in a small valley practically invisible to motorists speeding along the A465 between Abergavenny and Hereford. For those who do make the long trek across the fields, it is usually just to visit the parish church, which has been in the care of Friends of Friendless Churches since 2007. The forlorn little building incorporates some early twelfth-century masonry, but was altered in later years and subjected to a vigorous restoration in 1895. It is likely that the church is a pre-Norman foundation (the place-name suggests a connection to the Welsh saint Tyssilio who died around AD 610) and if it was the focal point for a native settlement, then this might explain why the castle was located here in the first place. There seems no other reason why such a low-lying valley with poor natural defences and restricted views should have been chosen; the nearby mottes at Walterstone and Rowlestone are far better situated for surveillance and defence.

At the time of Domesday, Llancillo was one of three churches in the possession of Roger de Lacy, the largest landowner in Herefordshire. His father had established a strong motte-and-bailey castle within the earthworks of a Roman and Anglo-Saxon fort a short distance away at Longtown, and this became the head of the Marcher lordship of Ewyas Lacy. In 1095 Roger was involved in an abortive rebellion against the king and was exiled as punishment, but his lands passed to his brother Hugh (d.1115). Either Roger or Hugh de Lacy could have been responsible for raising the primary castle at Llancillo to defend the southern borders of the lordship, but perhaps it is more likely to have been the work of a tenant, one Richard de Esketot, who was granted the land in fee. The property was retained by his descendants until 1243.

At first glance the castle appears to be just another earthen motte, but a closer examination reveals half-buried masonry and a scree of tumbled stones. Llancillo has long been known as a stone castle, but the extremely poor condition of the remains has kept antiquarians guessing as to its original form. The mound rises 8m above a boggy ditch, and has a dished summit enclosed by a fragmentary wall about 1.8m thick and up to 17.6m in external diameter. It has been suggested that it was a round keep, but these dimensions point to an improbably large

The dished summit and fragmentary stonework remains of Llancillo

How Llancillo may have appeared after the timber defences had been replaced with masonry

structure, far in excess even of the great tower that the Lacys built for themselves at Longtown, and in all likelihood it was a shell-keep. A few visible footings indicate that the wall was polygonal in shape, and so it would have resembled the better-preserved structures at Cardiff and Wiston (see p. 20). It seems to have had a number of semi-circular buttresses or turrets on the external facade. The foundations of one can be seen beside the entrance gap, and its companion on the other side is buried under a tree. There may have been another two, along with the footings of a garderobe drain on the east flank. Rounded buttresses also appear at Longtown, which might suggest that the same architect was involved or that the builder wanted to copy aspects of his lord's castle. But there is some similarity to Snodhill in the Golden Valley (see p. 270), where the entrance into the keep is also flanked by solid turrets. Given the similar layout and scale to Llancillo, we might envisage the same arrangement here as well – a ground-floor storage chamber with a residential apartment above, the massive floor and roof beams perhaps being supported by a central pillar. Excavation would doubtless reveal more of the plan, for much of the structure remains buried in its own debris.

There was a bailey on the side facing the church and it is evident that it, too, was walled in stone since masses of half-buried rubble have been exposed by stream erosion. Within the bailey is a mound of stones marking the site of a small building, measuring approximately 9m by 12m. This was perhaps a modest hall, and it is only thanks to the roots of a yew tree that these scant fragments have managed to survive at all. The rest of the outworks have been largely ploughed away. On the opposite (east) side of the motte is a low linear earthwork that has been interpreted as the remains of a second bailey, but it could be a post-medieval garden feature or field boundary, connected with the adjacent house.

Further uncertainty exists about the provenance of the many pieces of dressed stone that have been used to repair the graveyard wall. Some historians have suggested they came from the castle, but none appear to be particularly early and some are clearly ecclesiastical in origin (in all likelihood they are leftovers from the 1895 restoration of the church). Given the scant evidence available, it is impossible to pinpoint a construction date for the castle, other than to suggest a period sometime in the late twelfth to early thirteenth centuries. If so, then the rebuilding would have taken place in the lifetime of Richard de Esketot III (d.1220) or perhaps his son Walter (d.c.1243). The inheritance was thereafter split between two heiresses and Llancillo passed to the Eylesford family. It is mentioned in 1337 and was presumably still inhabited, but its subsequent history is uncertain.

Location & access
The site is located on the north side of the Monnow Valley, halfway between Pandy and Pontrilas. A private road branches off the A465 and leads to Llancillo Court via a tunnel under the mainline railway. Public access is usually allowed this way (ask permission at the house), but official rights-of-way start from Rowlestone church and from Walterstone Common. These paths cross several fields and descend into the valley towards Llancillo church (OS map ref: SO 367 255). The castle is on private land but clearly visible from the adjacent footpath and churchyard.

References
RCHME; Phillips (2005); HAN Vols 40 (1982) & 53 (1990)

Mynydd-brith, *Dorstone*

This is another of the numerous small castles that dot the landscape of the Golden Valley, but this one was considered important enough to warrant a costly rebuilding in stone. It is a typical flat-topped grassy motte, up to 5m high where best preserved, and partly surrounded by a silted-up ditch. Natural slopes gave added protection to the mound, and areas of scarping have been interpreted as the remains of a bailey extending around the landward approach. However, these earthworks are far less defined than normal and have been greatly disturbed by the road and adjacent farm buildings, so only excavation would confirm if there was indeed a genuine bailey here. The motte is easily seen from the roadside, and the stone foundations around the top can also be glimpsed.

Unfortunately for castle students, much controversy exists over the authenticity of the stonework. A previous owner, aided by an enthusiastic local historian, Roger Stirling-Brown, carried out unofficial excavations here. The top of the motte was dug into and the exposed masonry was rebuilt before a proper survey could be carried out. In 1994 the County Archaeological Service investigated the disturbance caused to the Scheduled Monument, and noted that the stonework marked out a polygonal shell-keep up to 18m across, the interior being divided by thinner cross-walls to form at least three small rooms of irregular shape. The amount of damage caused by the earlier foray into amateur archaeology is now difficult to assess, and the end result may be considered either a tolerably accurate restoration of what was found, or an imaginative reassembling of the rubble unearthed. To give the benefit of the doubt, it would seem that the former is perhaps more likely than the latter. The stone phase would therefore have consisted of a multi-sided curtain wall (similar to Llancillo), containing a number of cramped little rooms.

There is much uncertainty about why and when the castle was established in this remote part of Ewyas Lacy lordship. There is another motte at Nant-y-bar farm just 500m away in an even more elevated location, so why were two castles needed on the border? Were they contemporary, or were they built at different times and for different purposes? In Domesday, Mynydd-brith was a small settlement comprising nine villagers, four slaves, a priest and a blacksmith. There was a mill nearby, and apparently a chapel too. Slight terraces and platforms in the field beyond the road may be the remains of

The scant remains at Mynydd Brith

that settlement. No castle is mentioned, but that doesn't necessarily mean there wasn't one here already, which had perhaps been established in the wake of fitz Osbern's incursions into this region. The hamlet would then have grown up beside it or, alternatively, the motte was added later by one of the de Lacy tenants to protect the settlement and enforce Norman authority on the locality.

Location & access
The mound stands in a valley west of Dorstone village off the B4348 to Hay-on-Wye. Just outside the village take the fork signposted to Mynydd-brith, follow it for about 3.5 km then take the left turn to Michaelchurch. Part-way up the hill is Mynydd-brith farm (OS map ref: SO 280 414). The site is on private land, but visible from the roadside.

References
CAS Report 253 (1994); Phillips (2005)

Newcourt Tump, *Bacton*

Newcourt is yet another Golden Valley castle about which virtually nothing is known; and, like Mynydd-brith above, has also been studied in some detail by Roger Stirling-Brown. In 1086 the land was held by a sub-tenant of Roger de Lacy named Gilbert, but whether he built the castle is perhaps unlikely, for it has neither the shape nor scale of early-Norman foundations, so it probably belongs to a later generation. Ecclesiastical documents of 1132–34 mention a 'Roger de Bachingtona' who may have been the owner at that time, and in 1166 a William de Bacton is recorded owing a knight's fee here.

In the Herefordshire Inventory of 1931, the RCHME took a cautious approach to this site, classifying it vaguely as a 'fortified enclosure'. It is marked on modern OS maps as a 'motte and bailey', but it clearly isn't. The site has been created by digging a 3m-deep ditch in a straight line across the edge of the hillside, leaving a

Aerial view of Newcourt Tump

triangular enclosure containing the outlines of a rectangular building and an irregular mound. The mound is too small to be a motte and has a scooped-out interior that suggests it could be the remains of a collapsed tower. The rest of the enclosure is protected by natural slopes and boggy springs. Stirling-Brown published an imaginative plan suggesting this was a small and compact masonry castle with a round keep, internal buildings, a gateway and several flanking towers. There is no sign of any fallen rubble or foundations today, and the landowner (who used to play on the hill as a child) does not remember seeing stonework either. If there is indeed a masonry castle deeply buried under the soil, then it is going to take a lot of trowel-work for future archaeologists to bring it to light.

Location & access
The site is located off the B4347 midway between Ewyas Harold and Peterchurch, in the Golden Valley. Head north past Abbey Dore and 300m after the road makes a sharp right bend, there is a leafy footpath on the left that borders the wood. Follow this for 1.4 km, around the back of Newcourt Farm, and up the open hillside. The earthworks will be seen across the valley to your left. There is an alternative path through the woodland (OS map ref: SO 371 335). The site is on private land, but visible from the footpath.

References
RCHME; HAN Vol. 50 (1990); Phillips (2005)

PAINSCASTLE

This site could hardly be termed a 'forgotten' castle, for the massive earthworks are not only well-preserved and refreshingly clear of undergrowth, but they occupy a very obvious and prominent position in the middle of the little village. Painscastle is included here as an example of those sites that were originally substantial masonry structures but, either through neglect, demolition or stone-robbing, have been wiped from the landscape. Anyone looking at Painscastle today – or for that matter, the neighbouring strongholds of Builth, New Radnor and Knucklas – would never realise that these grassy mounds were major stone castles in their day.

Painscastle's setting in a rural upland area may seem 'off the beaten track', but in fact it stands on one of the main routes from England into Radnorshire. Earlier invaders than the Normans may have established a foothold here, for mosaic remains were reportedly found in the nineteenth century, that may have come from a Roman building (perhaps a villa or a fort). The castle was built in the early twelfth century by Payn fitz John as the administrative and military caput of the surrounding lordship of Elfael – and, like many border strongholds, it frequently suffered in the oscillating politics of the Marches. When Payn was killed in 1137 the territory was recovered by the Welsh and remained in native control until 1195 when Matilda, wife of William de Braose III, led an army to regain the castle and inflict a bloody defeat upon the Welsh. Painscastle was then rebuilt and renamed *Castrum Matildis* in honour of this ferocious woman, but the new name didn't stick. The works carried out must have been quite substantial, for the castle withstood two further Welsh attacks before the century was out. William's exalted position among the Marcher lords came to a sudden and dramatic end in 1208 when the capricious King John turned against him and forced him to flee the country. Matilda and her young son were not so lucky, and both were captured and starved to death in a royal dungeon.

For some years the lordship was held by a Welsh ally of the Crown, but when Llywelyn the Great attacked in 1231, Henry III personally intervened and undertook to rebuild the strategic base. The royal army encamped here for three months in the summer as building work commenced on this one castle (while Llywelyn destroyed ten others, as a chronicler sarcastically noted). The driving force behind the refortification of Painscastle was surely Hubert de Burgh, Henry's able and ambitious minister, who had built up a power-base in the Welsh Marches and was anxious to keep Llywelyn out of the neighbourhood. Hubert's works at the royal fortress of Montgomery, and at his own castles of Grosmont and Skenfrith in Monmouthshire, remain as testament to his skill at fortification design, and so it is regrettable that nothing survives here today.

Some of the royal accounts are missing so there is no complete record of what was done, nor the costs incurred. We do know, however, that the castle was 'splendidly rebuilt in stone and lime' and renamed *Maugre Lewelini* – which roughly translates as 'in spite of Llywelyn'. A borough was also founded alongside the castle to bring economic growth to the area, and the townsfolk had the right to hold weekly markets and an annual fair. Hubert was toppled from his pre-eminent position in 1232 due to the influence of powerful rivals and a series of military setbacks. Painscastle was granted to the Tosnys, but it fell to Llywelyn ap Gruffudd in 1265, and only after the first defeat of the prince in 1277 could Ralph Tosny order the defences to be rebuilt. The lordship subsequently passed to the Beauchamp earls of Warwick and the last recorded use of the castle occurred in 1401 when a garrison of 36 was installed during the Glyndŵr rebellion. The fate of the castle is not known (probably it was little more than a precarious English enclave in hostile Welsh territory) and after the war was over it was left to fall into decay. William Camden's *Britannia* of 1586 refers to this and other Radnorshire strongholds as 'almost buried in their own ruins'.

Aerial view of the well-defined contours of Painscastle

Despite this catalogue of destruction and costly rebuilding, all that remains of Painscastle today is a series of earthworks on a ridge south of the village. As 'earthworks' they must be described, even though just beneath the topsoil the collapsed footings of masonry buildings await rediscovery. There is a hummocky motte at the furthest point of the ridge with a roughly rectangular bailey in front, surrounded by a large ditch and counterscarp bank. Semi-circular barbicans gave access into the courtyard from the east and west sides. Aerial photographs of the site clearly show the outlines of buried buildings and the scars of robber trenches along the rampart, while the uneven summit of the motte probably conceals the base of a substantial tower. On the east side of the castle is a derelict house that has also played a role in the history of Painscastle. Within the whitewashed stone walls of Upper House are the remains of an early fifteenth-century timber-framed aisled hall, one of the finest examples surviving in Wales. Just like Cefnllys (p. 221), here at Painscastle we have a clear sign of the shift in power from the castle to an undefended nobleman's residence. The fact that the hall juts into the outer ditch means that the castle had by that time lost its military purpose, and was just a war-worn pile of rubble to be ransacked for building materials.

Location & access
The castle lies beside the village of Painscastle on the B4594 approximately 5 km east of the Erwood off the A470 to Builth Wells (OS map ref: SO 17 462). The site is on enclosed farmland with no public access. The earthworks are visible from the road.

References
AC (1923); HKW (1963)

Pencelli Castle, Pencelli

Pencelli Castle in the Usk valley near Brecon is more familiar as a caravan park and camping site than as a historic monument, for only a few fragments of the ancient masonry survive here. There are other forgotten castles displaying far more extensive and impressive remains, but what is so remarkable about Pencelli is that less than three centuries ago, a major ruined fortress existed here; it has almost wholly disappeared in a period when one might have expected it to have been preserved as a landscape feature, or at least valued as a ruin of historic importance. Were it not for the visual evidence provided by the Buck brothers, Pencelli might be otherwise considered a fairly insignificant site. The engraving they produced in 1741 shows a long stretch of curtain wall with a typical thirteenth-century twin-towered gatehouse (see overleaf). The position of loopholes suggests that the gatehouse stood at least two storeys high, probably three, and the arched window openings in the adjacent curtain wall mark the position of a two-storeyed building set against the inner wall. Within the courtyard stands an Elizabethan mansion, while towering over all is a fragment of a substantial internal tower. Of these features only the house remains today.

Pencelli was an important castle and valued at the service of four knights to the lord of Brecon, but there is not a great deal of documentary evidence to outline its history. It was founded by Ralph de Baskerville who had fought at Hastings and received lands along the Herefordshire border.[6] Ralph supported Bernard de Neufmarché's conquest of Brycheiniog in 1093 and so gained further territorial rewards for his services. Probably the castle was founded at this time, although an earlier date is not unlikely since the Normans had been attempting colonisation of this part of Wales in the 1080s. The chosen site was a triangular ridge jutting into the Usk valley, adequately defended by natural slopes on two sides, with the man-made defences massed on the more vulnerable southern flank. This side of the castle was also overlooked by higher ground, a factor that may have restricted the effectiveness of Pencelli as a major stronghold in later years. In the early days of the Norman invasion it was nevertheless a secure location and the few remaining earthworks that have survived later landscaping suggest it was quite a sizeable one too, perhaps encompassing as much as three acres.

Remnants of the castle today

The more secure tip of the ridge seems to have been worked up into a low motte (or perhaps a ringwork, the earthworks are now too mutilated to be sure). This served as the base for a stone keep probably erected at some point in the twelfth century. Only a handful of toppled masses of masonry remain above ground, but it is probable that these fragments formed part of the tall structure depicted by the Bucks.[7] Some years ago, unofficial excavations uncovered the foundations of this keep, which is estimated to be 14m square with walls 3m thick. The base of a square turret (probably for a garderobe) projects out from the north corner, while alongside it is a long narrow secondary chamber that might be the lower level of a forebuilding. Close to the west side of the keep is a fallen fragment of a semi-circular structure, perhaps the remains of a flanking tower. There are vestiges of a stone wall encircling the motte and more rubble has been exposed by erosion along the flanks of the bailey enclosure, but the extent and form of the twelfth-century castle will only be revealed by proper excavations.

When the last of the Pencelli Baskervilles died around 1210 the estate briefly passed to the Le Wafre family, before it was seized by Reginald de Braose in 1215 in the course of his rebellion against King John (as described in the entry on Blaenllynfi). Around this time Reginald married Gwladys Du, the young daughter of his current ally Llywelyn the Great, and settled the property on her in exchange for some lands in mid Wales. A short time after Reginald died in 1228, Gwladys married the heir of another great Marcher dynasty, Ralph Mortimer II, thereby alienating Pencelli from the de Braose line. Before long Ralph not only had to contend with other members of the de Braose family trying to reclaim Pencelli, but with the far more serious threat from his father-in-law. In 1231 the *Brut y Tywysogion* reports that Llywelyn destroyed Radnor, Hay and Brecon, before moving on to Caerleon. For some reason he seems to have ignored Pencelli on this occasion, but two years later destroyed the castle along with the neighbouring strongholds of Brecon, Blaenllynfi and Castell Dinas. The castle was recovered and must have been repaired, although the extent of work carried out is uncertain. It may still have consisted of a masonry keep with a stone-walled inner ward at this time, along with timber outer defences.

The ownership dispute was finally laid to rest with the marriage of Ralph's son Roger Mortimer III to Matilda de Braose in 1247, and the castle is claimed to have been significantly refurbished in the ensuing years with the addition of the curtain wall and gatehouse. While this is possible (we have already seen that Roger was an enthusiastic castle-builder) the details shown in the Buck engraving would not be incompatible with a later date. Between 1262 and 1276 most of Breconshire was in the control of Llywelyn ap Gruffudd and his allies, and the fate of Pencelli is unknown. Even if it was still in English occupation and had not fallen to the Welsh, it would not have been a suitable time for Mortimer to undertake extensive rebuilding. More likely the works were carried out as a precautionary measure once Llywelyn had been defeated and driven out.

Pencelli is mentioned again in 1322 as a Mortimer holding seized by King Edward II, when Roger IV was imprisoned for rebellion, but it was returned to the family once the unfortunate monarch's troublesome reign was over. The lordship passed to the Crown in the fifteenth century and was granted to various noblemen before being split up into smaller holdings in the sixteenth century.[8] Most of the estate passed to a branch of the Herbert family and remained with this important local dynasty until after the Civil War when it was conveyed to Thomas Powel of Llanishen, who had married a Herbert heiress. The condition of the castle during this period is not known. Perhaps some of the buildings were still occupied, but by 1583 a new house had been built in the courtyard, reputedly incorporating the remains of the castle chapel dedicated to St Leonard.[9] The Herbert house still survives more or less intact, although there have inevitably been improvements

An extract of the Buck engraving of Pencelli Castle, showing the lost gatehouse and outer walls

The house built in the castle courtyard before 1583, which reputedly contains parts of the castle chapel

and alterations, particularly around 1800 when it was given a castellated facade. Nevertheless, it is a fascinating building in its own right, one of the earliest examples of a 'double-pile' house in Wales, and strikingly similar to Newton in Brecon, which is linked to the family and possibly the work of the same architect. The builders of the Herbert house utilised some of the abundant masonry lying around, and fragments of reset Norman stonework can be seen in the walls.

There was still a substantial amount of the old castle left when the Bucks visited almost 160 years later and it cannot be just coincidence that the gatehouse was still standing then, for it would have served as an imposing entrance to the courtyard. But by the time of the 1840 tithe map all the ruins had gone. The map shows the house, an extensive range of outbuildings, and a large open space skirted by the turnpike road that doubtless marked the position of the outer bailey. The Breconshire historian Theophilus Jones makes no mention of masonry here *c.*1800 nor does he record the tradition of any, so it is likely that the last vestiges of the castle had been pulled down long before his time, probably soon after the Bucks' visit. The Georgian owners evidently had no further regard for the noble facade and swept it away, filling in the great ditches and using the leftover stonework to construct the stables and barns that still remain a prominent feature of the site today.

Urishay, *Peterchurch*

Some similarities exist between this site and the above mentioned Pencelli – both were early castles established by the Normans as they wormed their way into Welsh territory along the river valleys, and both were reoccupied by wealthy landowners in more civilised days. Here the castle mound is crowned by the gutted shell of a seventeenth-century mansion, visible through the encircling screen of trees. Next to the road stands the old chapel, which is reckoned to be the earliest surviving ecclesiastical building at any Herefordshire castle. Excavation has revealed that it was originally a single cell building with a rounded chancel (a feature that still survives at nearby Peterchurch and Kilpeck churches). It probably dates from the very early twelfth century, and would have been used by the inhabitants of the castle and any neighbouring settlers. The building underwent considerable reconstruction work in later years, before it was abandoned and then put to various degrading uses (such as a kennel and blacksmith's forge). In 1978 the ruin was taken over by the Friends of Friendless Churches and partly restored.

The place-name is assumed to derive from one Ulric or Urrie 'of the hay' ('hay' meaning a field or hedged enclosure). The site has been identified in Domesday Book as *Alcamestune*, which had been established on 'waste' (i.e. barren or previously unsettled land) by Hugh de L'Anse (d.1101), a supporter of William fitz Osbern. It is one of a string of forts along the valley of the River Dore, and a glance at the Ordnance Survey map will show that almost every village here has its own castle, ranging from modest earthworks to a substantial masonry fortress at Snodhill (p. 270), which was Hugh's main seat in the area. Few of these castles have any documented early history and they could have been built at any time within the century or so after fitz Osbern's conquest of the region.

Wide aerial view, showing the remains of Urishay Castle in its landscape setting

The substantial motte at Urishay rises just over 6m in height to a level summit about 50 m across. It is still surrounded by a wide and deep ditch, although the side facing the modern farm buildings has been largely filled in. Documentary evidence and slight surviving earthworks indicate that a bailey extended in an arc around the north and east sides and enclosed the chapel, while in the fields downhill are traces of what may be a deserted settlement. However, most of the earthworks have been considerably affected by later landscaping work, and it is likely that the motte was originally much higher before the house was built over it.

By the fourteenth century Urishay was in the hands of the de la Hay family, and their descendants were to retain possession of the estate until the dawn of the twentieth century. No doubt the original timber buildings were replaced in time with more durable masonry, but the gaunt ruin that now crowns the motte is clearly not medieval. Nevertheless, it appears to have been constructed with materials recycled from an earlier building on site, and pieces of chamfered stone dressings of tufa (a natural calciferous formation) have been incorporated into the walls.

The mansion was a three-storey block with two projecting wings on the main frontage, overlooking a series of terraces and walled gardens extending to the east. Access was provided by a stone causeway across the ditch (which was flooded at the time), and there was also an elegant stone staircase that linked the house to the gardens. A sketch dating from 1865 shows an attractive stone building with clusters of diagonal chimney stacks and mullioned windows, reflected in

How Urishay Castle and house may have looked around 1700 (the old chapel can be seen on the left)

the placid waters of the moat. However, by 1900 the house had undergone some radical renovation, the effects of which are still apparent today. The bare masonry was concealed under concrete render and the mullioned openings were replaced with larger windows to let in more light. The motte was transformed by additional revetment walls, so that from the east side it looked like a tiered wedding cake, as old photographs attest.

In the event, this was to be a short-lived revival. An economic downturn in agriculture before the First World War had a severe impact on the landed gentry and their estates, and Urishay was an early victim of the fate that befell many country houses. The family had already vacated the property when it went on the market in 1913, but the house proved difficult to sell, even after a second auction in 1919, and so the building was stripped of any valuable architectural fittings and deliberately gutted. Some of the beautiful stained-glass windows and intricately carved wainscoting ended up at Baker University in Baldwin City, Kansas.

Urishay is often cited as having been a fortified manor rather than a true castle, but the presence of the chapel and the scale of the mound (truncated though it is) suggests that it began life as a major Anglo-Norman stronghold and plantation settlement intended to control and exploit the uplands around the Dore valley.

A drawing of Urishay in 1865 by Lady Francis Harcourt, reproduced in
The Castles of Herefordshire and Their Lords by C.J. Robinson (1869)

The gaunt remains of Urishay House, with concrete rendered walls from the c.1900 renovations

Location & access

The castle remains are 2.5 km south-west of Peterchurch village, which lies on the B4348 from Pontrilas to Hay. At the crossroads in the village take the signposted turning to Urishay, continue across the valley and up the hill. There is very limited parking next to the semi-ruined chapel. The site is on private land and there is no public access, although the adjacent chapel can be visited.

References

RCHME; ewyaslacy.org.uk.website; Woolhope (1938) pp. 141–59

OPPOSITE: The ruinous and unstable surviving stonework of Alberbury Castle

5 The Middle Marches

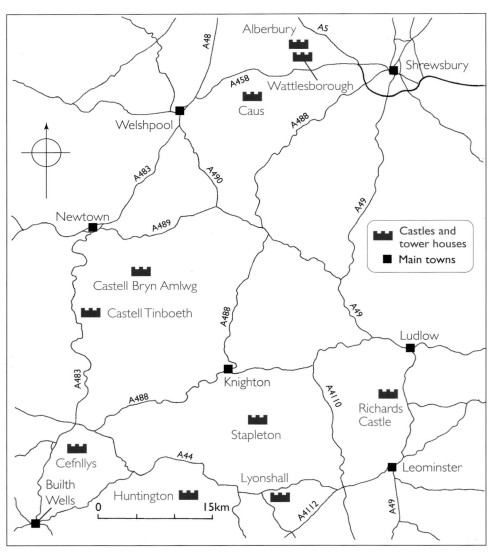

Alberbury

A5

Shrewsbury

A48

A458

Wattlesborough

Caus

A488

Welshpool

A483

A490

A49

Newtown

A489

Castell Bryn Amlwg

Castell Tinboeth

A488

Ludlow

A483

A49

Knighton

A488

Stapleton

A4110

Richards Castle

Cefnllys

A44

Lyonshall

Leominster

Builth Wells

Huntington

0   15km

A4112

A49

| Castles and tower houses |
| ■ Main towns |

5

THE MIDDLE MARCHES

ALBERBURY

As medieval castles go, Alberbury was a fairly modest building, just a rectangular block 17m by 11m, containing a basement store and upper domestic chamber, with an adjoining walled courtyard; but as it was valued at just a knight's fee, then the limited accommodation was probably considered sufficient. It lies within the immaculately-kept private grounds of Loton Park Hall, immediately adjacent to the imposing parish church of St Michael and All Angels – and yet in contrast to these august relics, the castle is a shamefully neglected ruin with heavily overgrown and dangerously unstable walls. It has been on the *Heritage at Risk Register* for a long time and English Heritage have so far been unable to progress negotiations to ensure its preservation.

At the time of Domesday, Alberbury was held by Roger Corbet, whose main base was further south at Caus (see the next entry). It was one of several castles established alongside the westerly routes out of Shrewsbury and into the wilds of Wales. The estate was soon enfeoffed to one Ralph the Fat, but from at least 1170 it had been acquired by the Fitzwarin family, who were to retain possession of Alberbury well into the fourteenth century. The Fitzwarins were extremely unimaginative when it came to naming their offspring (all the sons were called Fulk) and the most famous member of the dynasty was Fulk Fitzwarin III (d.*c*.1258). His long and adventurous life was chronicled in a French Romance entitled *Fouke le Fitz Waryn*, which survives in a manuscript dating from the early fourteenth century, in the

The neglected ruin of Alberbury Castle today

British Library. It contains a heady mix of fact and fantasy, with lots of derring-do, damsels in distress, and a few dragons thrown in for good measure.

The historical Fulk was fiercely defensive of his rights and privileges, and stood up to anyone who dared to oppose him, whether they be neighbouring Marchers, Papal envoys, Welsh warriors or meddling monarchs. He strove long and hard to regain the family's ancestral rights to the castle and lands of Whittington near Oswestry, but when King John steadfastly refused to support his claim, he and his followers rose in rebellion in 1201. Fulk eventually submitted and received a pardon, and finally gained his inheritance in 1204; but even so, this rare act of generosity on the king's part did not stop him from joining the rebel cause as the reign descended into turmoil.

The upswing in the family fortunes probably encouraged Fulk to invest in new stone buildings at his castles. He was allowed to refortify Whittington in the period 1220–22, though the young Henry III was suspicious of his loyalty and insisted that the works should only be on a scale sufficient to keep the Welsh at bay, and nothing more. It is presumed that he also built Alberbury around the same time, or even a little earlier, but because of the parlous condition of the ruin and the absence of any distinctive architectural details, it is difficult to pinpoint a date. According to the Romance, it was where his mother Hawise lived and amassed 'great treasure'. Fitzwarin took the loot to support himself and his followers whilst on the run.

Aerial view of the ruins of Alberbury Castle, with the church of St Michael and All Angels beyond

With his outlaw days behind him, Fulk was keen to cement his place in Marcher society, but endured some conflict with his litigious Corbet overlords and full-frontal hostility from Llywelyn the Great, who attacked his castles in 1223. As a Marcher he took the usual step of seeking divine kudos by establishing a monastic property on his land. The little priory he founded on the banks of the Severn, close to Alberbury, became one of only three houses of the French Grandmontine Order established in Britain (the others were at Craswall near Longtown, and Grosmont in Yorkshire). It was only ever a small foundation and was suppressed during the frequent wars between England and France, although the church was retained as a chantry until the Reformation. The few remains of the priory buildings have since been incorporated into a private house.

After a very long life, (he may have been in his nineties when he died)[1] Fulk was laid to rest beside his two wives in the priory church, and his inheritance was split between his sons. The senior line decamped to Whittington, while a cadet branch resided at Alberbury until that line died out in 1347. The subsequent history of the castle is uncertain. It may have been used as a lodge to serve a more congenial manor house established close by (and now represented by the seventeenth-century buildings of Loton Hall), and was certainly in ruins by Leland's time.

The existing building is often described as a keep, but it is quite different to the typical Anglo-Norman constructions to be seen at Bridgnorth (Shropshire), Goodrich (Herefordshire) and nearby Wattlesborough (p. 241) for instance. Indeed, the massively-buttressed tower of the parish church looks far more keep-like than the castle does. It is therefore best described as a fortified hall, and would have greatly resembled Newhouse in distant Pembrokeshire (see p. 70). Like Newhouse, Alberbury had a ground-floor storeroom accessed from outside, and a residential chamber on the first floor with its own entrance, probably reached by a timber stair. This large single chamber had a fireplace, several windows, and presumably a garderobe in the missing end wall. There was a spiral stair in one corner that seems to have connected all floors and rose up to the battlements. As mentioned above, it is difficult to suggest a date for the present building, but sometime in the early thirteenth century is plausible. There would have been less inclination to spend money on improving Alberbury once the Fitzwarins had settled at Whittington.

Adjoining the hall block is a well-preserved walled courtyard of polygonal plan. It appears to be an addition, but its antiquity has been called into question. The masonry varies in thickness, there is no sign of a strong gatehouse, and one arched doorway bears the inscribed date 1646. The current thinking is that the entire court-yard is post-medieval work intended to enhance the ruin as a landscape feature. However, some parts of the wall are strong enough for defensive purposes, and at the north corner are the foundations of a demolished flanking tower, apparently of D-shaped plan. It is therefore likely that the castle did indeed have a contemporary outer curtain, and that sections of it remain incorporated into the much-altered boundary wall.

Location & access
The castle is located beside the village of Alberbury on the B4393 to Four Crosses, 9 km west of the A5 Shrewsbury by-pass (OS map ref: SJ 357 145). The remains are on private land with no public access, although they are clearly visible from the roadside.

References
Wright (1855); Eyton (1858); Salter (1988)

CAUS, *WESTBURY*

Caus is one of the largest abandoned medieval settlements in Britain – a major castle and bustling market town now reduced to empty fields and overgrown earthworks on a hilltop. During the medieval period the original wooden fort was lavishly rebuilt in stone, then fell into neglect. It was revived as a Tudor country retreat, before finally being abandoned during the English Civil War. The damage caused by the inevitable slighting was exacerbated by stone-robbing and quarrying, so that now only a few foundations and fragments of masonry hint at the grand buildings that once stood here. Even less remains of the simple timber-framed dwellings of the townsfolk, other than faint terraces and worn-down tracks crossing the hillside. No proper excavations have been carried out here, but a recent survey of the surface features has made it possible to deduce the basic plan, and to hint at the structures that still lie hidden below ground.

Caus Castle is set on a narrow and steep-sided ridge that forms an extension to the Long Mountain range. The man-made defences are quite prominent when viewed from the roadside, and the enormous 11-acre enclosure is thought to have been an Iron Age hillfort that was reused and modified to shelter the fledgling town. The founder was either Corbet the Norman (d. before 1086) or his son Roger Corbet (d. before 1134), both being tenants of the earls of Shrewsbury. The castle was named after the family estate of *Pays de Caux* in Normandy, and their surname is believed to derive from the either the Latin *corvus* or the Anglo-French word *corb*, meaning crow. The family were later to adopt a coat of arms featuring two ravens.

The huge ridge-top site of Caus, possibly utilising a pre-existing Iron Age hillfort

Caus is not mentioned by name in the Domesday survey of 1086, either because it was included among the estates of the manor of Worthen, or it was masquerading as the large estate of *Alretone*, which had formerly belonged to Edward the Confessor and was held from the earl by the service of 5 knights. Some historians, however, consider the latter assumption to be wrong. The first certain reference to the castle occurs as late as 1140.[2]

The importance of the castle is testified by the interest shown in its maintenance by the Crown. In 1196 Richard 1 authorised the sheriff of Shropshire to provide Robert Corbet (d.1222) with financial aid for the 'king's service' in this region, and two years later another sum was provided specifically for the upkeep of the fortifications. It is assumed that these grants mark the start of the transition from wood to stone. The adjoining town was already in existence by this time, for in 1200 King John formally granted Robert the right to hold a weekly market here, and then in 1248 his son Thomas (d.1274) received a charter for a yearly fair. The borough served the needs of the castle dwellers and was doubtless intended to bring some measure of economic prosperity to this area of the March. Although it was in potentially hostile frontier territory, Caus was ideally situated to benefit from a trade route between Shrewsbury, Montgomery and mid Wales. There were at least two gates into the town: one behind the modern house on the east side, and another on the south-west called the Wallop Gate (named after the nearby village to which it led).

The borough grew and thrived, and had its own chapel, dedicated to St Margaret, in 1272. Prior to that date the burgesses would either have worshipped in the castle chapel of St Nicholas, or travelled to the parish church at Westbury 2.5 km away. In 1273, 28 burgages were recorded, and this number had increased to 58 by 1349; but the Black Death was cutting its devastating path through the countryside and the military need for a castle was fading. With the death of the last direct male heir, the Corbet estates were split between heiresses, and after 1347 Caus ended up with the Stafford family, with whom it remained for the next two and a quarter centuries.

The Staffords were very wealthy and had a large portfolio of estates elsewhere, so Caus was of less concern (a story repeated with many Marcher castles that had passed into the control of absentee owners). It was not entirely neglected, for there are accounts of work carried out during the fourteenth century, and a 'new tower' is referred to in 1379. In 1395 'Grymbald's Tower' was repaired, and records also speak of a *Wolvesgate* (which might have been a postern into the castle). However, it is not always easy to determine from such records if these are separate structures, or alternative names for existing buildings.

An intriguing episode took place at Caus during the early fifteenth century, when the castle was being provisioned against Glyndŵr. The Welsh constable and his sons changed allegiance and joined the rebels, thereby forfeiting their estates. One of the sons, Sir Gruffudd Fychan, served in the French wars and there is legend that he helped save the life of Henry v at the battle of Agincourt. He was certainly involved in the capture of the renegade Lollard leader Sir John Oldcastle in 1417, for which he was duly rewarded and regained the family honour.[3] But then in August 1443 he was accused of the murder of his master, Christopher Talbot, one of the sons of the earl of Shrewsbury. It seems that while the two were staying at Caus, the young man was stabbed through the heart with a lance.

The exact circumstances surrounding the incident are unknown to this day, so we cannot be certain if it was a premeditated act or the outcome of a violent fracas. Since Talbot was renowned as a champion jouster, it might even be speculated that it was a practice joust that went badly wrong – nevertheless, Gruffudd was deemed guilty and spent the next four years on the run with a price on his head. Eventually, he was lured to Welshpool Castle under the promise of safe conduct, but no sooner had he entered the gate than he was seized and beheaded on the spot without judge or jury. The Welsh bard Dafydd Llwyd bemoaned the treacherous end of the old warrior and the 'perfidy' of the 'double-tongued' English.

By that time the town of Caus was dying. The cramped hilltop location doubtless impacted on its potential for future growth, and only 20 houses were occupied in

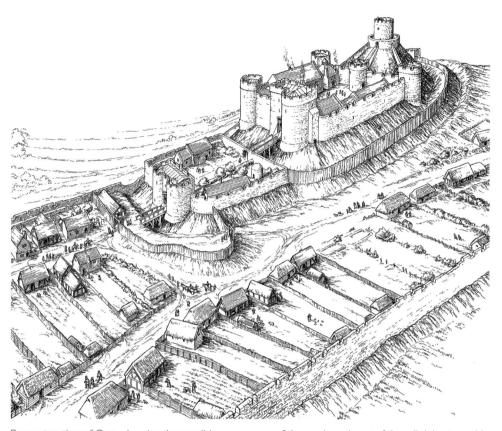

Reconstruction of Caus, showing the possible appearance of the castle and part of the adjoining township

1455. By 1540 rents from just nine dwellings were being collected, and the remaining buildings were reportedly decayed. There were four cottages left in 1581 (and only one was still occupied), and a reference to a newly-built house in 1614 seems to have been the last gasp. The castle was no longer the beating heart of a complex and widespread lordship, it was just a platform on which to display the wealth and standing of the current owners. Although the medieval buildings had decayed by 1521, the site was revived in the 1540s and a new brick mansion was built alongside the castle. The upper floor of the outer gate was also converted into a courthouse.

Lord Stafford sold the castle in 1573 but did not vacate for some years, and it was only after much legal wrangling that Caus was occupied by the wealthy courtier John Thynne (d.1604). Thynne carried out further rebuilding to make it suitable for the refined lifestyles of the Elizabethan gentry, but in 1580 he inherited his father's palatial mansion of Longleat House, and thereafter spent most of his time in Wiltshire.

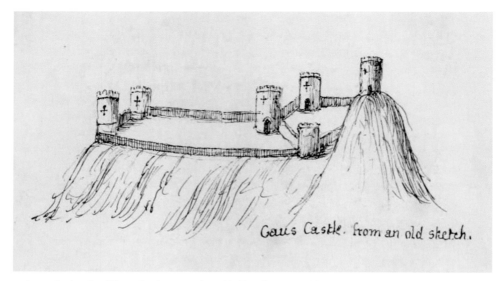

An early sketch of Caus Castle, reproduced in *The Garrisons of Shropshire during the Civil War* (1867)

During the Civil War the castle was held for the king and was garrisoned with 300 men. It was described as 'a place of great strength ... standing on a rock', but surrendered after a six-day siege in June 1645. An intriguing sketch of the castle survives, and shows it to have had a rectangular bailey with four round towers on the corners and a circular keep on the motte. A walled courtyard is shown at the foot of the motte, with a fifth tower that appears to have been a forebuilding guarding the entrance up to the keep. The provenance of this sketch is unclear, and it is undated. It may have been drawn in the early-1500s before the mansion was built, or after the depredations of the Civil War, and represent a more imaginary view of what the castle might have looked like.[4]

Today, the massive earthworks of the Norman castle and town are best appreciated in winter or spring, when the undergrowth is low and the trees are bare of leaves. The steep southern flank of the castle was defended by a single bank and ditch, but the remaining sides had a much more substantial double line of ramparts and ditches, in places deeply-cut through the natural bedrock. On the summit is a steep-sided motte, up to 12m high, with a 17m diameter summit on which there are traces of a masonry round keep. However, as the upstanding fabric incorporates reused stonework, it is thought to be the remains of a post-medieval summerhouse or folly tower (there is no trace of a ditch at the foot of the motte either, suggesting it had been filled in to make access to the mound easier). The surface of the rectangular bailey is covered with earthworks delineating a number of buildings ranged against the inner walls, and the outlines of a large structure set against the south wall doubtless represent the site of the great hall. Rubble mounds at the north-easterly end of the courtyard mark the remains of the gatehouse, which was probably a typical twin-towered structure (although the recent survey has suggested that it had a more asymmetrical plan, as shown in the reconstruction drawing).

Beyond the castle gate lay a small outer bailey, in which the chapel of St Nicholas is traditionally said to have stood. It is also where the recorded kennels and stables may have been situated, and was perhaps also the location of a garden and dovecot mentioned in 1274. From the outer bailey another gate led into the town. Most of the earthworks on this side of the castle (overlooking the modern farm) seem to have been modified in post-medieval times. There are rectangular enclosures on the slopes that could represent garden features associated with the last phase of the castle's history. It has been suggested that the Tudor mansion stood in a sunny and commanding position within the outer bailey, providing the wealthy occupants with expansive views over the gardens to the open countryside beyond.

Location & access
Caus lies 16 km south-west of Shrewsbury off the B4386 to Montgomery. Just past Westbury village take the right turning signposted to Wallop and Rowley. The castle is on private land and not accessible, although a public footpath skirts the edge of the hill, and the outer earthworks can be seen from the road.

References
Eyton (1858); MC (1998); CMHTS (2005); CSG report (2016)

CASTELL BRYN AMLWG

The modern name of this site translates as 'castle of the prominent hill', which is something of a misnomer because it is not very prominent at all, being overlooked by much higher ground on the south and east. It is, however, more obvious when seen from across the valley to the west, and that was probably the reason it was built here. Castell Bryn Amlwg is so remote from any town that it could only have served as a border defence of the Marcher lordship of Clun, which juts into the Welsh territories of Ceri and Maelienydd. The stream running below the castle still acts as the boundary between Wales and England to this day.

There are no early documents relating to this site and so supposition and conjecture must be cautiously used to piece together its history. In all likelihood, it was

A view northwards over the isolated earthworks of Bryn Amlwg

established as an outpost of the much larger and better-documented castle of Clun further east. Clun had been founded by Picot de Say before 1086, to control the lands that had been granted to him by Roger of Montgomery, earl of Shrewsbury. In the 1140s, during the turbulent reign of King Stephen, Helias de Say and his neighbour Hugh Mortimer were carrying out murderous attacks on the native rulers of Maelienydd. This would be a logical time to establish a castle at Bryn Amlwg (if it had not already been built) in order to reinforce Anglo-Norman authority in this upland region.

In 1155 Helias' daughter was married to William Fitzalan (d.1160) lord of Oswestry, and Clun was retained by this family for the next 420 or so years. After William's death the lands were held for a time by the king during the minority of his heir. Royal documents make mention of the Fitzalan castles at Oswestry, Clun and Rhuthin, and over £216 was spent on the upkeep of these three castles in 1161–64. Now, the latter site cannot be the Ruthin in north Wales, but there was a hamlet of that name in the vicinity of Bryn Amlwg, so it has been suggested that it was the original name for this castle. The name probably derives from *Rhudd-din* or 'red fort', and there are still several 'red' place-names in the vicinity. The walls of the castle were also built from locally-obtained red sandstone.

If this interpretation is correct, then Bryn Amlwg was probably the 'Castell Coch' that was overthrown by Llywelyn the Great during a campaign against the Fitzalan lands in 1233. This site has never been convincingly identified by historians, and in contemporary chronicles it bears the alternative names of Hithoet or Hychoet; names which were probably incorrectly transcribed from the Welsh *Is Coed* or *Uwch Coed* (presumably referring to the hunting preserve of Clun Forest). Llywelyn ap Gruffudd was in control of much of this contested region in the period 1267–76, and in 1274 an informer in Roger Mortimer's pay reported that the prince was thinking about building a new castle in Clun Forest. A suggestion has therefore been made that parts of Bryn Amlwg are Welsh work; however the architectural evidence is not very convincing.

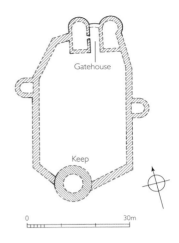

Interpretive plan of the castle

The wealth and standing of the Fitzalans received a major boost when John II (d.1267) inherited the Arundel estates in Sussex through his mother. His grandson Richard (d.1302), was the first to be officially titled earl of Arundel, thereby propelling the family to the upper ranks of the aristocracy. It is now considered that Richard built the great Norman-style keep that rises proud over the little town of Clun. The Fitzalans retained the earldom until 1580 (when it passed by marriage to the Howard Dukes of Norfolk), but by that time the family had long decamped to their huge fortress home at Arundel. The depredations of Glyndŵr badly affected the locality, and the prosperity of the town declined. According to John Leland, Clun was 'somewhat ruinous' by 1540, and in all likelihood the same fate had befallen Bryn Amlwg, but perhaps at a much earlier period considering its remote location and small size. Alternatively, it may have lingered in use as a hunting lodge, for as Leland notes, the Forest had 'very fair and good game'.

Today, Castell Bryn Amlwg looks like a shapeless green mound, scarred by ditches, rubble banks and quarry pits; but these marks are the palimpsest of buildings that remain hidden beneath the soil. Small-scale excavations in 1963 revealed that this was a substantial and complex little fortress, displaying several stages of construction between the twelfth and the thirteenth centuries, although insufficient evidence was recovered to firmly date the various phases. It began life as an oval ringwork carved out of a natural knoll, and protected by an outer ditch and counterscarp bank. A round tower, measuring almost 11m in diameter, was built at the southern end of the courtyard (see Figure **A** overleaf). Then the earthen rampart around the courtyard was replaced with a polygonal curtain wall

2m-thick and built from local stones bonded with inferior quality mortar (Figure **B**). The next phase saw the addition of small D-shaped flanking turrets jutting out from the east and west sides of the courtyard, followed by two rounded towers constructed with better quality mortar on either side of the gateway (Figure **C**). This was subsequently reconstructed and extended back into the courtyard area, thereby increasing the internal accommodation and creating a more typical twin-towered gatehouse design (Figure **D**).

There is no evidence for when the masonry was added, but a date in the first half of the thirteenth century for most of the fabric is likely. In layout and scale, the work compares closely to what another Marcher lord, Hubert de Burgh, was building further south at Grosmont and White Castle in the period 1219–39. This would place the building of Bryn Amlwg in the lifetime of John Fitzalan I (1216–41); and, to take another conjectural step, it could have been the castle that Llywelyn destroyed in 1233. Interestingly, the excavators considered that the second gatehouse (shown in **D**) had been built over the ruins of its predecessor – though whether this was indeed the result of an attack, or merely structural decay, might only be fully determined by undertaking further archaeological work at this remote site.

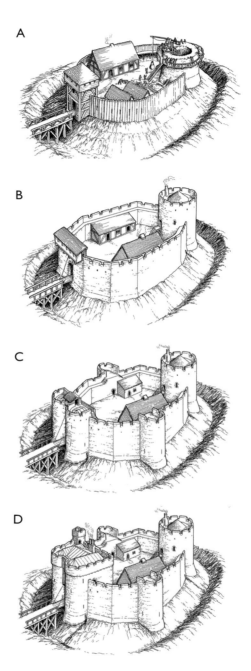

Stages in the development of Bryn Amlwg, through the twelfth and thirteenth centuries

Location & access
The site lies 15 km west of Clun, on the B4368 road to Newtown; or 11 km south-east of Newtown on the same road (take the A489 to Ludlow and turn off past Kerry village). The B4368 passes through the little hamlet of Anchor. Just past the Anchor Inn there is a signposted footpath across the fields that leads past the farm buildings and along an old track for about 400m. The castle is in the field to the right. There is another path through the forestry plantation on Bettws Hill. The site is on private farmland but is visible from the footpath.

References
MC Vol 60 (1967–8); SHA Vol 77 (2002); AC Vol 164 (2015)

CASTELL TINBOETH, *LLANBADARN FYNYDD*

Few documentary facts have survived to outline the history of this forgotten castle, and over the years antiquarians and historians have offered many theories to fill the gaps. What can be said with some certainty is that Castell Tinboeth was a thirteenth-century stronghold belonging to one of the most powerful and long-lasting dynasties to rule in the Welsh Marches – the Mortimers of Wigmore. Some members of this family were so closely connected to the royal bloodline that their lives were dogged with suspicion and misfortune, bringing the dynasty to a premature end in the first quarter of the fifteenth century.

Close-up of the rampart of Castell Tinboeth (left), and aerial view of the massive earthworks (right)

A birds-eye view of Tinboeth as it might have appeared around 1300

Their rise to power began in 1075 when Ralph Mortimer I (d.*c*.1115) was granted a portion of the forfeited territories of the earl of Hereford, who had been ousted for rebelling against the king. The earl's castle at Wigmore near Leominster became the new Mortimer seat and a springboard for further conquests. To the west lay a tempting group of Welsh cantrefs, principally Elfael and Maelienydd, which formed a territory known as *Rhwng Gwy a Hafren* ('between the Wye and the Severn'). In the great offensive against the Welsh in 1093, Ralph moved into Maelienydd and built a motte-and-bailey at Cwm Aran (Cymaron), which was to serve as the main Norman power-base in the region for the next two centuries. The chronicles record the frequent capture, destruction and rebuilding of that castle; but by 1200 the territory was more or less firmly under Mortimer control. The rise to power of Llywelyn the Great posed a serious threat to their success in the middle Marches, even though Ralph Mortimer II (d.1246) had made a politic marriage with the prince's daughter Gwladys Du. To reinforce his hold on the area, Ralph ordered the construction of new stone castles at Cefnllys and Knucklas in 1242, but as he was serving in Gascony at the time the work was very likely overseen by his eleven-year-old son and heir Roger III (d.1282) – an early start for what was to be a long military career.

Tinboeth, just like Cefnllys and Knucklas, was built on a high, steep-sided hill that coupled natural defences with a strategic viewpoint, to the detriment of any domestic comfort. The entire summit was scarped into an oval platform surrounded by an enormous rock-cut ditch, which is still a formidable obstacle today despite centuries of erosion and silting. There is a counterscarp bank around the rim of the ditch which swells out to form a narrow bailey or barbican on the east flank where an attack would most likely be directed. Around the summit of the platform an earthen rampart probably covers the footings of a stone wall, laid out in straight stretches to enclose a courtyard of polygonal plan. Antiquarians have suggested that there were flanking towers as well, but the low mounds that can be seen today appear too small for towers, though they could be the remains of semi-circular buttresses. A solitary fragment of upstanding masonry is all that remains of a typical twin-towered gatehouse, the rest of the building having tumbled into the ditch. No other structures can be seen above ground today, but excavation would doubtless reveal more of the plan.

There is no record of the castle's construction, and lingering theories that it might have built by the de Braose family back in the twelfth century can be dismissed, for the site is too substantial to be anything other than a thirteenth-century fortification. The assumption that the first buildings were of wood, and only later replenished with masonry is debateable, for the scale of the ditches and the vast amounts of shale that must have been produced make it more probable that the castle was stone-built from the start. Furthermore, the often-repeated suggestion that the castle sits within an Iron Age hillfort is questionable too, and may only be proven by excavation. The hill is scarred with a number of earthworks, but none form a coherent defensive scheme and are probably due to quarrying or mining activities.

Some additional confusion has been caused by the place-name. During the medieval period the site was known as Dinbod, Dynbawd, Tynbot and other

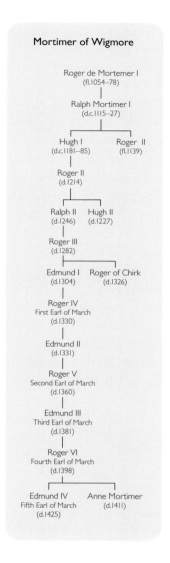

Mortimer of Wigmore

Roger de Mortemer I
(fl.1054–78)

Ralph Mortimer I
(d.c.1115–27)

Hugh I   Roger II
(d.c.1181–85)   (fl.1139)

Roger II
(d.1214)

Ralph II   Hugh II
(d.1246)   (d.1227)

Roger III
(d.1282)

Edmund I   Roger of Chirk
(d.1304)   (d.1326)

Roger IV
First Earl of March
(d.1330)

Edmund II
(d.1331)

Roger V
Second Earl of March
(d.1360)

Edmund III
Third Earl of March
(d.1381)

Roger VI
Fourth Earl of March
(d.1398)

Edmund IV   Anne Mortimer
Fifth Earl of March   (d.1411)
(d.1425)

variations – names which have been realistically interpreted as *Din-baud* or 'Maud's fort', giving rise to the tradition that it was built by Roger's widow, Matilda de Braose.[5] This is not an unlikely suggestion, for Matilda was no shrinking violet but a resourceful woman fully capable of aiding and abetting her ambitious husband. However, the idea of a sorrowful widow building a castle to defend her family land is unlikely, no matter how appealing it sounds, because we know that the castle was already in existence when Roger died, as *Dynbaud* was listed among the places garrisoned during the war of 1282–83. Five horsemen and 30 soldiers were stationed here during the emergency.

This is the first reliable mention of the castle in contemporary records and, taken at face value, strongly suggests that it was a late foundation established by Roger himself. Bearing in mind the trouble that Llywelyn caused over Mortimer's nearby castle at Cefnllys (see below), then the most likely period for Roger to have built Tinboeth would have been in the years immediately following the prince's first defeat in 1277. If it had been built earlier then it could hardly have escaped a mention in the chronicles, nor avoided Llywelyn's bellicose attention.

In the early fourteenth century the castle seems to have passed into the ownership of one of Roger's younger sons, who styled himself William of Tinboeth (d.1297), but the Mortimer estates were seized by the Crown in 1322 when another Roger (the most notorious member of the family to bear that name), was imprisoned for taking part in a rebellion against King Edward II. The estates were restored, but confiscated again when Roger was executed in 1330 for his part in the downfall and death of that monarch. While these events of national significance were being played out, Castell Tinboeth quietly slipped into obscurity, and the lack of any further records suggests it had a very short life. A remote and inconveniently-sited castle such as this could only function as a military base, and when that need had passed it was quickly abandoned.

Location & access
The castle lies on a hill 2.5 km north of Llanbister village on the A453 from Llandrindod Wells to Newtown. Past the signposted turning to Bwlch-y-sarnau, there is a lay-by beyond a house. Park here and follow the track opposite (a public footpath) that slants up through the woods to the hilltop (OS map ref: SO 090 754). The castle is on enclosed farmland, but accessible via a stile from the footpath.

References
Brut; AC (1858, 1967); Remfry (1996)

CEFNLLYS CASTLE, *LLANDRINDOD WELLS*

Like Tinboeth, this was another Mortimer stronghold built to consolidate their claim to Maelienydd, and was similarly built on a steep-sided hilltop. The English were so determined to secure possession of this region that *two* castles were eventually built here, in the course of a long and bitter struggle against Prince Llywelyn ap Gruffudd.

The history of Cefnllys begins in 1241 when the Welsh of Maelienydd attempted to dislodge Ralph Mortimer II, but the uprising failed and the following year he built a new stone castle on a high ridge within a loop of the river Ithon to forestall any further trouble.[6] These natural defences coupled with high stone walls must have made Cefnllys a seemingly impregnable fortress, and it is significant that when the Welsh rose again in revolt in 1262, the castle was only taken 'by treachery'. According to the *Brut y Tywysogion*, once the invaders had been allowed inside, they killed the gate-keepers and captured the constable and his family before setting the buildings on fire. The chronicle implies this was a random act by the local populace, but some historians have considered that the attack was instigated by Llywelyn as part of his scheme to weaken Mortimer support in the middle Marches.

A large force under the command of Ralph's heir, Roger Mortimer III, aided by Humphrey de Bohun of Brecon, soon arrived at Cefnllys. Llywelyn, though, was determined that this strategic base should not remain in English hands, and sent forces to blockade the troops within the ruined walls. Besieged, undermanned and short of supplies, the outcome to the conflict could have been very grim indeed, but Llywelyn allowed Mortimer and Bohun to make an ignominious retreat. Was this a chivalrous gesture, or a deliberate ploy to avoid staining his growing political status with unnecessary bloodshed? Once the English had left, Llywelyn presumably completed the destruction of the castle.

Within a few years the prince had reached the pinnacle of his power with the signing of the Treaty of Montgomery in 1267, in which Henry III acknowledged his pre-eminent position. One of the clauses of the treaty concerned the vexed question of ownership of Maelienydd. The territory was effectively under Llywelyn's control by right of conquest, but Mortimer was nevertheless allowed to repair Cefnllys in advance of any lawful settlement of his claim to the land. It did not take long for this legal loophole to be exploited.

Instead of carrying out repairs, Mortimer started work on a second castle here, evidently stronger than the first. Because of this, the angry prince wrote to the new king Edward complaining that the terms of the treaty had been exceeded. Llywelyn's specific complaint was that Mortimer had 'constructed a new work, not merely a fence, as has been suggested to the king, but a wide and deep ditch, and stones and timber have been brought to construct a fortress'. Not surprisingly, the king showed little enthusiasm for reining in Mortimer, and by 1277 Llywelyn was no longer in a position to make demands. Work on the second castle continued, presumably utilising materials from the first site. A small borough was also established here to encourage some economic growth in the area. This urban venture was to last long after the medieval period, and only declined with the rise of the nearby spa town of Llandrindod Wells in the eighteenth century. The town may have lain within the defended hilltop or, more likely, at the foot of the slope beside the surviving church of St Michael.

In October 1282 Roger Mortimer died, barely two months before his enemy Llywelyn, and Cefnllys passed to his son Edmund. There was another uprising in 1294 and Edmund was subsequently obliged to offer some concessions to his Welsh tenants, and grant them the right to be heard in court under English law so long as they did not rebel against his ownership of Cefnllys. Edmund died in 1304 and the inheritance passed to his son, the notorious Roger Mortimer IV, reputed lover of Queen Isabella and the driving force behind the deposition of King Edward II. A monarch in all but name, Roger enjoyed his exalted position to the full, claiming for himself the controversial title of 'Earl of March' in 1328. Never before had a whole region been claimed for an earldom, instead of a specific county or town, but it clearly signposted his overweening ambitions and the source of his power in the Welsh borderlands. But fortune's wheel turned swiftly for Mortimer, and just two years later he was swinging at the end of a rope, the victim of a coup launched by the young King Edward III in retaliation for his father's death.

The Mortimer estates were confiscated, but soon returned to Roger's heir by the forgiving king, and they remained with the family until the death of the last direct male heir, Edmund Mortimer IV, in 1425. Thereafter, the inheritance passed to his nephew Richard, duke of York. In 1461, during the Wars of the Roses, Duke Richard's son and heir (Edward, Earl of March) was crowned King Edward IV, thereby bringing Cefnllys and all the former Mortimer estates into royal ownership.

The castle in the meantime was probably in decay, although it was not abandoned as Tinboeth seems to have been, probably because the existence of the town made it a necessary fixture. During the Glyndŵr rebellion Cefnllys was garrisoned with 12 spearmen and 30 archers. An account claims that the surrounding land was laid waste by the rebels, but historians are uncertain whether the castle itself was taken. The site nevertheless remained inhabited, and sometime around the middle of the fifteenth century the itinerant poet Lewys Glyn Cothi wrote four poems in praise of the hospitality of the constable

Aerial view of the precipitously-sited Cefnllys showing the site of the earlier castle in the foreground and the later castle beyond

of Cefnllys, Ieuan ap Philip and his wife Angharad. The poems allude to Ieuan's new timber-framed hall, which presumably stood on the level ground between the two castles and is now marked by a series of earthworks. The manorial function of the court was soon transferred to another building nearby, and Cefnllys was finally abandoned. John Leland was here around 1539 and saw 'great ruins of two castles. The one is called Tynbot ... the other is called Kevenlles ... now down, it belongs to the duke of York'.

All the buildings of Cefnllys have collapsed into heaps of rubble so large and shapeless that it cannot be said with any certainty what stood here. The hummocky mound of the first castle stands at the north end of the ridge and could represent the buried remains of a central tower surrounded by several walled enclosures. Aerial views appear to show a large forecourt with a gatehouse facing the northern approach along the hill.

The second castle lies at the opposite end and is a separated from the rest of the ridge by a deep rock-cut ditch (evidently the one referred to in Llywelyn's complaint to the king). Beyond the ditch is a roughly-rectangular walled platform, possibly with corner towers, and a central mound marking the collapsed remains of another keep. A few tantalising clues to the appearance of this lost castle may be gleaned from the poems of Lewys Glyn Cothi:

> *A white castle above a full white lake*
> *An eight-sided fort above the bank of Ithon,*
> *A Greek fort in twelve encircling bands*[7]

The reference to white walls suggests lime plaster or whitewash, and the 'eight-sided fort' might suggest the keep was octagonal in plan. The 'Greek fort' may be an allusion to the imagined strongholds of classical antiquity, while the 'twelve encircling bands' could be a reference to a multi-sided enclosure. But in truth, any sort of castle could be conjured up from such poetic hyperbole, and so Cefnllys must keep its secrets buried in rubble until such time as proper excavations are carried out here.

Location & access
Cefnllys lies 3 km east of Llandrindod Wells town centre off the A483. At Fiveways roundabout take the signposted turning up Spa Road past the County Hall and Library, and continue along this minor road until it descends into the Ithon valley. There is parking beside the river at the entrance to the forestry (OS map ref: SO 089 615). A public footpath from the car park crosses a bridge to St Michael's church, from where several paths lead up the steep sides of Cefnllys hill.

References
Brut; Radnor (1932, 1972); Remfry (1996); Cefnllys (RCAHMW); CSGJ No 35 pp.82–104

HUNTINGTON, *KINGTON*

The early history of this major castle and failed borough is very obscure. It is listed in Domesday as *Hantinetune,* and valued as waste land belonging to the king – but whether there was a castle here at that time is uncertain. There was certainly a royal estate nearby, centred on Kington, which had its own castle. This estate was granted out to monarchical favourites in return for the service of five knights. A number of small earthwork castles survive at Cwmmau, Hengoed and Lower Hergest (among others) and probably represent the fortified homes of these sub-tenants. The earthworks at Huntington are quite substantial and could represent an early foundation established by the earl of Hereford, William fitz Osbern, or even Bernard de Neufmarché (who conquered Brecon in the 1090s). The castle lies right on the border with Wales, facing the cantref of Elfael, so was well-situated for a westwards push into native territory. But the presence of another castle here, barely a mile away, muddies the waters significantly.

The undocumented site of Turret Castle consists of a well-preserved flat-topped mound up to 24m across and almost 7m high, set on a steep-sided ridge between two streams. Deep ditches cut off the vulnerable approach from the west, while the tip of the ridge has been scarped and strengthened with ramparts to form an irregularly-shaped bailey. Despite some loose surface stone, there is no convincing sign of any masonry here, so the buildings may only ever have been of timber.[8] Given its exceptional size and strength, it has been reasonably suggested that Turret Castle was the earliest Norman base in the locality, and that it was supplanted by a new castle at Kington, or by Huntington itself at a later date. Either way, the significance of this site and its relationship to the other castles in the neighbourhood may only be understood by archaeological evaluation.

Aerial view of Turret Castle motte-and-bailey

And so, while Huntington may have been an early foundation, it only gained prominence at a much later date, when Kington was destroyed in the civil wars of King John's reign. William de Braose (d.1211) had claimed the lordship for a while, but was ruthlessly ousted by his royal master. His son Reginald de Braose (d.1228) then recovered the family lands and was very active in this area during the rise to power of Llywelyn the Great (as described in the previous entries on Blaenllynfi and Pencelli). He was busy cutting down trees for building works in 1217–24, and this may be the time that the existing timber defences of Huntington were upgraded with masonry.

Upon Reginald's death, the castle was briefly taken over by the king, before being returned to his son and heir William de Braose v. But he had little time to enjoy his inheritance, for just two years later in 1230, William was caught in a compromising situation with Llywelyn's wife while on a diplomatic mission to the Welsh court, and was hanged for his impudence. This signalled the end for the main branch of the family and their estates were split up between four daughters and their husbands: Abergavenny went to William de Cantilupe; Builth to Llywelyn's son, Dafydd; and Radnor to Roger Mortimer iii. As Huntington was now included with the larger lordship of Brecon, it passed to Humphrey de Bohun iv, earl of Hereford, and, despite a hiatus in the 1260s when the split was challenged by Roger Mortimer, the lordship remained with that family until the death of the last earl in 1373. Thereafter, it passed via an heiress to the earls of Stafford (who later became dukes of Buckingham).

The castle was spruced up in 1403 as a precaution during the Glyndŵr revolt (records mention the keep being re-roofed with lead and shingles, and the gates and palisades being renewed), but it seems that no major damage was caused by the Welsh, who contented themselves with stealing cattle and burning the mill on their rampage through the area. Further repairs were carried out in 1415, but by 1460 it was reported to be 'beyond repair' and abandoned as a residence. The story is the same with many of the Marcher castles that passed into the hands of rich and powerful noblemen – with so many better and more convenient properties elsewhere to spend their immense wealth on, why bother with an old fortress in the troubled borderlands? Huntington eventually ended up back with the Crown when Henry viii had the last duke of Buckingham executed for alleged treason in 1521. By then the castle was in decay, although Leland notes that one tower was kept up for use as a prison.

The site is now covered with mature trees and only a few fragments of masonry remain standing. Regardless of the various theories concerning its origin, Huntington has every appearance of being a classic motte-and-bailey converted into a stone fortress. It was protected on one flank by a stream valley, while deep ditches and counterscarp banks enclosed the remaining sides. There was even a man-made lake on the southern approach – although it is perhaps more likely that its real purpose was to enhance the appearance of the castle in the landscape (as well as provide fish for supper). There were attempts to encourage the growth of a borough here, for Henry III granted Humphrey de Bohun the right to hold a market on a Friday and a three-day

A fragment of one of the towers

horse fair every July (the fair continued to be held until 1953). There were 47 tenants recorded here in 1299, but all that remains of the borough today are the later houses and farm buildings that line the road to the thirteenth-century parish church. The prominent rectangle of lanes south of the castle may delineate the extent of the abortive settlement.

The scant remains of the castle are almost impossible to closely date, but it may be assumed that the stonework was raised by Reginald de Braose, and enhanced during the long tenure of the Bohuns. Much masonry still remains hidden below ground, but the few visible fragments indicate that the oval-shaped inner bailey was walled in stone and had at least three flanking towers, one of which was typically D-shaped in plan. There is a tall, narrow motte in one corner, though much of its height is probably made up from the collapsed remains of a stone keep. Stafford documents of the early fifteenth century refer to an 'octagon', which could mean that the keep was of multangular plan. The castle gate was on the east side where a modern causeway leads to a large outer bailey, which is fortunately clear of trees but impinged upon by a modern house. The terraces and linear earthworks still visible in this area could be the remains of an abandoned settlement, or alternatively garden features dating from the castle's more sedate times. It would appear that the layout was not all that dissimilar to Richards Castle, and so the reconstruction drawing of the latter on p. 234, gives some idea of how Huntington might have looked in the 1400s. Records also mention other buildings, including the Countess' Tower, the Reeve's Tower, the Prison Tower, a wine cellar and a large barn (perhaps standing within the outer bailey). There was also an extensive deer park – a necessary adjunct to any lordly residence of the period.

Location & access

The site lies 6 km south-west of Kington town centre, off the signposted road to Brilley and Hergest. A right fork just beyond Hergest industrial estate leads via Mahollam Road up to the village. There are alternative routes off the B4594 Painscastle to Gladestry road (OS map ref: 249 538). The remains are on private land, but there is a public footpath from the village hall enabling access to the site.

References

AC (1869); RCHME; HAN Vol 50,66 & 70; Remfry (1997)

LYONSHALL, *KINGTON*

About 14 km north-east of Huntington is the site of another major castle, now reduced to tree-covered earthworks within a muddy moat beside the parish church. Despite the uninspiring remains, Lyonshall was a substantial and expansive fortress encompassing around 2.7 hectares (7 acres) of land. The moated ringwork occupies just one corner of a sub-rectangular ditched enclosure that extends northwards towards the modern farmhouse that lies within a further annexe. Historians are uncertain whether these extensive outworks belong to a fortified enclave predating the founding of the castle, or are later modifications designed to strengthen the Norman defences.

The principal feature of the castle is the near-circular earthwork about 50m across, surrounded by a water-filled moat now crossed by a modern bridge (presumably marking the site of the original entrance). There are a few fragments of an angular curtain wall that once enclosed the courtyard, and some footings of internal buildings. At the north corner is the base of a collapsed round keep about 11m in external diameter, with ragged breaks marking the position of three loopholes. The keep sits on a low mound, but it is unclear if this is the remains of a motte or whether the surrounding ground has been purposely raised. It may simply be that the base of the tower is buried in its own spoil. The keep is partly surrounded by the remains of a well-built polygonal curtain wall, in which can be seen a blocked postern door and an external garderobe shaft. The rest of the masonry is reduced to foundations, so that the complete plan will only be understood by excavation at a future date.

These few remains were in a very poor state until conservation work in 2018, when the repointed walls were 'soft capped' with earth (this method is increasingly used

Remains of the round keep at Lyonshall, with the parish church in the background to the left

today and contrasts with the more traditional types of wall conservation that leaves the masonry easier to see, but more exposed to damage from the elements). It was noted that in places the walls had been rebuilt and thickened during medieval times, and that there was a building (presumably the hall) immediately adjacent to the tower. There are few visual clues to the age of the building, but the keep has a splayed base topped with a projecting string course, a detail that also appears at Bronllys, Clifford, Dinefwr and Skenfrith, all of which are dated to the early thirteenth century. The polygonal wall that partly surrounds the keep could be contemporary, but alternatively it might have been a much older shell-keep that was cleared of internal buildings and replaced with the central tower (a similar development took place at Tretower, and also further afield at Launceston in Cornwall).

There is no mention of a castle here in Domesday, although the surrounding land was occupied by Walter D'Evreux (Devereux) a sub-tenant of Roger de Lacy, chief lord of the surrounding barony of Weobley. Roger was exiled for rebellion in 1095 and it is likely that the castle (if it had been built by then) came more firmly under the control of the Devereux family. Baring a number of lengthy interruptions, Lyonshall remained with this line into the seventeenth century. They were connected to some of the major Marcher families of the day, not just to the Lacys, but to the Badlesmere, Braose and Marshal dynasties, and the de Vere earls of Oxford. Some members served as sheriff of Herefordshire, and by and large they were loyal servants of the Crown. King John, desperate to retain baronial support while the country was wracked by civil war, unctuously referred to his 'dear and faithful' ally Stephen Devereux (d.1228). Stephen was granted the right to hold a weekly market and annual fair here. His son William also rode high on royal

favour, but incurred substantial debts and made a last-minute (and fatal) decision to support the wrong side at the battle of Evesham in 1265. A later descendant was killed at Bosworth in 1485 fighting on behalf of Richard III.

Given the lack of dateable evidence, the masonry buildings cannot be attributed closely to any one family member, though Stephen would seem to be the likeliest person to have built the tower at the very least. He held Lyonshall between *c*.1197 and 1228, and may well have wanted his rising status to be commemorated in stone and mortar. It is just possible that the works were carried out by his successor William, but he was a minor until about 1236, so it is unlikely that any money would have been spent on improving the castle until after that time.

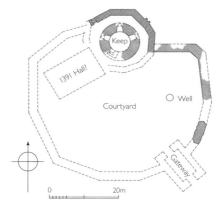

Interpretive plan of the remains and (top) a reconstruction of Lyonshall in the 1390s

Thanks to the fortuitous survival of a document dated February 1391, we know that further building work took place at the castle, even though the scanty remains

The base of the keep

do not permit these works to be identified today. In that year, John Devereux (d.1393) had regained his family seat after a long hiatus in the hands of the king and his favourites, and evidently felt that the castle was in need of some serious refurbishment. Indeed, just three years earlier it was considered to be of no value.

John commissioned a Hereford mason to build a hall at the castle, and provided specific instructions for what he wanted. It was to measure 44 by 26 feet internally, and was to have buttresses, four carved stone doors and three windows. One of the windows was a projecting oriel of ten lights, so it must have been a very impressive structure filled with expensive glass, and was doubtless intended to illuminate the high table. The gate was also rebuilt and enlarged, and provided with a portcullis, a vaulted passageway, a spiral stair, and a side door for the porter's use. On the upper levels there were two chambers, each provided with a window, a fireplace and a privy. The battlements were crenelated and machicolated (the forward parapet jutted out on stone brackets creating holes through which the defenders could drop things on any unwelcome visitor below). This document is typical of the building contracts that survive from the late Middle Ages, and, despite the reference to a few military features, it reveals that domestic comforts were uppermost in the mind of the builder. The drawing opposite is therefore an imaginative view of the castle as it might have looked following the rebuilding, the decorative new work contrasting with the much plainer, older fabric.

Despite this makeover, it is unlikely that Lyonshall was valued as the main seat of the family at the time, and they would have had other properties elsewhere. Though the castle declined in importance, it was still sufficiently useful to be manned during the Glyndŵr rebellion, when the king ordered landowners in

Herefordshire to ensure their castles were up to scratch, or risk forfeiting them. It has been suggested that the outer earthworks might have been added at this time to reinforce the defences. Nevertheless, by 1540 the castle was a derelict shell, and John Leland wrote that 'nothing remains of it but the old walls'. Yet even he considered it to have been 'a noble structure', and so there must have been a lot more to see at the time for that most succinct of antiquarians to voice such an opinion.

Location & access

The castle lies in a field behind the parish church in Lyonshall village, 3 km east of Kington on the A44 to Leominster (OS map ref: SO 332 563). The castle is on private land and is not accessible to the public, although the exterior can be viewed from the churchyard.

References

RCHME; CSGJ No 30; Herefordshire Council Archaeology Report No 384; Zaluckyj (2017)

RICHARDS CASTLE, *LUDLOW*

Richards Castle is a village of two halves. The present settlement clusters around the main road to Ludlow and retains the name of its predecessor, but the original foundation lies further away, along a narrow lane winding up into the hills. Here, the natural defences offered by a steep-sided ridge were exploited by the builders of the castle and also served to shelter a small borough alongside.

What makes this site so interesting is that it is believed to be one of the very few castles that were built in England *before* the Norman invasion of 1066. According to the *Anglo-Saxon Chronicle*, a castle had been built somewhere in Herefordshire by 'foreigners', who 'did much harm and insulted the king's men thereabouts'. A power struggle had been brewing for some time between King Edward the Confessor and some of his earls, particularly the powerful and ambitious Godwin family. Edward had blood ties to the ruling house of Normandy and had spent much of younger days in the duchy, therefore he had little compunction against employing Norman mercenaries when occasion demanded. Sometime between 1047 and 1050 one of these 'foreigners' was charged with protecting Herefordshire from Welsh attack, and set about organising the region's defences along the same lines as in Normandy. Unfortunately, this did not go down well with the locals nor with the earls, who were violently opposed to the king's cosmopolitan attitude. In

Aerial view of Richards Castle, with the church occupying the slope to the left

the turmoil that followed, the Godwins were exiled, though they soon returned and forced the king into a compromise. They regained their lands and privileges as the price of peace, and the hated Normans were kicked out of England.

How many castles were built in those few years is a matter of contention. One was mentioned in 1051, and another in 1052 (though whether it was the same site or a different one is not clear). The latter belonged to Osbern Pentecost, and has traditionally been identified as the large mound on the hill above Ewyas Harold village. Hereford is also believed to be a pre-Norman foundation, and Richards Castle is probably another. Some historians have identified further mottes in the region that could be contemporary – but in reality, it is impossible to pin a precise date on an overgrown earthwork, without good documentary or archaeological evidence to back up the claim.[9]

Richards Castle derives its name from the founder Richard fitz Scrob (or Scrope) who, it seems, was not expelled from England in 1052 but stayed on, and later supported his countrymen in their programme of enforced settlement. His son Osbern fitz Richard (d.c.1137) was in possession of a castle here at the time of Domesday, where it is believed to be the entry called *Avretone* (Overton) and where 23 people

Reconstruction of Richards Castle as it might have appeared around 1300

were recorded living within the *castello*. There were in addition 34 villagers, 6 small-holders and 10 slaves. It consisted of a substantial motte with a large kidney-shaped bailey defending the more level approach along the ridge. The useable area of the bailey was very much smaller than it now appears, because a lot of space was taken up by a great ditch that encircled the motte (since filled in on the courtyard side). The whole site was surrounded by an outer ditch with a counterscarp bank, and another rampart was later constructed to enclose the parish church and a small borough lying on the ridge to the east. It has been suggested that this outer enclosure started life as a second bailey of the castle, before being reused and enlarged to protect the town. The adjacent fields are still marked by slight earthworks that define the linear boundaries and house platforms of the vanished borough.

The property remained with the descendants of fitz Scrob until about 1187 when it passed through marriage to the de Say family of Clun, and then again through marriage when Margaret de Say married Robert Mortimer in 1211. However, he was not a member of the powerful Wigmore dynasty that has so frequently been mentioned here (even though both castles are only about 10 km apart), but a scion of a lesser-known branch that hailed from Attleborough in Essex.[10] In 1216 Robert was granted a charter to hold a weekly market and annual fair here (though this

Fragments of the surviving walls of Richards Castle, climbing uphill to the motte

may just have been official recognition of an existing arrangement). There were 103 burgesses residing in the town at the time the last of Robert's descendants died in 1304 (reputedly poisoned by his wife). The lordship was then split between two daughters, one receiving Richards Castle, the other Stapleton (see the next entry).

For several generations, Richards Castle passed through marriage to another great warrior dynasty, the Talbot earls of Shrewsbury. The later history of the site is rather obscure. The town and market were still a going concern in 1382, but it is thought that decline set in the following century, as people migrated to a more amenable location lower down in the valley. By 1540 the castle was in decay and the bailey was used for agriculture, as Leland writes that 'the keep, the walls and the towers of it yet stand, but going to ruin. There is a poor house of timber in the castle garth for a farmer'. The church remained in use for much longer, and it was not until the 1890s that a replacement was built down in the village.

Richards Castle therefore displays the classic Norman layout of castle, church and defended town. The proximity of the church to the castle might be considered a blind spot in the defensive circuit (such an arrangement also occurs at Kilpeck, Lyonshall and Urishay), but it is important to appreciate that churches were usually extended and rebuilt in later years, so a little edifice of the 1100s would not have greatly impacted on the effectiveness of the castle at the time. It is one of a number of Herefordshire churches with detached bell towers, and which, it has been claimed, served a defensive function adjacent to the castle. Admittedly, the evidence is not very convincing, and the tower is thought to date from *c.*1300, but it could have offered some shelter to the townsfolk during an emergency.

At some stage in the late twelfth century, the timber buildings and stockades of the castle began to be replaced with masonry. This development is very similar to what took place at Huntington, although much more of the layout of Richards Castle is known through excavations carried out here in the 1960s (even though precise dating for the various phases is lacking). The motte is estimated to be about 14m high, but much of this height is due to the collapsed remains of a massive tower on the summit, revealed to be of octagonal plan 13.4m across with 3.6m thick walls. A semi-circular annexe had been added to one side, which has been interpreted as a chapel, or a forebuilding guarding the entrance to the tower. Perhaps it was a combination of both, as other Norman keeps are known to have contained small private chapels within their walls. A square gate-tower controlled access into the bailey, and the courtyard was surrounded by high walls that linked up with the keep on the motte. The northernmost section of the curtain wall was later in date than the southern segment and was better defended, having several flanking towers that can perhaps be attributed to thirteenth-century Mortimer work. A large tower on the main east front was certainly an addition, and might have been used as a solar to a vanished hall alongside. Today, though, only some exposed foundations and a few upstanding sections of the curtain walls can be seen of the masonry defences, and many of the features revealed by excavation are once more concealed below ground.

Location & access
Richards Castle is 5 km south-west of Ludlow town on the B4361 road from Ludford to Leominster. In the village beside the Castle Inn a turning leads up to the church and castle (OS map ref: SO 484 703). Since recent conservation work the site is now accessible to the public and reached via a path from the churchyard.

References
RCHME; CSGJ No 30; a detailed English Heritage report (2000) is available on the Historic England website

STAPLETON, *PRESTEIGNE*

Much like Urishay (p. 198), Stapleton is a genuine medieval site that was superseded by a grand mansion, and it is the ruins of this later building that now overlook the town of Presteigne and the floodplain of the river Lugg (that here defines the border between England and Wales). The early history of Stapleton is bound up with Richards Castle (see above) to which it belonged, even though it was geographically separated from it by the lordship of Wigmore. By 1086 Osbern fitz Richard had extended his presence westwards as far as Presteigne, where a ringwork castle was built on a hill above the village. Whether he also built a castle at Stapleton at this time is uncertain, and the general view is that this did not occur until the anarchy of King Stephen's reign. As self-seeking warlords changed sides for material gain, and lands and castles were taken and lost, Presteigne was seized by the earl of Hereford around 1144 and annexed to Huntington. Osbern's heirs still needed a foothold in this strategic area, so a substitute stronghold was established at Stapleton, and this in time became the centre of a new lordship.

The castle was situated intimidatingly close to the old base across the river, on a steep-sided hill flanked by stream valleys (the eastern brook was later dammed to form a millpond). Since the hilltop has been overbuilt by the later mansion, the extent of the original castle is unclear, but there are very obvious remains of

Aerial view of the remains of Stapleton Castle

Aerial view of the fragmentary shell of Stapleton Castle as it is today

Stapleton   1850

Drawing of Stapleton Castle as it appeared in 1850, as depicted in Charles J. Robinson's
A History of the Castles of Herefordshire and their Lords, published c.1869

rock-cut ditches enclosing a rounded enclosure on the summit, with an angular bailey extended northwards to protect the more level approach along the ridge. There are platforms, terraces and half-buried foundations scattered across the hill, and a subsidiary summit on the north side also appears to have been shaped into an additional bailey. However, because the hill has suffered so much post-medieval disturbance and landscaping, the age and purpose of these outworks must be viewed with some caution. Nevertheless, the remains imply that Stapleton was an extensive and important castle at one time.

The first documented reference to the site occurs in 1207 when it was briefly under King John's control. In 1216 Robert Mortimer of Richards Castle (a distant relative of the Mortimers of Wigmore) applied for a grant to hold a market here. This seems to have been a deliberate attempt to boost the importance of Stapleton, and by the start of the fourteenth century there were 34 recorded burgages; however, the town faced stiff competition from Presteigne across the river and never thrived. Presumably the fledgling borough lay at the foot of the hill alongside the road that led down to the bridge over the Lugg. One of the houses, Carter's Croft, is the oldest building in the area and has a cruck-framed hall at its heart, that was probably standing when the last of the Mortimers was in residence at the castle.

With the death of Edmund Mortimer in 1304 the lordship was split between his two daughters and their husbands, and Stapleton passed to the Cornwall family, who retained possession for the rest of the medieval period. Notable members of the family included Sir John Cornwall, who was ordered in 1403 to garrison the castle against Glyndŵr and who later fought with Henry v at Agincourt. During the English Civil War in 1645, Sir Gilbert Cornwall feared that the castle would not be able to withstand a siege, since the water supply was inadequate, and at the instigation of Sir Michael Woodhouse (the Royalist governor of Ludlow) the defences were deliberately demolished to prevent them being used by either side. After the conflict had ended, a new house was built over the ruins. The last of the Cornwalls moved out of Stapleton Castle in 1675, and in 1706 it was sold off to the Harley family, before gradually declining to the status of a tenanted farmhouse.

In C.J. Robinson's *History of the Castles of Herefordshire and their Lords* (1869), there is a drawing of the west front of the house as it appeared in 1850. It shows a typical seventeenth-century mansion in terminal decline, the crumbling walls overgrown with vegetation. On the left side is a three-storey cross-wing with a buttress and an arched gateway, so at least some early masonry was retained in the later building. While this was the most interesting and picturesque side of the house, it is now the worst-preserved part. None of the features shown in the drawing are still standing, other than a piece of thick masonry that formed part of the above mentioned gate. This fragment has a drawbar hole that would have held a sliding beam to secure the door against intruders, and would have originally led either into the courtyard of the medieval castle, or into one of its buildings that must now lie buried beneath the house.

In total contrast to the higgledy-piggledy rear elevation, the main east front of the house had a very formal facade with rows of spacious arched windows (some having been blocked up to avoid paying Window Tax).[11] The sheer number of openings and the liberal use of brickwork are clear indications of major renovations carried out during the Harley tenure. The reconstruction drawing on p. 43 attempts to show how the castle may have looked in its final guise as an elegant mansion, all hints of its medieval predecessor decorously hidden from view. It is based on the existing remains, various archive photographs, and a landscape painting (1833) by J.M. Ince. There was a 'gothic colonnade' along the main front-age, but this could have been a later addition and has been omitted from the drawing for the sake of clarity. In 1992 the local historian and castle enthusiast Roger Stirling-Brown carried out a survey of the site and believed that much more medieval work survived here than first appearances suggest. He considered that there was a polygonal curtain wall or shell-keep surrounding the mansion, as well as a barbican and several flanking towers. There is certainly much fallen stonework and foundations all about the hill, and masses of rubble have been exposed in rabbit burrows; but whether these remains are actually part of the original castle, or just post-medieval features associated with the mansion, will only be resolved by future archaeological investigations.

Location & access
The castle is prominently situated 0.8 km north-east of Presteigne (between Kington and Knighton on the B4355), follow a signposted road from the town centre to Stapleton and Lingen (OS map ref: SO 323 655). There is no public access to the hill, but the ruins can be seen from the roadside. Guided tours can be arranged during open days at Stapleton Castle Court Garden.

References
RCHME; HAN Vol 58 (1992); CMHTS (2005)

WATTLESBOROUGH, *SHREWSBURY (SJ 355126)*

By a quirk of alphabetical ordering, Alberbury and Wattlesborough find themselves at opposite ends of this section of the book, even though geographically they are just 2 km apart. Both belonged to the Corbets of Caus (see p. 208) and guarded the outlying approaches to Shrewsbury from the west. Although it is almost engulfed by modern farm buildings, the sole surviving tower of Wattlesborough occupies a surprisingly dominant position and can be seen from afar – which was no doubt the intention of the original builders. There are traces of a rectangular moat in the fields to the west, and antiquarian hints of further towers and walls, but everything else has gone apart from the derelict keep. It has long been on the *Heritage at Risk Register*, but remains substantially intact and displays a wide range of architectural details indicative of a very long life.

In Domesday it is listed as *Wetesburg*, and the 'burg' element has led to the suggestion that it might occupy the site of a pre-Norman fortification. The subsequent descent of the property is rather confused due to the many intertwining branches of the family tree and the repetitive use of the same forenames, but according to Eyton's *Antiquities of Shropshire* (1858), Wattlesborough was held by a cadet branch of the main Corbet dynasty for a knight's fee. In the early thirteenth century one of the sons married into the Toret family of Morton Toret, which is located on the opposite side of Shrewsbury. This estate was subsequently renamed Morton Corbet, and the Corbet line established there was to last well after the feudal age was little more than a distant memory. The ruins of their castle and grandiose Elizabethan mansion are now in the care of English Heritage.

But to return to Wattlesborough, in 1272 King Henry III granted Robert Corbet (d.1300) the right to hold a weekly market and an annual three-day fair, so there must have been more than just a castle here to warrant such a move. A village is said to have stood

The surviving tower of Wattlesborough Castle, now adjoined by a farmhouse

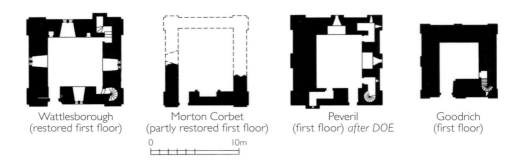

Wattlesborough
(restored first floor)

Morton Corbet
(partly restored first floor)

Peveril
(first floor) *after DOE*

Goodrich
(first floor)

0   10m

Comparative planes of: Wattlesborough, Morton Corbet, Peveril and Goodrich

in the featureless fields to the east, and the fair was last held in 1857. Towards the end of the fourteenth century the estate passed by marriage through several owners until about 1471 when it ended up with the Leighton family. They improved the accommodation at the castle, either refurbishing or building anew the hall that adjoins the tower and still remains occupied to this day. Around 1565 the herald and bard Gruffudd Hiraethog paid a visit and recorded the many coats of arms that were emblazoned on the walls and windows.

A generation later, Sir Edward Leighton (d.1593), sheriff of Shropshire and Montgomeryshire, entertained the flamboyant and ill-fated earl of Essex here for several weeks in 1584. His descendent, another Edward, abandoned Wattlesborough in 1711 in favour of Loton Hall at Alberbury. The building remained in use as a farm, but was certainly not neglected by the wealthy owners, for a painting dated 1796 shows it had been transformed into an ornamental folly. The battlements had been replaced with a pyramidal roof crowned with a balustraded cupola, from where extensive views of the surrounding countryside could be enjoyed. The tower seems to have remained inhabited well into the nineteenth century and the roof lasted until the 1950s. Thereafter it was abandoned and all access into it from the adjoining hall blocked off.

The actual age of the tower has been the subject of much debate. The 'official' view is that it was probably built at the end of the thirteenth century by the aforementioned Robert Corbet, in a deliberately antiquated style to associate himself with the older noble families of the Marches. The towers at Clun and Hopton (Shropshire) are similarly thought to be examples of architectural nostalgia among the medieval aristocracy. But Wattlesborough sports too many archaic details for this view to be tenable. In fact, when all the later additions, insertions and alterations are stripped away, we are left with a late-Norman keep, and not a late-medieval pastiche. The buttresses, string course, simple unglazed window openings and carved doorway with tympanum, are all typical of the period. It has a strong similarity to the royal castle at Peveril (Derbyshire), built by Henry II in 1176–7, and there is a resemblance to Bridgnorth (Shropshire), which may even date back to the reign of Henry I. Some details also appear at Morton Corbet itself.[12]

A cutaway reconstruction of the keep at Wattlesborough as it might have looked at the end of the twelfth century. The interior decorations are conjectural, and it may even have had a grander stone staircase than the timber one shown

While the keep certainly appears very imposing, it is relatively small structure, barely 6m a side internally, with 2m-thick walls faced with finely-dressed blocks of masonry. It belongs to a class of towers that castle students have termed 'solar-keeps' – in other words, it was not a massively-defended stronghold bristling with soldiers, but rather a secure private apartment for the lord of the castle, whose main accommodation would have been provided by an adjacent hall. The tower originally contained just one habitable chamber over a dark basement store, and was accessed by an external stair leading up to the impressive carved stone doorway. There was just the one room inside, lit by four unglazed windows and heated by a portable brazier (as there was no original fireplace). One door gave access to a garderobe, and another led to a spiral stair climbing to the battlements, which rose high above the gabled roof. Such countersunk roofs are another feature of Norman castle architecture, and may have been intended to fool outside observers into thinking the tower was more substantial than it really was.

A residential tower of Robert Corbet's time would never be so ill-equipped when domestic comfort was increasingly influencing the design of English castles. The keep was undoubtedly built by an earlier member of the family, probably at the very end of the twelfth century, and by the Richard Corbet who appears to have held the property between c.1180 and 1225. Subsequent owners had to carry out major alterations to improve the spartan accommodation here, including the insertion of an extra room in the attic, building an adjoining chamber block, and the welcome addition of fireplaces and glazed windows. The architectural details suggest these changes took place over a long period of time between 1300 and 1600. Last to be added was the existing hall, which seems primarily to be of seventeenth-century date, though it may well incorporate material recycled from the other domestic buildings that must once have existed here.

Location & access
The castle lies roughly 9 km west of the A5 Shrewsbury by-pass along the A458 to Welshpool. A lane on the right side between the hamlets of Rowton and Wattlesborough Heath leads up to the hall (OS map ref: SJ 354 127). The castle is privately owned with no public access. A distant view of the tower can be obtained from the main road.

References
Eyton (1858); AJ (1868); AC vol 35 (1880); Mercer (2003) pp.95–6; CSGJNo 35 pp.82–104

OPPOSITE: The shattered, hilltop remains of Castell Carndochan

6   NORTH WALES

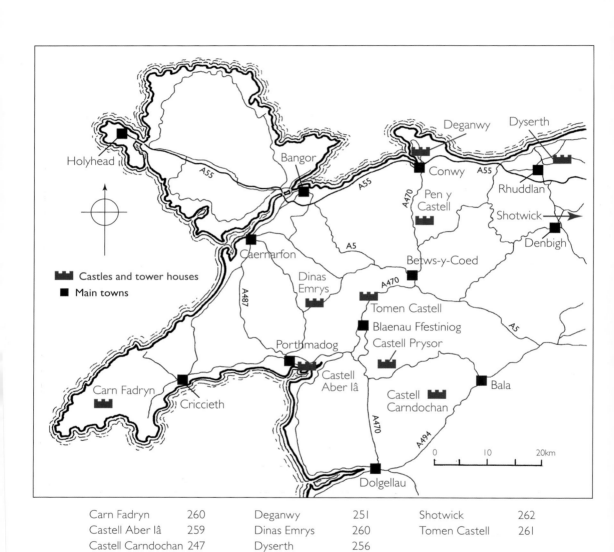

Carn Fadryn	260	Deganwy	251	Shotwick	262
Castell Aber Iâ	259	Dinas Emrys	260	Tomen Castell	261
Castell Carndochan	247	Dyserth	256		
Castell Prysor	249	Pen y Castell	260		

6

NORTH WALES

CASTELL CARNDOCHAN, *BALA*

THIS enigmatic scatter of rubble on a high crag has no recorded history, but it undoubtedly marks the remains of a native stronghold built to control one of the strategic roads across the bleak uplands of Gwynedd. The Welsh were rather slow to adopt the Norman practice of castle-building (the first attempt is not recorded until 1111) and their earliest efforts were copies of the mottes that proliferated throughout the twelfth century. They took to using masonry defences with a similar lack of enthusiasm, and the few stone castles that appear to predate 1200 are very primitive structures indeed (see p. 260). However, a more complete understanding of the early development of native stone castles is hampered by the lack of documentary evidence and the paucity of surviving remains. It seems that the concept of building castles did not fit in well with the Welsh predilection for guerrilla warfare, but it is also clear that the princes did not have the revenues or manpower to attempt large and complex fortifications like their Anglo-Norman contemporaries.

It was not until the reigns of Llywelyn the Great (d.1240) and his grandson Llywelyn ap Gruffudd (d.1282) that the period of native castle-building reached its high point. Expensive stone strongholds were deemed necessary to hold back the encroachment of the Marcher lords and bolster their princely status among the lesser rulers of Wales. The architectural features still to be seen at the more intact sites of Castell y Bere,

Aerial view of Castell Carndochan

Reconstruction of Castell Carndochan as it may have appeared in the thirteenth century

Criccieth, Dolwyddelan and Dolforwyn (all in the care of Cadw) reveal how the Welsh borrowed and adapted ideas to create something new. None can be said to be masterpieces of military planning, for they are little more than haphazard arrangements of towers, yet they display an idiosyncratic approach to castle building, particularly with the use of the apsidal or D-shaped keep. This design was similar to the half-round flanking towers used in English castles, but was usually larger and more elongated.

The most complete example of an apsidal keep can be seen at Ewloe near Flint, which was reportedly built by Llywelyn ap Gruffudd in 1257 to control the borders of his expanding dominions. However, the design seems to have originated with his grandfather, Llywelyn the Great, who built *two* apsidal towers at the large mountain fortress of Castell y Bere, begun in 1221. Among the rubble of Carndochan can be seen the foundations of another apsidal tower, comparable in size to those Llywelyn had built elsewhere, and very likely his work as well. He had seized the surrounding land from its native ruler in 1202 and perhaps felt that a new castle was needed here to signal the change of ownership. The tumbled stonework demarcates an oval enclosure at the end of a rocky ridge overlooking a river valley draining into Llyn Tegid. There was a small square building within the courtyard, a circular tower on the cliff edge, a rounded turret beside the simple gateway, and the much larger apsidal tower that jutted out to meet any attacker head-on. Recent excavations have revealed that the main towers, with their better-quality masonry, were additions to an earlier and simple castle. It may be that Carndochan was built and altered over a lengthy period of time, and that specialist masons may have been drafted in to carry out the work, leaving the rest of the defences to be built by less skilled local labourers. Few other details were discovered and regrettably no precise dating evidence was found, although traces of burning suggests the castle came to a fiery end, perhaps destroyed by the forces of Edward i, or deliberately slighted by the retreating Welsh.

Location & access
The remains lie in the Lliw Valley 3 km west of the village of Llanuwchllyn. On the A494 towards Bala, take the left turning signposted to Trawsfynydd, and continue along this for about 2 km. By the red telephone kiosk, cross over the bridge and take the right turning down a narrow lane that passes several farms and skirts the edge of the crag on which the castle is situated. There is limited parking at the entrance to the forestry just across a stream (OS map reference: SH 847 306). The site is on private land, but with permitted access, and can be reached by a steep track through a gate and up the open hillside.

References
Merioneth (1955); Davis (2007 & 2021); AC (2020)

CASTELL PRYSOR, *TRAWSFYNYDD*

From a distance Castell Prysor hardly looks like a castle at all, just another of the many natural outcrops that dot the rocky landscape of this region. And basically, that is what it is: Castell Prysor is a natural tor which has been heightened and clad in clay-mortared walling to create a motte-like fortification. The stonework is now very ruinous, but it is still possible to make out sections of revetment that formerly encased the knoll and rose to support a stone tower on the summit. This seems to have been reached by a path or stairway curving around and up the side of the mound. At the foot of the knoll two rubble banks link up with another natural outcrop to create a tiny oval enclosure. This has been termed a bailey, but it is absurdly small and could only have functioned as a barbican to protect the access stair to the motte. The expected ancillary buildings are located on the south side of the knoll in a slightly sheltered hollow, where the foundations of two

Aerial view of Castell Prysor (left) and as it might originally have looked

rectangular buildings and enclosure walls can be seen. There is a third building on the other side of the knoll, but it is better preserved and could be the ruins of a later farmstead.

King Edward I wrote a letter from Prysor in 1284 while travelling through the recently conquered heartland of Gwynedd. This is the one and only mention of the castle in medieval records, but should not be taken as evidence that Castell Prysor was English work of the late-thirteenth century, just that it was a convenient staging-post across the mountains. Presumably the king and his army were encamped here, for it is hard to believe that this modest little fort offered suitable accommodation for a passing monarch. The primitive nature of the castle suggests a far earlier Welsh origin, perhaps dating back to the turbulent years following the death of Owain Gwynedd in 1170 and the breakup of centralised power in north Wales. Gerald of Wales considered it noteworthy that the Welsh princes had built new stone castles by 1188 (which will be discussed further on) and it may be that Prysor was also constructed around the same time by Owain's heirs, desirous to secure the boundaries of their fragmented realm.

Location & access
The castle lies in the valley of Cwm Prysor, east of Trawsfynydd village, off the A40 Dolgellau to Porthmadog road. At the village take the A4212 signposted to Bala and continue for about 5 km. The castle mound can be seen in a field beyond the river, on the left hand side of the road (OS map ref: SH 758 369). The castle is on private land and there is no official public access.

References
Brut; AW (1998); Davis (2007 & 2021)

Deganwy, *Llandudno*

Until the end of the thirteenth century, this natural outcrop of volcanic rhyolite beside the estuary of the river Conwy marked the high tide of English expansion into north Wales. A mighty castle was built on the summit to symbolise the royal power that threatened the independence of the native princes. Now, there is just a scatter of broken walls and buried foundations, the meagre remains supplemented by spectacular views across the estuary to the mountainous heartland of Gwynedd. It is not hard to see why this outcrop was ideally suited as a fortification: it rises over 100m above the sea to a roughly level summit 60m across, protected on most sides by inaccessible cliffs. The less severe slope on the eastern flank served as the main approach and also formed a natural saddle linking up with a second, smaller peak.

The larger of the two summits was utilised as a settlement site long before the Norman Conquest. Excavations carried out here between 1961 and 1966 produced finds dating from the first to the third centuries AD and, more significantly, imported Mediterranean pottery of the fifth and sixth centuries, which supports the literary tradition of a royal citadel of the Dark Ages. The *Brut y Tywysogion* records the destruction of the settlement 'by fire of lightning' in AD 812, and again in 823 by the less-divine intervention of Anglo-Saxon raiders.

However, the building of the first true castle here was the work of one of the earliest Norman invaders, Robert of Tilleul, cousin to Earl Hugh of Chester. Robert was given *carte blanche* to plunder westwards and by 1073 had reached the banks of the Clwyd, where his motte-and-bailey at Rhuddlan served as a secure base for further advance, as well as providing him with a surname with which he is familiarly known – Robert of Rhuddlan.

'For 15 years he severely chastised the Welsh and seized their territory ... making inroads into their country, through woods and marshes, and over mountain heights' wrote the chronicler Orderic Vitalis in his *Historia Ecclesiastica*. 'He inflicted losses upon his enemy in every shape. Some he butchered without mercy like herds of cattle as soon as he came upon them. Others he threw into dungeons, where they suffered a long imprisonment, or cruelly subjected them to shameful slavery'. He aided, and then double-crossed the squabbling rulers of Gwynedd, and by 1080 had reached the line of the Conwy where the rock of Deganwy offered a superb defensive position. For Robert to have built an earthen motte here (as he had at Rhuddlan) would have been a waste of time, and bearing in mind the geology of the site there is no reason why his castle was not stone-built from the start, perhaps utilising the simple defences of the earlier fort and having a central stone hall or tower.

Aerial view of the twin summits of Deganwy, with the river Conwy beyond

In 1086 Robert was listed in Domesday as ruling all of north Wales for a yearly rent of £40. In reality this must have been a nominal acknowledgement rather than an enforceable claim. His violent career came to a sudden end during an attack by either Welsh or Norse raiders. When news reached him of the arrival of enemy ships, he recklessly charged down from the castle before all his troops could arrive, and was promptly shot full of arrows. The ships sailed away into the sunset with his head on a mast. For the beleaguered Welsh, this was only a temporary respite, for Earl Hugh now took command of the offensive and pushed beyond the Conwy as far as Caernarfon and Anglesey. The Norman takeover of Gwynedd seemed inevitable, but then in 1094 a series of Welsh counterattacks took place and the invaders were pushed back across the river, leaving the land west of the Conwy as the core territory of the royal House of Gwynedd. The land to the east, the four ancient *cantrefs* of Perfeddwlad, remained in disputed ownership.

The castle was an obvious thorn in Welsh flesh, a visible symbol of English power just out of arrow-shot across the water, and a stumbling block to any expansionist schemes. By 1210 Llywelyn the Great had removed that obstacle from his path. The current earl of Chester hastily rebuilt the castle to reinforce his claim to Perfeddwlad, and the following year received an encouraging visit from

Reconstruction of the possible appearance of the castle c.1256; the main citadel is on the left, with Mansell's Tower on the smaller peak (right)

King John and his army to counteract Llywelyn's advance. The *Brut y Tywysogion* boasts how this show of military might ended in ignominy when the army was blockaded at Deganwy and suffered such food shortages that 'it was a luxurious feast for them to have the flesh of their horses'. Nevertheless, John succeeded in crossing the Conwy and humbling the prince, and it was to take another three years for Llywelyn to regain his position from this setback. In 1213 Perfeddwlad once more passed under Welsh control and Deganwy was rebuilt as a native stronghold and palace.

Unfortunately, subsequent works have removed all certain traces of that structure apart from a section of revetment wall and the base of a small round turret on the north side of the rock. A few other foundations underlying the later masonry might also belong to this period. During the 1960s excavations a finely-carved stone bracket was discovered here, which depicts a bearded and crowned head, perhaps a likeness of the great prince himself. It would originally have supported one of the roof beams of the hall or some other grand building, and is now on display at the National Museum of Wales.

Whatever the size, scale and splendour of Welsh Deganwy, the castle did not long outlive its builder. When Llywelyn died in 1240 his legitimate heir Dafydd failed to hold onto power with the same ruthless efficiency, and as the English began to reclaim their territories, Deganwy was purposely destroyed in a scorched earth policy. Dafydd was brought to heel and forced to concede all the lands between the

Dee and the Conwy to King Henry III. To counteract any Welsh resurgence, the king ordered the construction of a new castle at Dyserth (see p. 256) and then began to transform the shattered walls of Deganwy into a major royal stronghold. It was a task that was to take ten years and cost a huge sum of money. However, despite being claimed to be the strongest castle in the kingdom, it was never completed.

Royal accounts provide an overview of the building scheme. The work was undertaken on the king's behalf by John Lestrange, Justiciar of Chester, who was ordered to use the best masons available. But progress was slow in the face of repeated opposition and harassment from the Welsh – so much so that the king himself had to arrive with an army in 1245. It was still unfinished when he left two months later. The principal tower was not started until 1247 and was still under construction in 1249, as well as another tower on the second summit (which was named after the king's clerk and counsellor, John Mansell). The small bailey between the two outcrops was only protected by timber palisades and rock-cut ditches, and so in 1249 the order was given to upgrade the defences with masonry.

Work began the following year on the south side of the bailey, which was provided with a twin-towered gatehouse containing two upper floors of heated chambers. The north side was intended to have the same defences, but although a start was made on the gatehouse (now marked by a solitary upstanding fragment) it appears that the scheme was never finished. In the meantime the King's Hall was completed, Mansell's Tower was heightened by another storey and roofed with lead, and then a start was made on building a ring wall around it. While all these works were going on a small borough was established beside the hill, and a charter of rights was issued in 1252. Each burgess was to have a half-acre plot for building a house and two acres of arable land beyond the limits of the settlement. The earthworks of that urban venture can still be seen today. Ironically, the town managed to outlast the castle and was still occupied at the beginning of the fourteenth century.

Meanwhile, the garrison of the incomplete stronghold faced a grave crisis. Llywelyn ap Gruffudd had succeeded where his uncle Dafydd had failed, and by 1256 had united Gwynedd under his rule. Perfeddwlad was once more in Welsh control and the hated royalist strongholds of Deganwy and Dyserth were isolated outposts in enemy territory. For seven years they were intermittently besieged and relieved, before the situation became so hopeless that the garrisons had little choice but to surrender. Both castles were then taken and thoroughly demolished: 'not one stone was left upon another' wrote the scribe of the *Annales Cambriae*. Llywelyn could have kept Deganwy and refortified it for his own use, but instead he opted for savage destruction. Was it simply too big for the more modest Welsh armies to effectively garrison, or was the symbolic status of this royal castle too much to bear?

Llywelyn's workmen were particularly enthusiastic in rendering the castle indefensible. At the foot of the hill some sizeable chunks of tumbled masonry can be seen, but most of Deganwy has been reduced to foundations and scrappy fragments. By piecing together this jigsaw of rubble it is possible to make a tolerably accurate reconstruction of the castle, although many details are forever lost. The main part of the castle was known as the donjon, which in this instance does not mean a solitary keep but the whole of the larger summit. A curtain wall was built in straight stretches around the cliff edge, linking up with the irregular outcrops and incorporating some of the older ramparts. There were various buildings set against the wall (indicated by the position of garderobe drains) and a large central quarry where most of the building stone came from. The pit might later have doubled as a cistern to collect rainwater. On the highest part of the hill there stood a long block, almost certainly the King's Hall of 1250. A mass of rubble at its west end has been interpreted as the remains of a tower, perhaps a keep dating back to the earliest days of the castle. There are more certain remains of a half-round tower jutting out from the opposite corner of the hall. This, presumably, was the 'principal tower' built in 1247–49. Despite the extremely ruined state, it is still possible to see pieces of dressed stone that would once have formed part of the base of the tower. Regardless of the rushed construction, it seems King Henry wanted a few architectural flourishes to grace his new fortress, and no doubt the principal chambers were similarly decorated.

From this tower the garrison could overlook anyone climbing the steep path up from the bailey towards the gateway. If an enemy broke through the first barrier they would have entered a narrow killing ground hemmed in between the southern slope and the upper curtain wall, with another gate at the far end. The main gatehouse down in the bailey was a more typical structure for the time but this was not started until 1250, along with a curtain wall that climbed

The smaller peak seen from the main citadel

the precipitous side of the eastern summit to link up with Mansell's Tower. Some form of defence on this smaller peak was a prerequisite from the start, and it seems to have taken the form of a relatively large tower of apsidal plan. Some historians have compared its shape and size to the Welsh keeps at Ewloe and Castell y Bere, suggesting it was a leftover from Llywelyn's fortress. While this is possible, the name of the tower and the documentary accounts make it more probable that it belongs entirely to Henry's scheme.

In the course of Edward's first war against Llywelyn, the royal army encamped within the rubble of Deganwy, but when the king finally defeated his enemy in 1283 he decided to build a completely new castle on the opposite side of the river, a significant step beyond the natural barrier that had so long marked the boundary between Welsh and English lands. Edward's castle at Conwy was positioned right on the water's edge so that even if the overland routes were in enemy control, ships could dock below the walls and bring in men and supplies. Stones from Deganwy were said to have been used in the building of Conwy, and this may have been more than just a practical method of recycling materials; for elsewhere the king dismantled the residences of his vanquished foes and incorporated them into his mighty new castles – a symbolic conquest expressed in architectural terms.

Location & access
The rock of Deganwy lies 3 km south of Llandudno beside the A456 road to Conwy, off junction 18 of the A55 (OS map ref: SH 783 795). The site is freely accessible. There are several footpaths to the hill, the easiest by a signposted lane at the top of Gannock Park Road, off York Road from the A456.

References
Brut; HKW (1963); RCAHMW (1956)

DYSERTH, *PRESTATYN*

The story of Dyserth parallels that of Deganwy, for this was another royal castle built to take advantage of a downturn in native fortunes. However, unlike ancient Deganwy, the history of Dyserth extends to a mere 22 years, and now, thanks to an unwarranted act of commercial vandalism in the early twentieth century, there is virtually nothing left to see. Photographs taken around 1911 show an extensive ruin on the summit, with upstanding fragments of walls and towers, but quarrying for limestone had already started, and by end of the First World War the castle had been practically obliterated. All that now remains are the overgrown banks and ditches of the outworks, just visible at the back of some private gardens.

Conjectural reconstruction of the original appearance of the inner ward, based on antiquarian surveys

The castle was built by King Henry III in 1241 to consolidate English authority in north-east Wales. Llywelyn the Great was dead and his son and heir Dafydd had been defeated and forced to relinquish all his lands between the Conwy and the Dee. Henry's masons were directed by John Lestrange, Justiciar of Chester, to build the castle on the summit of a steep rock overlooking the Vale of Clwyd. The site was variously known as Caerfaelan, Castell y Garreg and Dincolyn, and occupied the remains of an Iron Age hillfort.[1] Henry's army soon pushed further west and

began to rebuild Deganwy, but both royal castles were to be short-lived. Dafydd besieged Dyserth in 1245 but was repulsed by the arrival of an army from Chester, and he died the following year. Building work continued for some time to come, and royal accounts mention the purchase of lead to complete the roofs in 1246. However, the bailey was unfinished, and the King's Hall and chapel within the courtyard were only started after 1250.

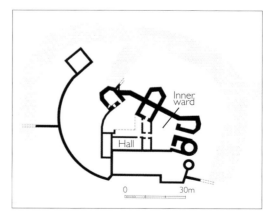

Interpretive plan of Dyserth Castle (after Edwards et al)

By 1256 Perfeddwlad was under the control of Llywelyn ap Gruffudd and both Deganwy and Dyserth faced seven long years of intermittent siege before they were taken and destroyed in 1263. Dyserth may have been sited on a seemingly impregnable rock, but it had no direct link to the coast for it to be effectively maintained when the overland supply routes were in Welsh control. It was a lesson that Henry's successor Edward learned well. When Llywelyn was first defeated in 1277, Edward chose to build a completely new castle at Rhuddlan with a river route to the sea, rather than repair the broken walls of lofty Dyserth.

The form and appearance of this short-lived castle can now only be recovered from archive material and the results of minor excavations here before its destruction. It was clearly a very unusual thirteenth-century castle, but some of the conclusions reached by the archaeologists are suspect, and the veracity of the excavation reports can no longer be confirmed on site. The main feature was a small inner ward with thick curtain walls and two large multangular towers on the side most vulnerable to attack. It appears the main walls were never built on the remaining flanks, perhaps because the planners deemed the steep rocky slopes to be sufficient protection. Entry to the ward was through a gatehouse of asymmetrical plan, flanked on one side by a polygonal tower and by a round tower on the other. Most of the courtyard was occupied by an L-shaped range of domestic buildings, which seems to have been connected to one of the flanking towers by a covered walkway. The south-facing side of the castle was further protected by a thin-walled outer enclosure with two towers of round and square plan, perhaps as an afterthought to improve the negligible defensive strength on this flank. From the gatehouse a drawbridge led across a rock-cut ditch to an outer bailey defended by a rubble rampart, ditch and counterscarp bank, and this is now the only substantial part of the castle still surviving.

In some respects, Dyserth is comparable to Montgomery Castle (Powys), which had been built by Henry some 20 years earlier. This too has a compact, heavily defended inner ward with a twin-towered gatehouse and a series of outworks; but the use of multangular towers is quite unusual at a time when round towers were almost universally adopted by the castle-building elite. It is not clear where the influence for the design came from. Multi-sided towers are not at all common – solitary examples had appeared in English castles such as Odiham (*c.*1174), Dover (*c.*1180), the Tower of London (*c.*1190) and Corfe (*c.*1204) – but it is easier to find later examples than earlier. More than 40 years were to pass before anything similar to Dyserth was built (at Caernarfon and at Denbigh for instance). Regardless of whether the decision to construct such unusual towers was a deliberate choice of the king, or just a fad of the architect, there can be no doubt that the end result would have been a striking and unusual symbol of English power in the face of Welsh resistance.

GERALD'S CASTLES

In 1188 the Archbishop of Canterbury travelled around the country recruiting soldiers for the Crusades, and was accompanied in this task by the Archdeacon of Brecon, Gerald de Barry, better known to history as *Giraldus Cambrensis*, or Gerald of Wales. The outcome of their journey was subsequently written down by Gerald and serves as a window into late twelfth-century life and customs in Wales and the Marches. While travelling through Gwynedd, Gerald made a point of commenting on two stone castles that had recently been built by the Welsh: one was called Deudraeth, and was 'situated in the Eifionydd area facing the northern mountains'. Timber castles were still commonly used by the Welsh at this time and masonry fortifications seem to have been something of a novelty. Deudraeth has been identified as **Castell Aber Iâ**, located on a headland separating two estuaries (the 'two sands' or deu-draeth of the place-name). Gerald tells us that it had been built by Gruffudd and Maredudd ap Cynan, grandsons of the great prince Owain Gwynedd, to secure this portion of the divided territories.

The castle site is little more than an overgrown knoll with a rock-cut ditch isolating the rounded summit, but among the undergrowth can be glimpsed fragments of drystone revetment, the last vestiges of the masonry defences. Antiquarian accounts suggest there was some kind of tower here, but the remains were largely robbed for building stone in the nineteenth century. The estate was subsequently acquired by Sir Clough Williams-Ellis who, from 1925 onwards, transformed the hamlet into the architectural hodgepodge now known as Portmeirion. Sir Clough built the mortared walls around the summit of the rock, and also incorporated some of the remaining stones into his Italianate campanile above the village.

The other castle Gerald mentions is **Carn Fadryn** on the Llŷn peninsula further west. This is an isolated rocky hill crowned with one of the largest Iron Age forts in Wales. Just below the summit itself is a tumbled drystone enclosure of roughly triangular plan, now very ruinous and somewhat hard to distinguish from all the pre-Roman remains scattered about. It could have served as a small bailey to a vanished tower that might have stood on the very top. It is such an odd structure that if it wasn't for Gerald's writings it might no doubt be passed off as a small fort of Iron Age or Dark Age date.

Elsewhere in north Wales there are a number of similar primitive stone forts that might be broadly contemporary with Gerald's castles. The aforementioned Castell Prysor is one; **Pen y Castell** near Llanrwst is probably another. The remains of the latter are shrouded in a dense forestry plantation high above the Conwy valley, which makes it very difficult to appreciate the layout. There seems to have been a series of drystone walls and revetments that strengthened the natural outcrops to form a long and narrow enclosure subdivided by a rock-cut ditch. On the highest and most northerly part of the site is a more substantial circular structure, 17m across, and surrounded by a thick drystone wall that still stands 2m high in places. Despite its small size, this looks more like an enclosure rather than a tower, and perhaps sheltered some internal timber lean-to buildings originally.

Whether this was a twelfth-century castle, or much earlier fortified homestead, may only be determined by excavation at some future date. There is little doubt about the two final castles looked at here. **Dinas Emrys** is a rugged hill of consid-erable archaeological importance, located in the Gwynant valley near Beddgelert. It figures prominently in early myths and legends, and excavations here in the 1950s confirmed that the rock had formed a defended outpost in Roman times and during the Dark Ages. Unfortunately, the remains of this early fort are not very prominent today and have become obscured in places by more modern walls. Unlike most hillforts there was no con-tinuous circuit, but rather short lengths of stonework that linked up with natural outcrops and crags to form an effective, albeit intermittent, line of defence. In medieval times the hill was reoccupied,

Aerial view of the keep at Dinas Emrys

and a stone keep erected near the summit. The stones were bonded in clay rather than mortar, and only the lower courses survive today, outlining a rectangular basement 7m by 9.8m. There was probably just one upper chamber, and quite possibly the rest of the building was timber-framed. How old the tower is, and who built it, are questions that will probably remain unanswered. The most popular contenders are Owain Gwynedd or Llywelyn the Great, but it could well have been one of the minor princes in the hiatus between the two reigns.

Further east, beyond Betws-y-Coed, the imposing keep of Dolwyddelan looks like all self-respecting castles should, bristling with battlements and glowering down from an unassailable crag; but this appearance is due entirely to restoration work in 1848–50 when the fragmentary remains were practically rebuilt from the first floor up. Dolwyddelan is not the 'forgotten' castle looked at here, but rather its inconspicuous predecessor known as **Tomen Castell** in the valley below. Like most

The possible appearance of the modest tower of Tomen Castle (it is here assumed that the stone foundations supported a timber superstructure)

of these small castles, it is a natural outcrop of rock which has been augmented with stonework, and was designed to guard one of the upland routes. The pine-covered knoll stands between the river and the road and carries the last vestiges of an oblong keep of irregular shape, much like the one at Dinas Emrys. The summit could only have been reached by a zigzag path climbing the steep southern flank of the mound. This modest tower may well have been built by Owain Gwynedd's son Iorwerth, who held this territory and whose own son, Llywelyn the Great, enhanced his birthplace by building the new castle of Dolwyddelan nearby.

Location & access

Aber Iâ lies in woodland west of Portmeirion, off the A487 near Porthmadog, and can be reached by a footpath, subject to admission to the village itself (OS map ref SH 588 372). Pen y Castell is on National Trust land 4 km north of Llanrwst, off the A470. At Maenan Abbey hotel and caravan park, take a right turn signposted to Cadair Ifan Goch, and continue up the steep and narrow road to the car park. Follow the well-marked path through the woods and up the side of the ridge, until it levels off; then double-back through the dense forestry and along the crest of the ridge, until the site is reached (OS ref: SH 793 667). Access to the hill of Dinas Emrys is via a footpath starting from the National Trust car park at Craflwyn Hall, 1.5 km east of Beddgelert on the A498 to Capel Curig (OS ref: SH 606 492). Tomen Castell is on private farmland, but can be seen from the car park at Dolwyddelan Castle on the A470 between Blaenau Ffestiniog and Betws-y-Coed, (OS ref: SH 724 521).

References

Gerald; AC (1927, 1960); RCAHMW (1956); Cadw (2004); Davis (2007 & 2021)

SHOTWICK, *CHESTER*

Shotwick is a borderline case for inclusion here, for not only is it in England (and therefore just off the map on p. 246), but there is not the slightest scrap of stonework to be seen today. It now looks like an ordinary motte-and-bailey in a field, one of many similar earthworks in the northern Marches, and yet it was a very substantial masonry building in its day. In that it resembles Painscastle (p. 191), another major structure that has been wiped from the landscape, but at least there the outlines of the buried buildings are still detectable on the ground; at Shotwick the earthworks are smooth and featureless.

The original castle was probably built by the formidable Hugh of Avranches (d.1101), first earl of Chester. Also known as Hugh the Wolf (and, less flatteringly, as

Aerial view of the surviving earthworks of Shotwick (taken on a frosty morning)

Hugh the Fat – though whether anyone dared use that name to his face is debatable), the earl extended Norman rule into North Wales and harassed the native princes in a series of long and bloody campaigns. Shotwick was doubtless intended to guard the lower reaches of the River Dee as it meandered down to the sea from the main base at Chester, and also overlooked a ford where the treacherous tidal estuary could be crossed on horseback.

Although it was never an important stronghold, Shotwick was used on occasion by the English kings during their campaigns against the Welsh. Henry II was here, as was Henry III and Edward I. The castle had become Crown property following the death of the last hereditary earl of Chester in 1237, but by the end of the century its days as a front-line fortress were over. In 1327 Edward III transformed the site into a luxurious hunting lodge with a deer park, ornamental ponds and formal gardens. His son the Black Prince was the last recorded royal visitor here, and in June 1353 he wrote to the Chamberlain of Chester to prepare for his visit; 'Make clean and prepare my houses of Shotwick' he ordered, '[for] I intend to stay and have sport in the park'. Clearly it was then valued as a manor house rather than a military fortress. Further work on the buildings was carried out in 1371. Control of the castle and park was usually granted out to royal favourites. Leland mentioned that it belonged to the king but unfortunately did not comment on its condition.

Speculative reconstruction based on Randle Holme's sketch plan and elevation opposite

However, by that time environmental changes were having a major impact on the region. The build-up of silt and the spread of the saltmarshes was choking the river and affecting maritime trade further upstream. By 1449 the quay at Shotwick was being used to alleviate the problems faced by the port at Chester, but the situation did not remain stable for long, and new docks had to be established lower down the estuary as the navigable waters receded. Even the enormous task of canalising the Dee in 1732 failed to revive Chester's status as a major trading port, and the city was soon eclipsed by the growth of Liverpool on the Mersey. Shotwick had long been abandoned in favour of a moated residence where Lodge Farm now stands, and in 1622 the historian William Webb described it as 'the ruins of a fair castle'. The last remaining stonework was carted away in 1756 for use in sea defences elsewhere. A poorly-recorded excavation by a local schoolmaster in 1876 confirmed the existence of substantial foundations buried under 2m of earth, as well as traces of a cobbled roadway leading to the gate.

So, what evidence do we have about the appearance of this vanished stronghold and aristocratic pleasure palace? Fortunately, a lot of information can be gleaned from a survey carried out towards the end of the seventeenth century by the Chester antiquarian, Randle Holme. Considerably more of the fabric remained above ground at that time, and Holme depicts a polygonal walled enclosure on the motte with six rounded flanking towers, two astride a gateway. The castle would therefore have resembled the

Randle Holme's plan and sketch of Shotwick

inner ward of Clifford (see p. 179) and conceivably might also have been of an early thirteenth-century date. There was an internal building (probably a hall or chamber block) with corner buttresses and what appears to have been a garderobe turret projecting beyond the curtain wall. His sketch also shows a much more substantial structure at one side of the courtyard, which appears to have been a typical Norman tower-keep with pilaster buttresses, presumably of twelfth-century date. A later account claimed that it stood five stories high, but this may be an exaggeration since most castle keeps rarely exceeded three floors.

Curiously, Holme's plan appears to indicate that the twin-towered gatehouse faced south (towards the river) rather than north (into the bailey) as might be expected. Presumably this was a simple cartographic error, for it seems most improbable that a gatehouse was needed on the side least likely to be attacked. There must have been a postern gate on the river side, so that supplies could be unloaded off boats, and an account written around 1810 claims that when the last vestiges were removed back in 1756, only the 'two round towers at the entrance to the castle from the shore' were still standing at the time. This confirms that there was a gate of sorts on this side, though it is rather unclear as to whether it was the principal gateway into the castle. The reconstruction drawing opposite is therefore highly speculative, and has been based on the assumption that the twin-towered gatehouse did indeed face towards the north. Holme gives no indication of whether the bailey was ever walled in stone, but it does seem likely, given the length of time that the castle was a royal possession. Another assumption is that the plan relates to buildings that once stood upon the motte, but there is a tantalising possibility that Holme is actually depicting the *whole* castle – in other words, the curtain wall and round towers enclosed the bailey, and only the keep stood on the mound. Such a hypothesis might only be proved or disproved by future archaeological investigations.

All that can be seen of Shotwick Castle today is the earthworks of a low motte, up to 40m across, with a crescentic bailey curving around the landward approach. Broad and deep ditches surround the site, which is sandwiched between two small streams for added defence. A survey carried out by the RCHME in 1996 revealed that the western stream had been dammed to form a series of ponds and walkways, and that the ditch flanking the motte on this side may have been enlarged, presumably with the intention of creating water features to enhance the visual aspect of the castle to approaching visitors. A faint checkerboard pattern on the ground revealed that the whole of the bailey had been turned into a formal garden.

All the grand buildings have now disappeared and only the earthworks remain. Not only has Man erased this forgotten castle from the landscape, but Nature has also transformed the surrounding environment in a geological instant of time. Where boats docked to deliver essential supplies to the castle gate, and where the turreted facade of the castle was reflected in the murky waters of the tidal estuary, an expanse of green meadow and marshland now stretches away toward the horizon.

Location & access
The castle earthworks lie in a field 1 km west of Saughall village, 6 km north-west of Chester city centre via the A540 or A548 (OS map reference: SJ 349 704). The land is a council-owned conservation area and can be reached along signposted footpaths from either Church Street or Seahill Road.

References
Chester City Council Archaeological Service News No 4 (1993); The Royal Manor and park of Shotwick, R Stewart-Brown (1912) pp. 82–142

~

LESSER SITES

Aside from the castles looked at in detail in the preceding pages, a number of other neglected sites almost qualified for inclusion in this book, but are either undergoing restoration work or are now partly open to the public. Therefore, the sites have been demoted to this appendix where, for the sake of completeness, they are briefly described below.

Hawarden, *Flintshire* (SJ 319 653)

A substantial motte-and-bailey castle with massive outer defence works was established here as a springboard for Norman advance into north Wales in the late eleventh century. In 1265 Llywelyn ap Gruffudd destroyed the castle, and after 1283 the earthworks were upgraded with masonry defences. On the summit of the motte was built a two-storey round keep, very much like the one at nearby Flint, and perhaps also the work of the same royal designer. The small bailey was enclosed with a curtain wall and later works include a barbican and a square tower jutting out from the east flank. The castle was refortified and garrisoned for the king during the Civil War, and subsequently slighted in 1647. Around 1810 nearby Broadlane Hall was transformed into a gothic mansion and renamed Hawarden Castle, the remains of the old castle then being preserved as a landscape feature. The mansion is privately owned, but the castle can be seen from the park and is open to the public on weekends in the summer.

Hay-on-Wye, *Powys* (SO 230 424)

The imposing ruins of Hay Castle dominate the marketplace of this famous book town, although not a great deal of the medieval fabric remains apart from the keep and gateway, now very overgrown and in a poor state of repair. The prominent multi-windowed edifice is a private mansion built in the early seventeenth century, which was gutted by devastating fires in 1939 and 1977. As a major border stronghold, Hay suffered many attacks by the Welsh. The first castle here was probably built by one of Bernard de Neufmarché's followers, subsequently passing to Miles Fitzwalter, earl of Hereford and then William de Braose II. It was a large ringwork castle, to which a square keep-gatehouse and curtain wall were added. Further works were carried out to strengthen the modest gateway, and the tower shows multiple phases of rebuilding; but much of the castle was lost when the grounds were turned into formal gardens, so that only future excavation will reveal the extent of the early structure. The Hay Castle Trust was formed to regenerate the site and, at the time of writing (2021), the castle buildings are undergoing essential conservation work prior to public access.

HOLT, *WREXHAM* (SJ 411 537)

This was one of the new strongholds designed to secure English victory over the Welsh princes, and it was built by the earl of Surrey, John de Warenne, who received the territories of Bromfield and Yale as a reward for his services. Holt was referred to as a 'new castle' in 1311, and in 1347 the lordship passed to the Fitzalans of Arundel. It was provisioned against attack during the Glyndŵr rebellion, but does not seem to have been taken, and towards the end of the fifteenth century the lordship was in royal ownership, and periodically granted to favoured magnates. Holt was not neglected in post-medieval times: John Leland saw 'a goodly castle' here in *c.*1539, and later surveys mean that we know considerably more about this lost castle than many other better surviving ruins. The plan consisted of a compact pentagonal enclosure with round towers on each of the five corners jutting out into the water-filled moat. A detached square gatehouse with a drawbridge defended the approach to the castle, and around the inner courtyard were ranged a series of lavish apartments. The building was unusual and highly ornate, making its loss all the more regrettable. It was captured in 1647 during the English Civil War and slighted, but the real damage was done by subsequent stone-robbing. For years, all that could be seen was a scrappy collection of fragments in a fenced-off quarry, and anyone would have been hard pressed to recognise it as a castle, let alone a major fortress of the Edwardian period. Fortunately, in 2015, after four years of excavation and consolidation work, the few remains have been preserved and reopened to the public.

KILPECK, *HEREFORDSHIRE* (SO 444 304)

The earthworks of Kilpeck Castle

Most visitors go to Kilpeck to see the remarkable twelfth-century church, enriched with some of the finest Romanesque carvings in Britain. Kilpeck is a historical gem for other reasons. It is a 'shrunken village', an archetypal medieval settlement that never fully developed its early promise. Earthworks beside the road mark the remains of the walled town, there was a little priory here (founded by the Benedictine monks of Gloucester in 1134), and a castle carved into the hilltop behind the church. It, too, was an ambitious structure testifying to the hopes of the founding family. The extensive and well-preserved earthworks comprise a motte with multiple baileys, which are likely to be the result of several phases of expansion. Probably by 1200 the mound had been crowned with a masonry shell-keep of polygonal shape. Only two upstanding fragments remain, one of which has fireplaces flues and a garderobe shaft marking the position of single-storey lean-to buildings ranged against the inner wall. King John stayed here on three occasions as a guest of the sheriff of Hereford, so the buildings must have been palatial enough to satisfy the tastes of that prickly monarch. By the middle of the fourteenth century the castle belonged to absentee owners and seems to have fallen into decay. It was in ruins by Leland's time. The site has recently been conserved and made accessible by a footpath from the village green.

Knucklas, *Powys* (SO 250 746)

Massive earthworks on a steep hill above the village mark the collapsed remains of a stone castle established here in the second quarter of the thirteenth century by Ralph Mortimer II to secure his claim to the territory of Maelienydd. In 1262 the castle was captured and destroyed by Llywelyn ap Gruffudd after besieging Cefnllys. It was rebuilt, for the castle was garrisoned in the war of 1282–83, but was soon afterwards abandoned and left to decay. The original appearance of Knucklas castle has become obscured by tons of debris accumulated over the centuries. A few vestiges of walling suggest it was a rectangular enclosure with round towers on the corners. The quarry on the west side may be a vast ditch that was intended to surround the stone castle but was never completed. It would have resembled Tinboeth (p. 217) if it had. The hill is leased to a community land trust and accessed by footpaths from the village and the B4355 Knighton road.

Llanddew, *Powys* (SO 055 308)

The meagre remains of the Bishop's castle at Llanddew near Brecon, comprise a length of curtain wall with an added half-round tower, a recess containing a well, and an attractive stone archway beside the village green. Within the vicarage garden is a large rectangular block containing a first-floor hall with a garderobe turret. However, a coherent plan of the site is hampered by later buildings and the loss of many early features. Llanddew was a fortified residence of the Bishops of St Davids, and when Gerald of Wales was appointed Archdeacon of Brecon between 1175 and 1203, he often stayed here, describing it as 'a tiny dwelling house ... convenient enough for my studies and work'. However, the building standing here today is thought to have been the work of Bishop Henry de Gower in the fourteenth century. By Leland's time it was an 'unseemly ruin'.

Newport, *Pembrokeshire* (SN 057 388)

This was the stronghold of the Marcher lordship of Cemais in north Pembrokeshire. It was established by William Fitzmartin around 1200, but was destroyed by the Welsh in 1215 and again in 1257. The defences of the original ringwork were subsequently replaced with masonry walls, a twin-towered gatehouse and three flanking towers. Two of the towers are now very fragmentary, but the third is a fairly well-preserved D-shaped structure boldly jutting out of the south flank. An adjoining chamber has an intact rib-vaulted undercroft. The castle may have been in decay from the time of the Glyndŵr rebellion, but around 1860 the gatehouse was rebuilt as a mansion and is still occupied today. The site is privately owned but just visible from the road alongside the parish church.

Ruthin, *Denbighshire* (SJ 121 580)

Edward I began the construction of Ruthin in 1277 along with Flint and Rhuddlan, but work was interrupted by the outbreak of war in 1282. The territory was later granted to Reginald de Grey and work was resumed at his expense, probably with some input from the royal masons. Building continued to the end of the century and resulted in a large and strong fortress of red sandstone surrounded by rock-cut ditches. The plan comprised a rectangular outer ward with a pentagonal inner ward, the corners capped by round or D-shaped towers. In 1400 the unscrupulous actions of another de Grey provoked Owain Glyndŵr into rebellion, and Ruthin town was the first target to suffer in the uprising. In the early seventeenth century the estate was sold to the Myddletons of Chirk and the decaying castle was patched up for use in the Civil War. After the inevitable slighting the remains were left to moulder until 1826 when a large part of the site was incorporated into a new mansion, which was extended 1848–53 with some interiors by William Burges, of Castell Coch fame. The surviving medieval remains were extensively altered and utilised as garden features. The mansion is now a hotel, and guests can explore the old ruins in the landscaped grounds.

The medieval remains of Ruthin Castle

SHRAWARDINE, *SHROPSHIRE* (SJ 400 153)

Located on a crossing of the Severn, Shrawadine was an important jumping-off point for campaigns against the Welsh. It belonged to the Fitzalan lordship of Oswestry, but was held and repaired by the Crown between 1171 and *c.*1240. In 1215 it was destroyed by Llywelyn the Great on his way to attack Shrewsbury. After the castle was recovered by John Fitzalan (see Castell Bryn Amlwg, p. 213) it was rebuilt and renamed Castle Isabel in honour of his wife. It was still occupied in Tudor times and was held by Royalists in the Civil War, but suffered a five-day siege in 1645 and was subsequently slighted.

The earthworks of Shrawardine

Material was taken to Shrewsbury to repair the town walls, and further stone-robbing depleted the masonry, apart from some foundations and revetment walls around the central mound. More walls presumably lie hidden below ground. Despite the sparsity of the remains, the quality of the masonry is very good, and it must have been an impressive and substantial structure in its day. Survey work in 1991–94 suggests that the castle consisted of a compact inner ward or shell-keep, with several rounded flanking towers, two possibly astride the gate (so it may have resembled Clifford and Shotwick). The masonry castle had an extensive series of outer wards that now only survive as earthworks. The site was purchased by the Montford Parish Millennium Green Trust as a public accessed space, and the few upstanding walls have been consolidated.

SNODHILL, *PETERCHURCH* (SO 322 402)

For years this little-known castle was on the *Heritage at Risk Register* and the crumbling walls were hidden by dense undergrowth. It would have been a contender for inclusion in the main section of this book, but now, thanks to the work of the Snodhill Castle Preservation Trust, the castle has been treated to some serious conservation work by Historic England and is accessible. At the time of writing the excavations are still proceeding, so further details about the castle's development may be forthcoming. Snodhill is a large motte-and-bailey scarped out of a natural hill overlooking the Golden Valley. It is assumed to have been founded by Hugh de l'Asne (see Urishay) under the direction of William fitz Osbern, and later passed to the Chandos family who held it from at least 1136 until 1428. They would have been responsible for upgrading the earthworks with masonry, but traces of an early keep have been detected on the motte, so it is possible that Snodhill was among the very few castles in Britain that was stone-built from the start. The motte is

Snodhill Castle, Peterchurch

crowned by a polygonal keep with an added twin-turreted gatehouse, while the bailey was also walled in stone. A substantial tower (almost a second keep) was added to the north curtain wall. The castle was reportedly in ruins by 1353 but later references to the site, along with the establishment of a deer park, suggest that some improvements were carried out. It was certainly capable of being garrisoned against the Welsh in 1403, but was thereafter neglected and by Leland's time was 'somewhat in ruin'. A detailed report (No. 76) has been published on the Historic England website.

Usk, *Monmouthshire* (SO 377 011)

A large and substantial hilltop castle that cries out to be properly excavated and adequately restored. The castle may have been founded by the earl of Hereford in the 1070s but is not mentioned in the chronicles until 1138 when the lordship was in the hands of the de Clares. Later in the century a small square gatehouse-keep was added to the inner bailey. William Marshal acquired the property through marriage and rebuilt the castle on a grand scale around 1216–20. Subsequent works have obscured Marshal's design, but the keep-like Garrison Tower and modest inner gateway reflects

The gatehouse-keep at Usk

his work elsewhere at Chepstow and Pembroke. Usk was subsequently regained by the de Clares and greatly enlarged and improved by Elizabeth (see the entry on Llangybi, p. 147). It fell into gradual decay after the Glyndŵr rebellion although the outer gate was later converted into a house. The Humphreys family lived here from 1908 onwards, carried out some excavations and turned the courtyards into formal gardens. The castle is now run by a local charity and there is public access most days of the week.

ENDNOTES

1 The excellent database of The Gatehouse website was used to reach these figures. The total of 720 castles in Wales will further increase if sites considered 'possible' or 'dubious' are also included.

2 For a further understanding of the history and development of the March, the reader is strongly recommended to head for the three-volume *Welsh Marcher Lordships* currently being published by Logaston Press.

3 A more detailed overview of early-medieval Wales and the archaeology of the native llys and castle, can be found in my own book *Towers of Defiance* (Y Lolfa, 2021).

4 Traditionally, Welsh surnames were taken from the father's forename; therefore, Gruffudd ap Cynan means simply Gruffudd, son of ('ap') Cynan; this method enabled families to trace their line back many generations.

5 The earliest use of the word 'keep' to denote a great tower, has been traced to late fourteenth-century documents, but it became more common in Tudor times, and the antiquarian John Leland used the spelling 'kepe' for several castles he visited.

6 For further information on shell-keeps and associated structures, see 'Shell-keeps revisited: the bailey on the motte?' By R. Higham (2015) available on the CSG website.

7 There has recently been a move to push the origin of round keeps in Britain well back into the twelfth century, and while there is some evidence to support this move, most learned opinion (backed by architectural detail), points to a proliferation after 1200. See Chapter 19 of *The March of Ewyas* (Logaston Press, 2020).

8 There is some controversy over the interpretation of the Chepstow gateway; the doors themselves have been securely dated to *c.*1190, but it has been suggested that the flanking towers are later modifications.

9 These three were Carew, Picton and Stackpole; only Picton now remains, making it one of the oldest continually inhabited buildings in Wales.

10 Castles Studies Group newsletter (1999–2000).

11 Quoted in Richard Avent's essay 'The restoration of castles in Wales; philosophy and practice' in *Archaeologia Cambrensis* (2007), an overview of the perils and pitfalls of restoration work.

1 West Wales

1 David Sweetman's *The Medieval Castles of Ireland* (Boydell Press, 1999) is an excellent source of further information on tower houses and similar fortified buildings on the Emerald Isle.

2 A reeve was usually elected by the lord on a yearly basis to manage his estate, and the name of David Hychyn appears twice in the records. Records relating to the Slebech estate (incorporating Newhouse) are available online at isys.llgc.org.uk

3 Alternatively (as the late Rick Turner of Cadw suggests), some timbered floors in medieval buildings could have been covered with flagstones to create a fireproof surface.

2 Glamorgan

1 This fabricated history was originated by Sir Edward Stradling (d.1609) of St Donats, who was desirous to push his family ancestry back to Norman times.

2 The full story behind the troubled construction of Morlais is given in pp. 235–42 of *Three Chevrons Red* (Logaston Press, 2013).

3 Regrettably, I have not been able to find out any further details of this intriguing episode, mentioned in John Lloyd's *History of Carmarthenshire* (1935).

3 MONMOUTHSHIRE

1   There is some uncertainty whether it was Maredudd or his son Morgan who was dispossessed by Gilbert.

2   Several publications and websites erroneously suggest that Llanhilleth was the 'Castell Hychoet' attacked by Llywelyn the Great in 1233; but this is due to a misreading of the chronicles, and the reference is to a completely different site (quite possibly Castell Bryn Amlwg – see p. 213).

3   Rick Turner of Cadw disagrees with my hypothesis and considers that the hall block was a freestanding completed structure.

4   Personal information from Dr Neil Phillips of APAC. Ltd.

5   Both accounts can be found in the respective pages of *Archaeologia Cambrensis* 1956 and 2003. The *Time Team* excavations were broadcast in episode 8, season 17.

6   A fuller account of the history of Tregrug and the connection with Bogo de Clare can be found in Chapters 9 & 10 of *Three Chevrons Red* (Logaston Press, 2013).

7   The lower walls of the passage have now been recognised as part of an older and smaller entrance that stood here before the gatehouse was built.

8   Rick Turner has pointed out that the number of garderobe shoots suggests there was only one upper floor in the gatehouse (per comm.).

9   A 2008 volume of the *Gwent County History* contains the statement that the great castle was 'left unfinished and empty, a monument to the over-ambitiousness of the Clare family'.

4 MID WALES & THE SOUTHERN MARCHES

1   To add further confusion to the family tree, there were another three Williams before the male line died out, some of whom we have already encountered: William v (d.1230); William vi (d.1291) and William vii (d.1326).

2   Only a handful of stone castles were built in Britain before 1100. Comparison of the Castell Dinas keep to the early hall at Chepstow (traditionally ascribed to Earl William around 1068) is no longer viable, since recent re-evaluation suggests it could belong to a later generation.

3   Jones claimed that Einion built Penpont castle in the fourteenth century after retiring from a long period of military service in France (*History of the County of Brecknock, 1805–09*).

4   The comparable details are the mural recesses in the gatehouse at Montgomery, and the string courses on the splayed bases of the towers, that appear at many of the round keeps in the region (including Bronllys, which is also considered to have been built by Walter Clifford).

5   In modern values this might be around £500,000. For comparison, Henry ii had built the keep at Scarborough for £650, and an entire castle (at Orford) for £1,415.

6   Incidentally, it was this family name along with local legends about a ghostly hound, that inspired Sir Arthur Conan Doyle's most famous literary work.

7   It may be due to their less than perfect draughtsmanship that the keep appears to stand in front of the house, rather than behind it. They probably also exaggerated its height.

8   This is the usual descent, but it is also claimed that Pencelli was owned by the Vaughans of Tretower from the fourteenth century and was left by Maud Vaughan in 1597 to her nephew Sir Richard Herbert (Brycheiniog 1978–9).

9   There are said to be medieval arches in the cellar of the house, and yet the chapel is also supposed to have been in the attic! Unfortunately, I was not permitted to carry out a survey of the house so cannot confirm the veracity of these claims.

5 The Middle Marches

1 This is an incredible age for medieval times. It is uncertain when he was born (dates between 1160 and 1178 have been proposed), and some biographers have suggested that there is a missing generation so that it was a different Fulk who died around 1258. However, as the Romance claims that he was blind for the last seven years of his life, it could be indicative of a great age.

2 It has been suggested that the first castle here was a ringwork at nearby Hawcocks Farm, which in 1361 was known as Aldescausefield ('Old Caus Field'). However, the scale of the earthworks on Caus hill are quite massive and typical of early Norman works, and it seems hard to believe that the founders should have ignored the defensive potential of this site and opt for a much weaker and low-lying position to establish their castle.

3 For further information about Oldcastle's career (the basis for Shakespeare's Falstaff), see *Sir John Oldcastle of Herefordshire* by Andy Johnson (Logaston Press, 2020).

4 The sketch is reproduced in *The Garrisons of Shropshire during the Civil War* (British Museum, 1867).

5 Maud is the vernacular of Matilda, and in medieval times the two names were often interchangeable. There may also be some confusion with another formidable Matilda (d.1210), wife of William de Braose III, who rebuilt Painscastle in Elfael in 1195 and which was renamed Maud's Castle in her honour.

6 Some authorities think that Mortimer rebuilt a pre-existing castle here. The *Brut y Tywysogion* merely states that the 'castle of Maelienydd' was fortified, but later references always refer to it as the 'new castle', making it more likely that it was a new foundation.

7 After translations by A.E. Brown, *Transactions of the Radnorshire Society*, 1972.

8 Roger Stirling-Brown (HAN Vol 50) suggested there was a shell-keep, walls and gatehouse here, but I saw no evidence of stonework that could not be attributed to natural geology or modern agricultural activity. Interestingly, the same arrangement of two large castles in close proximity occurs at Longtown in Ewyas Lacy lordship; the motte-and-bailey there has been revealed to have been an abortive foundation that was abandoned before the wooden buildings were added. Did the same thing happen to Turret Castle?

9 No actual evidence for a pre-Norman date was found at Richards Castle during excavations carried out in 1962–64; though there have been suggestions that the castle occupies the site of an earlier (Iron Age?) enclosure.

10 For greater detail on the labyrinthine genealogy of this dynasty, see the Mortimer History Society website.

11 Window Tax was first introduced in 1696 and only repealed in 1851. Initially the basis was a flat rate per property, plus a variable rate for houses with more than 10 windows. There seem to have been around 30 windows at Stapleton; curiously, some of the blind arches appear to have been ornamental features rather than former windows, for they show no sign of having been openings that were subsequently blocked up.

12 The Corbet connection with Morton Corbet castle began early in the thirteenth century when a Richard Corbet married Joanna, daughter of Bartholomew Toret. Only when Toret died around 1235 did the castle pass to his grandson Roger Corbet (d.c.1255). But there is also some doubt as to the age of this tower too; it is broadly dated to *c.*1200 so could have been built by the Torets, or even by the Corbets after 1235. Wattlesborough probably served as the model (though arguably the shared details are a regional style favoured by local masons, rather than a deliberate attempt at copying).

6 North Wales

1 Prehistoric and Roman finds have been made here and some of the rock-cut ditches may be early. Also, it seems that the builders commenced work at a nearby location, but Lestrange was ordered to start again at the present site.

SELECT BIBLIOGRAPHY, REFERENCES AND FURTHER READING

Aside from the publications specifically quoted as references at the end of the individual entries (and detailed below), there are a number of excellent books providing general information on castles and medieval Welsh history, including the following selection:

Castellarium Anglicanum, an Index and Bibliography of the Castles in England, Wales and the Islands, D.J. Cathcart King (New York, 1983).

Castle M. Morris (Pan, 2004).

Castles in Wales and the Marches, Essays in honour of DJ Cathcart King, (ed.) R. Avent & J. Kenyon (University of Wales Press, 1987).

Conquest, Co-existence and Change 1063–1415, R.R. Davies (Clarendon Press/ University of Wales Press, 1987).

The Decline of the Castle, M.W. Thompson (Cambridge University Press, 1987).

Destruction in the English Civil War, S. Porter (Sutton, 1994).

The Medieval Castle in England and Wales, a social and political history, N.J.G. Pounds (Cambridge University Press, 1990).

The Rise of the Castle, M.W. Thompson (Cambridge University Press, 1991).

Ruins, their Preservation and Display, M.W. Thompson (British Museum Publications, 1981).

The Revolt of Owain Glyndŵr, R.R. Davies (Oxford University Press, 1995).

A major new series on the Marcher lordships is currently being prepared by Logaston Press. *The Welsh Marcher Lordships* Volume 1, by Philip Hume (*Central & North: Montgomeryshire, Denbighshire, Radnorshire, North Herefordshire, Flintshire and Shropshire*), published in 2021. There are many internet sites dealing with the subject of medieval castles, but the most useful for those seeking factual details and references is the late-Philip Davis' *The Gatehouse* website: **www.gatehouse-gazetteer.info/home**

ABBREVIATIONS & REFERENCES

AC	*Archaeologia Cambrensis*, journal of the Cambrian Archaeological Association.
Austin	David Austin, *Carew Castle Archaeological Project (1994 interim report).*
AW	*Archaeology in Wales*, journal of the Council for British Archaeology.
BBCS	*Bulletin of the Board of Celtic Studies.*
Bradney	Joseph Bradney *History of Monmouthshire* (Vol 1–4 1904–33; Vol 5 ed. Madeleine Gray 1993).
Brut	*Brut y Tywysogion* (Chronicles of the Princes), Peniarth MS 20 version, trans by Thomas Jones (University of Wales Press, 1952).
Brycheiniog	*Brycheiniog*, journal of the Brecknock Society.
CADW	CADW Welsh Historic Monuments guidebooks: *A Nation under siege*, Peter Gaunt (1991); *Dyfed*, Sian Rees, (1992); *Glamorgan & Gwent*, Elizabeth Whittle (1992); *Clwyd & Powys*, Helen Burnham (1995); *Gwynedd*, Francis Lynch (1995); *Dolwyddelan Castle*, Richard Avent (2004).
CAS	Hereford & Worcester County Council Archaeological Services.
Coxe	William Coxe, *An Historical Tour of Monmouthshire* (1801).
Charles	B.G. Charles, *Place-names of Pembrokeshire* (National Library of Wales 1992).
CMHTS	Central Marches Historic Towns Survey 1992–96 (English Heritage 2005).
CSGJ	Castle Studies Group Journal.
Davis	Paul R. Davis *A Company of Forts* (Gwasg Gomer, 2000); *Castles of the Welsh Princes* (Y Lolfa, 2007); *Three Chevrons Red* (Logaston Press, 2013); *Towers of Defiance* (Y Lolfa, 2021).
Davies	John Davies, *A History of Wales* (Penguin Press, 1990).

DAT	Dyfed Archaeological Trust (sites & monuments record & website).
Eyton	R.W. Eyton, *Antiquities of Shropshire* (London, 1858).
Fox & Raglan	Cyril Fox & Lord Raglan, *Monmouthshire Houses* (volume 1, 1951).
HKW	*History of the King's Works*, ed. H.M. Colvin (HMSO, 1963).
Gerald	Gerald of Wales, *The Journey through Wales & the Description of Wales*, trans. Lewis Thorpe (Penguin, 1978).
Goodall	John Goodall, *The English Castle* (Yale, 2011)
GCH	*Gwent County History* volume 2, ed. Ralph Griffiths (University of Wales Press, 2008).
HAN	*Herefordshire Archaeological News.*
Homfrey	Jeston Homfrey, *Castles of the Lordship of Glamorgan* (Cardiff, 1828).
Jones	Francis Jones, *Historic Houses of Pembrokeshire* (Brawdy Books, 1996).
Jones	Theophilus Jones *History of the County of Brecknock* (1805–09).
Knight & Johnson	Jeremy Knight & Andy Johnson (eds.) *Usk Castle, Priory and Town* (Logaston Press, 2008).
Leland	John Leland, *Leland's Itinerary in Wales 1536–39*, (ed. Lucy Smith London, 1906).
MC	*Montgomeryshire Collections* Journal.
Mercer	Eric Mercer, *English Architecture to 1900: the Shropshire Experience* (Logaston Press, 2003).
Merioneth	*Journal of the Merioneth Historical Record Society.*
Morgan & Wakeman	Octavius Morgan & Thomas Wakeman, *Notes on Wentwood, Castle Troggy and Llanfair* (Newport, 1863); *Notes on the Ecclesiastical Remains at Runston, Sudbrook, Dinham and Llanbedr* (Newport, 1856).
Pevsner	'Pevsner' guides to the Buildings of Wales: Edward Hubbard *Clwyd* (Penguin, 1986); John Newman *Monmouthshire* (Penguin, 2000); Thomas Lloyd, John Orbach, Robert Scourfield, *Pembrokeshire* (Yale University Press, 2004).
Phillips	Neil Phillips, *Earthwork Castles of Gwent and Ergyng AD 1050–1250* (University of Wales, 2005).
Porter	Stephen Porter, *Destruction in the English Civil War* (Sutton Publishing, 1994).
Radnor	*Transactions of the Radnorshire Society.*
Remfry	Paul Remfry, *Castles and History of Radnorshire* (Logaston Press, 1996); *Huntington Castle* (SCS 1997); *Castles of Breconshire* (Logaston Press, 1999).
RCAHMW	Royal Commission on Ancient and Historical Monuments (Wales): *Pembrokeshire Inventory* (HMSO, 1925); *Caernarfonshire Inventory* volume 1 (HMSO, 1956); *Glamorgan Inventory* volume 3 part I (HMSO, 1991) part II (HMSO, 2000); *Cefnllys Castle, David Browne & Alastair Pearson*.
RCHME	Royal Commission on Historical Monuments (England): *Herefordshire Inventory* Vol 1 (HMSO, 1931), Vol 3 (HMSO, 1934).
Salter	Mike Salter, *Castles & Moated Mansions of Shropshire* (Folly Publications, 1988).
SHA	*Shropshire History & Archaeology* Journal.
J.B. Smith	J. Beverley Smith, *Llywelyn ap Gruffudd, Prince of Wales* (University of Wales Press, 1998).
Smith	Peter Smith, *Houses of the Welsh Countryside* (HMSO, 1988).
TCNS	*Transactions of the Cardiff Naturalists Society.*
Thompson	Michael Thompson, *The Decline of the Castle* (Cambridge University Press, 1987).
Tree & Baker	Michael Tree and Mark Baker, *Forgotten Welsh Houses* (Hendre, 2008).
Woolhope	*Transactions of the Woolhope Naturalists Field Club.*
Wright	T. Wright (trans.), *The History of Fulk Fitz Warine* (London, 1855).
Zaluckyj	Sarah & John Zaluckyj, *A History of Lyonshall* (Logaston Press, 2017).

INDEX

Numbers in **bold** refer to the main entry for the castle; in *italics* to illustrations